1 MONTH OF
FREE
READING

at

www.ForgottenBooks.com

By purchasing this book you are eligible for one month membership to ForgottenBooks.com, giving you unlimited access to our entire collection of over 1,000,000 titles via our web site and mobile apps.

To claim your free month visit:

www.forgottenbooks.com/free911812

ISBN 978-0-265-93253-7
PIBN 10911812

CITIZENS' BUSINESS

BUREAU OF MUNICIPAL RESEARCH 1919

ISSUED WEEKLY AT 805 ₹ FRANKLIN BANK BUILDING
PHILADELPHIA. ENTERED AS SECOND CLASS MATTER
JUNE 7, 1913 AT THE POST OFFICE AT PHILADELPHIA,
PA., UNDER THE ACT OF AUGUST 24TH, 1912 —
SUBSCRIPTION FIFTY CENTS THE YEAR·

A Municipal Creed

By THOMAS L. HINCKLEY

Formerly Director of
Milwaukee Citizens' Bureau of Municipal Efficiency

No. 345   January 2, 1919

The subject-matter of this number was contained
in CITIZENS' BUSINESS No. 134, Dec. 17, 1914, and
is reprinted in response to a number of requests.
   The author, according to latest reports, is now a
lieutenant in the U. S. Army in France.

Said the Spirit of the Modern City:

I Believe in myself—in my mission as a defender of the liberties of the people and guardian of the light of civic idealism.

I Believe in my people—in the sincerity of their hearts and the sanity of their minds—in their ability to rule themselves and to meet civic emergencies—in their ultimate triumph over the forces of injustice, oppression, exploitation and iniquity.

I Believe that good food, pure water, clean milk, abundant light and fresh air, cheap transportation, equitable rents, decent living conditions and protection from fire, from thieves and cut-throats and from unscrupulous exploiters of human life and happiness, are the birth-right of every citizen within my gates; and that in so far as I fail to provide these things, even to the least of my people, in just this degree is my fair name tarnished and my mission unfulfilled.

I Believe in planning for the future, for the centuries which are to come and for the many thousands of men, women and children who will reside within my gates and who will suffer in body, in mind and in worldly goods unless proper provision is made for their coming.

I Believe in good government and in the ability of every city to get good government; and I believe that among the greatest hindrances to good government are obsolete laws—which create injustice; out-grown customs—which are unsocial; and antiquated methods—which increase the cost of government and destroy its efficiency.

I Believe that graft, favoritism, waste or inefficiency in the conduct of my affairs is a crime against my fair name; and I demand of my people that they wage unceasing war against these municipal diseases, wherever they are found and whomsoever they happen to touch.

I Believe that those of my people who, by virtue of their strength, cleverness or thrift, or by virtue of other circumstances, are enabled to lead cleaner lives, perform more agreeable work or think more beautiful thoughts than those less fortunate, should make recompense to me, in public service, for the advantages which I make it possible for them to enjoy.

Believe that my people should educate their children in the belief that the service of their city is an honorable calling and a civic duty, and that it offers just as many opportunities for the display of skill, the exercise of judgment or the development of initiative as do the counting houses and markets of the commercial world.

Finally, I Believe in the Modern City as a place to live in, to work in, and to dream dreams in—as a giant workshop where is being fabricated the stuff of which the nation is made—as a glorious enterprise upon whose achievements rests, in large measure, the future of the race.

Reprinted by courtesy of The Survey and with the permission of the author.

Pol, Sci

CITIZENS' BUSINESS

BUREAU OF MUNICIPAL RESEARCH

ISSUED WEEKLY AT 805 FRANKLIN BANK BUILDING
PHILADELPHIA. ENTERED AS SECOND CLASS MATTER.
JUNE 7,1913 AT THE POST OFFICE AT PHILADELPHIA,
PA.,UNDER THE ACT OF AUGUST 24TH,1912 —
SUBSCRIPTION FIFTY CENTS THE YEAR

OVERPAID?

No. 346   January 9, 1919

"Wisdom is the principal thing: therefore get wisdom and with all thy getting
get understanding."

Now that this campaign for increasing the salaries of teachers is waging, how many are voicing the sentiments of the gentleman whose letter to one of our newspapers was published recently? He says that the teachers are "very liberally paid for their short hours and comparatively easy work. They are subject to no physical fatigue and their mental strain is over only a few hours of the day." Or, how many people of our city maintain an attitude of absolute indifference? In sharp contrast to these two classes is another whose interests in the movement have been keenly aroused and who are now working for the betterment of our whole school system. **To which of these classes do you belong?**

In other cities, those outside of Pennsylvania, an increase in salary has been given to the teachers several times in the past few years. For example, in Cleveland from 1915 to 1918 elementary teachers' salaries show an increase graded up to about 30 per cent with a maximum salary of $1600. In New York, salaries show an increase graded up to about 15 per cent with a maximum of $1920. In Chicago, the increase is from 9 per cent to 14 per cent with a maximum of $1500.

In Philadelphia, teachers have had no increase in salary since 1914. There are in this city 7136 school teachers, principals, and clerks. They receive yearly a salary of $6,476,330, an average of $907.54. The elementary teacher's salary to begin with is $600. Just think of it! Could you live today on $600 a year? Each year the teacher receives an increase in salary. Do you know what that increase is? It is a princely sum, $3 per teaching month or $30 per year for five years; and then, if she qualifies, $50 per year. After ten years of hard work, she obtains her maximum, $1000. If she is fortunate and is assigned a grammar grade, in ten years' time she will receive a maximum of $1100.

Let us consider what is expected of this teacher in our elementary schools. She must be alert, enthusiastic, able to hold the attention of 35 to 65 children for the full five hours' time. She must read, attend lectures, and study. She must be able to teach adequately and well at least ten branches and at the same time to discipline many and various temperaments. She has in addition a vast amount of clerical work to perform in connection with reports, roll sheets, attendance cards, and truant slips. Lessons must be planned for two weeks ahead of time; a program for the day's work must be in readiness; a great number of papers must be corrected and marks registered. And what does she receive for this amount of work, Mr. Citizen? Suppose you had labored faithfully for five years would you think that you were sufficiently paid if you received a salary of $750 or even $850?

Here is another item of interest. There are in our schools about four hundred janitors and engineers. They receive an average pay of $1453.50 from which must be deducted the amount spent for supplies and help. Even considering this, however, the usual pay of a janitor is considerably more than that of a teacher. Without reference as to whether janitors are suitably compensated or not—is this fair?

Let us have a few more figures in comparison. The bonus paid to teachers in 1918 was $5 per month for ten months 5.5 per cent of their salary. The bonus paid to janitors in 1918 was 13 per cent of their pay and supplies. The bonus declared for janitors covering the period to December 31, 1919 is 15 per cent of their salaries and supplies.

"Wisdom is the principal thing: therefore get wisdom." Our children are our future citizens. They must be taught. Their training, moral, physical, mental, is largely in the hands of the teacher. They are directly under her care for at least five hours a day. She is entirely responsible for them during that time and much is expected of her. Are not her services worth much more to us than we are paying at present?

Let us finish our Biblical quotation, "And with all thy getting get understanding." If you think the salaries are high, look into the real conditions. If you do not feel interested, investigate so as to **get** understanding. If you **are** interested, then work for the makers of our future citizens of Philadelphia.

JUST A POSSIBLE ECONOMY

The city's printing bill for the year 1919 will probably be not less than $400,000. This is a guess, based on the consumption of the commodity in years past. It is costly, isn't it?

The Philadelphia Commercial Museum finds it advisable to do all its own printing. The amount of its work is relatively small, in comparison with the official city work—but it figures that its saving *is not less than* 30 *per cent*—with more satisfactory service.

How about a little standardization in printing, through the medium of a city print shop?

CITIZENS' BUSINESS

BUREAU OF MUNICIPAL RESEARCH

ISSUED WEEKLY AT 805 FRANKLIN BANK BUILDING
PHILADELPHIA. ENTERED AS SECOND CLASS MATTER
JUNE 7, 1913 AT THE POST OFFICE AT PHILADELPHIA,
PA., UNDER THE ACT OF AUGUST 24TH, 1912—
SUBSCRIPTION FIFTY CENTS THE YEAR

Let the People Rule!

No. 347	January 16, 1919

> But let us not be so hypocritical as to assume that every citizen is a student of the intricate mechanics of government.
>
> Public opinion is not spontaneous—especially on technical issues. It will respond, but it must be given time.

It's In the Air

˷These days of activity along the lines of charter revision have brought out some wholesome and interesting discussion, and throughout the legislative session we shall doubtless be treated to a substantial volume of oratory, and a goodly quantity of printed matter relative to the changes proposed for Philadelphia's government.

An interesting turn has been given to the preliminary skirmishing by one of the influential political leaders, in an interview in which he declared that the adoption or rejection of any measures advocated would depend on whether a given proposal was desired by the people.

This is precisely what ought to determine— if we really believe in democracy.

Is This What He Wishes us to Infer?

No doubt the astute political leader in question counted on there being no definite "desire" in the majority of the community for any *specific* changes in our charter and sought to create the superficial inference that our people are *hostile* to a better machinery of municipal government.

Is this the fact? Decidedly no! People struggling for a livelihood or wrapped up in the homely concerns of everyday life have no opinions—or very few—on the principle of the short ballot, on theories of budget-making, on the intricacies of municipal contracts, on how the council should be formed. They have, however, a *general* desire to get what is broadly known as "good government" and will, we believe, respond to intelligent *and disinterested* leadership.

After any group or groups tell their story, after there has been abundant discussion, after each suggested change has been tested by searching criticism, the mass of citizens *will* have opinions, and it will then be in order to ascertain their approval or disapproval of the suggestions before them.

* * * * * *

Our prediction is that, given a fair opportunity to present its plan, given an honest discussion without "red herrings" and without insincerity, any group will receive widespread support for a great many fundamental charter improvements.

Let us see.

"A lot of people will pick up their 1913-14 thoughts right where they laid them down."— *New York Evening Sun.*

BUREAU OF MUNICIPAL RESEARCH

ISSUED WEEKLY AT 805 FRANKLIN BANK BUILDING
PHILADELPHIA, ENTERED AS SECOND CLASS MATTER.
JUNE 7, 1913 AT THE POST OFFICE AT PHILADELPHIA,
PA., UNDER THE ACT OF AUGUST 24TH, 1912 —
SUBSCRIPTION FIFTY CENTS THE YEAR~

Where is our School Survey?

No. 348   January 23, 1919

"You cannot run away from a weakness;
You must sometime fight it out or perish,
And if that be so,
Why not now and where you stand?"
                        —*Robert Louis Stevenson.*

Why Educate, Anyway?

The end of all real education is service. The public school is not only a means of preparing pupils for college, it is not only a means of producing a high grade of scholarship and culture. Scholarship as an end of education may be a high ideal, but it is an outlived ideal. Scholarship and culture are by-products, **service** is the true object of education. If a school turns out steady, honest, manly boys and sincere, self-reliant, capable girls, that school is a good school, no matter what it may do otherwise. On the other hand, a school that fails to turn out such graduates is a poor school, no matter what it may do from the view-point of scholarship. How does our public school system measure up to this standard of efficiency?

Are Our Schools Perfect?

In order to portray truly our school system we must have "a moving picture not a photograph." **A school system is alive,** and like all other living things, it is constantly growing, developing, changing. We must know not only where we were yesterday, and where we are to-day; but most important of all, whither we are going to-morrow. What is the present status of our schools? Have they made progress in the past few years? In which direction are they going; what are their present tendencies? We, the citizens of Philadelphia, have the **right** to ask such questions; indeed, it is our **duty** to ask them; and, moreover, **we should expect answers.** If our school system is perfect, if it is all that we can desire or expect, we have a right to know; if it is not all that we want or expect, we have just as much right to know that also.

Would not a school survey answer these questions?

But how are we to learn the condition of our school system? A school survey would be the most natural answer to this query. An investigation made by trained specialists would meet the needs—an investigation effective but sympathetic, one that would point out the **good** of our system as well as the **bad.** The need of a survey has been felt here in Philadelphia for some time. We feel it still more now, as we face an **increase in our school tax rate.** Before the Board of Education is allowed the expenditure of more money, it is only fair that it should show that our schools are managed efficiently, economically, and progressively.

Mislaid—the Philadelphia school survey

More than a year ago a school survey was suggested, a thorough investigation of the schools to be made by trained workers, preferably disinterested, outside persons, so that we might benefit by new ideas. Funds were even offered to finance such a survey. This offer, however, was ignored. The Board of Education took no action at all in regard to the matter. Why, we wonder. In spite of discouragement by the Board, agitation for the inquiry continued. Last April, in response to the demand of large groups of people, a committee of members of the Board of Education was appointed, ostensibly to conduct this survey. Such a committee, although it obviously cannot possibly have the wide and unprejudiced view-point of a group of disinterested outsiders, unquestionably might have done something; but although it was appointed last April, so far as the public has been permitted to know, it has done nothing.

Where is our school survey?

MEASURING EFFICIENCY

Not by the number of words per hour—
    By the expansion of the children's concepts.
Not by the scores of children promoted—
    By the soundness of convictions formed.
Not by the stiffness of children's backs—
    By the hearts resolved to fight the fight.
Not by the yards of dry red tape—
    By the feet that hasten to meet the dawn.
Not by the acres of compositions marked—
    By the diameter of broadened horizon.
Not by the ancient tales retold—
    By the dreams of youth come true.
                —The American Teacher.

CITIZENS' BUSINESS

BUREAU OF MUNICIPAL RESEARCH

ISSUED WEEKLY AT 805 FRANKLIN BANK BUILDING
PHILADELPHIA. ENTERED AS SECOND CLASS MATTER
JUNE 7,1913 AT THE POST OFFICE AT PHILADELPHIA,
PA.,UNDER THE ACT OF AUGUST 24TH,1912—
SUBSCRIPTION FIFTY CENTS THE YEAR

Whaddye mean

HOME RULE?

No. 349   January 30, 1919

*Slogans are often more effective than
arguments.*

Sometimes slogans mean something.

THE slogan of the Philadelphia Charter Committee contains a reference to "home rule" as one of the objects for which the Committee is fighting.

The Governor of Pennsylvania in his inaugural address said he favored for Philadelphia "a greater degree of home rule."

Surely the experiences and needs of American municipalities must incline forward-looking citizens to concur in these sentiments.

But what *is* "home rule"?

There has never been any *real* home rule for cities in our State, and no one has yet proposed, during the present movement at least, that any considerable amount of local autonomy be granted us.

The proposals thus far outlined are for the legislature to set up, in considerable detail, not only the *structure* of our local government, but to no inconsiderable extent the *procedure* as well.

*　*　*　*　*

This is not by way of objection to the present legislative program; the charter revision proposals thus far announced appeal to us as offering highly desirable gains in our local machinery.

But we would be unjust to the present program if we did not permit it to focus our attention on the need for *real* home rule.

In some states, municipalities are permitted to frame their own charters. The usual procedure is for the voters of the city to elect a charter convention, which draws up a charter. This proposed charter is submitted to the electors for ratification or rejection—similar to the usual procedure for constitutional revision.

For Philadelphia, after the Charter Committee has finished all its labors satisfactorily, the "new charter" still has to be fought through a legislature, the majority of whose members are rural. In these other American cities, when a work similar to that of the present Charter Committee has been finished to the satisfaction of the committee, or convention, it is voted on by the voters of the city, and if a majority of them approve of it, that constitutes its adoption.

Some will claim that so complete a degree of "self-determination" for Philadelphia is undesirable, or, at any rate, unobtainable. However that may be, this more genuine "home rule" is a matter important to be thinking about in these days of proposed drastic changes in our structure of local government.

Does the Soldier Want Patronage?

The numerous schemes afoot to give to soldiers special preference in governmental jobs upon their return to civilian life is looked upon as petty politics by the soldiers with whom the writer talked while serving with them overseas. Their principal objections may be enumerated as follows:

1. Having been in the greatest game in the world they are averse to being manipulated or advertised in the smaller, less noble game of partisan politics. A healthy indication of self-respect.

2. Anticipating the closer competition of the coming period of reconstruction, they want to establish their economic independence to insure themselves and their families against possible lean years. A mere salaried job without guarantee of advancement will not suffice.

3. Patronage is not wanted, particularly that patronage which regards only the fact that the man has served in the great war. He wants to forget it. He wants recognition, not of the soldier, but of the man.

4. The democracy for which he has been fighting has been under his examination. He wants and will demand that the servants of his democracy be the best obtainable by training and inclination—in order that efficient administration may lighten the public burden. He does not want to be a mere job-holder at the public expense.

Undoubtedly some soldiers are experiencing the pinch of existing circumstances, but what the soldier *wants* is his *own* job at a remuneration adequate to protect his family against a possible recurrence of present conditions.

Is he right?

CITIZENS' BUSINESS

BUREAU OF MUNICIPAL RESEARCH

ISSUED WEEKLY AT 805 FRANKLIN BANK BUILDING
PHILADELPHIA, ENTERED AS SECOND-CLASS MATTER
JUNE 7, 1913 AT THE POST OFFICE AT PHILADELPHIA,
PA., UNDER THE ACT OF AUGUST 24TH, 1912—
SUBSCRIPTION FIFTY CENTS THE YEAR

A Cure Worse than the Disease

No. 350   **February 6, 1919**

The Bureau of Municipal Research first printed
this message on THE POLICE IN POLITICS in
November, 1917. Proposals now before the public
seem to indicate that it is just as applicable today
as it was then. Maybe more so.

SOME thirty years ago champions of municipal reform were pointing out what they believed to be the solution of the whole question of corruption and inefficiency in city government. They held that if we only elected the *right men* to office, ALL our ills would cease and all our civic problems would be solved.

City after city had its wave of "reform," only to lead, in most cases, to bitter disappointment. Careful observers of the "good-man" type of reform have long since discarded it as inadequate. Goodness alone is not enough: there must be skill, technique, training, in public administration.

Other remedies have from time to time been tried. One of the most trusted of these has been legislative action by the states. These enactments were usually restrictive—on the theory that maladministration can be prevented by law.

Looking to the legislatures for statutes designed to insure good city government has also proved futile. Indeed, this way instead of merely proving inadequate has been of positive detriment, for all the carefully designed checks have proved to be drags when officials tried to do a good job, and in almost every large American city the best administrations have chafed under constitutional and statutory restrictions on the freedom of municipal action.

The arguments for home rule of cities are so numerous and so widely known that repetition is unnecessary.

A LOCAL APPLICATION

We have been having a bad dose of police in politics here in Philadelphia—or at least such is the judgment of all the newspapers, a large part of the police force itself, and of a number of discerning citizens.

Nobody defends police in politics—the director of public safety and the mayor insist that such conditions are contrary to their definite instructions.* Politicians of all shades of opinion outvie each other in protestations of horror at utilizing the police in such an illegal and immoral way, and certainly the great public does not desire that its paid protectors should divert their energies to other channels.

Hence it should seem easy, with such virtual unanimity of expression, to remove the police from politics *and keep them out.*

A suggested remedy—originating with the district attorney—that the police force be turned over to a commission outside the city government has certain surface appearances of a good proposal and has already met with considerable approval. *Let us look at it more closely.*

In the first place, such a commission would not, in our opinion, be possible of creation in view of Article III, Section 20, of the Constitution of 1873.

But aside from that, is such a move *desirable in itself,* regardless of legality or constitutionality? Would this be a step forward or a step sidewise? Mere *change* is not progress.

*Reprinted exactly as originally written (Nov. 8, 1917).

The most admirable feature of the Bullitt Bill is the concentration of power in the hands of the mayor, with the major municipal functions entrusted to *responsible department heads*. The experience of Philadelphia, as well as of most other American cities, bears witness to the superiority of this organization over those formerly in vogue, in which power and responsibility were deliberately diffused over a number of officials.

What reason have we to feel assured that in the years to come *Harrisburg* will give us a police administration less "political" than that which we have given *ourselves?* It certainly is plain that the municipal home rule for which so many of our citizens, and some of our best officials, have been pleading for years is here threatened with a serious setback. *We want less Harrisburg, not more!*

No amount of complicated governmental machinery can take the place of continuous, intelligent citizen interest, the kind that gets active on the prosaic, unspectacular, every-day matters of government. Instead of whirling like Charlie Chaplin from pillar to post in the hunt for a panacea and dodging the responsibility for failures in government, our citizens have got to buckle down and help and guide officials in the big job of making government a success.

* * * * * * * *

The way to keep an official on his good behavior is to fix responsibility on him and then turn on the non-partisan publicity.

CITIZENS' BUSINESS

BUREAU OF MUNICIPAL RESEARCH

ISSUED WEEKLY AT 805 FRANKLIN BANK BUILDING
PHILADELPHIA. ENTERED AS SECOND CLASS MATTER
JUNE 7, 1913 AT THE POST OFFICE AT PHILADELPHIA,
PA., UNDER THE ACT OF AUGUST 24TH, 1912 —
SUBSCRIPTION FIFTY CENTS THE YEAR.

What Should the 1918 Tax Rate Have Been?

No. 351   February 13, 1919

The $1.75 city rate produced more than four million dollars more revenue in 1918 than was needed to cover all of the city's expenses during the same year. A rate of $1.50 would have taken care of all of the expenses.

The Day of Reckoning

Now that the year 1918 is completely behind us, and the city's accounts for the year closed, and a preliminary report of the city's financial operations and condition presented to councils, the time is ripe for citizen-stockholders of our immense city-corporation to review the financial results of the past year's operations.

Our city is a huge business corporation organized for the common good. Unlike ordinary business corporations, it does not exist for the purpose of making monetary profits for its stockholders. Nevertheless, its financial operations are essentially the same as those of a railroad, a telephone company, a steel plant, or a department store.

Before a profit-seeking undertaking can show a profit for a given period it must obtain enough revenue, or earnings, or income, to cover all its expenses (including depreciation). In other words, it must maintain its net worth.

This brings us to what is, perhaps, the most important point to be watched in the city's fiscal operations.

Pay-as-You-Go.

It is contended—and admitted—on all sides that the city should pay-as-it-goes. Everyone seems to believe this to be the first canon of the city's financial program

But what is meant by pay-as-you-go? Like most popular slogans, this one does not define itself. Nevertheless, it is perfectly clear from the explanations that are elicited from time to time, and from the attempts that are made to force a pay-as-you-go policy, that it means obtaining sufficient revenue to cover expense—that is, to maintain the net worth.

The strong movement in various parts of the United States for limiting the term of bonds to the life of the assets acquired with the borrowed money is one of the many more or less crude means of seeing to it that expense is fully covered by revenue. The oft repeated assertion that the tax-payers should be required to pay for what they receive from the government is another form in which this slogan is defined.

It is obvious that cities, business undertakings, and individuals cannot be said to pay-as-they-go unless they avoid an impairment of their net worth. Maintaining net worth means simply obtaining sufficient revenue to cover expense—replacing expired value by earnings or income. Ordinary business undertakings recognize this without question. Cities and other governments are beginning to recognize it also.

Did We?

Let us now see whether in 1918 the city paid-as-it-went. Let us see whether or not the revenues equalled the expenses. An examination of the city controller's preliminary annual report for 1918, issued to councils on February 6, shows that *the city's revenue exceeded the city's expenses by more than $4,000,000.* In other words, the city not only lived up to a strict pay-as-you-go policy during 1918, but it *"got ahead"* by *more than $4,000,000.*

In view of the fact that in many previous years the city habitually got behind, this is a good showing. Of course, it is well to bear in mind that the city tax rate has been increased from $1.00 in 1916 to $1.75 in 1918.

If we assume that the city should have aimed

simply to obtain enough revenue to cover expense and not attempt to pile up an increased inheritance for future generations—an inference to be drawn from the attitude of a great many taxpayers when the tax rate was fixed—the city in effect levied $4,000,000 more taxes than it should have done. This more than $4,000,000 of taxes represents one-seventh of the taxes raised by the $1.75 rate and therefore is equivalent to twenty-five cents in the tax rate. *Had the city levied a tax just sufficient to provide revenue enough to meet expenses the tax rate would have been $1.50 instead of $1.75.*

A Question of Policy.

This Bureau is not advocating that the city limit itself to the securing of sufficient revenue to cover its expenses. A more exacting standard should, perhaps, be adopted and adhered to. The city positively ought not to be satisfied with any *less exacting standard.* It should see to it that its revenues at least equal its expenses. And what is of equal importance, the city should set up its policy in terms that are self-explanatory and that insure accomplishing the results sought.

One of the greatest boons to civil life that has thus far come out of the war is the excellent wartime repression of venereal disease and control of vice in civil communities. There is danger now that this control may relax if organized public opinion is not brought to bear in favor of strict law enforcement by all local authorities. The National Municipal League, the Council of National Defence, and a dozen more national organizations of dignity, conservatism and importance realize the gravity of the situation. Let Philadelphia, and Philadelphians, do their part!

CITIZENS' BUSINESS

BUREAU OF MUNICIPAL RESEARCH

ISSUED WEEKLY AT 805 FRANKLIN BANK BUILDING
PHILADELPHIA-ENTERED AS SECOND CLASS MATTER
JUNE 7, 1913 AT THE POST OFFICE AT PHILADELPHIA,
PA., UNDER THE ACT OF AUGUST 24TH, 1912—
SUBSCRIPTION FIFTY CENTS THE YEAR-

Borrow or Tax?

No. 352   **February 20, 1919**

Should the city borrow for current expenses?
Should the city borrow for non-self-supporting under-
    takings?
Should the city borrow at all?

THE Director of City Transit, in a recent address, sounded a note of warning against the present tendency in public finance to borrow for all kinds of public improvements.

According to the almost universally approved policies of recent years, the Director's position is rank heterodoxy and as such should receive an exposure of its error, or else it should prove a challenge to our present assumptions.

The *minimum* standard for the conduct of public business is that the municipal corporation, or other unit, shall not lose ground financially—that it shall not impair its *net worth*.

This minimum standard has been interpreted by many as meeting the requirements of a "pay-as-you-go" policy, as we made clear in CITIZENS' BUSINESS No. 351—February 13. And being content with such a minimum standard is by no means wholly without reasonable argument in its favor. In its behalf it is urged that it is unfair to charge the taxpayers of the *current* generation with the entire cost of property which *future* generations also will enjoy.

Is It Wrong to Borrow?

Now, there is no absolute right or wrong to the latter widely-accepted doctrine. So long as the city's capital or accumulated net property is left intact, it is a matter of policy to determine whether or not we shall *add* each year to our inheritance, and if so, *how much?*

Our view is that there are a number of factors to be taken into consideration when deciding upon a borrowing or non-borrowing policy for financing improvements.

The question of the nature of the proposed capital improvements—whether, for instance, they are utilities of a self-supporting character—is an important factor.

Then, the question of whether the existing debt is already large and whether it is burdensome, should be considered.

The money market and the relative advantages or disadvantages of floating securities on particular terms at any given time are matters that should play a part in making the final decision.

Above all, it must not be forgotten that interest on debt is, except during construction, *pure expense*. Whether that expense is more desirable than higher immediate taxes is the question to be decided.

Citizens Must Think

While no hard and fast rule can be laid down that will be applicable to all cases, the conservative policy would seem to lean toward the views of the transit director, that we are too much inclined to borrow.

The questions raised are among the most important that the public has to answer. They cannot be answered without a serious effort to understand our huge city-corporation in all its relations.

―――――――――――――――――――――

"It is a shame that here where liberty was cradled, the city should still be in the cradle stage."—F. B. Barnes, in Philadelphia *Public Ledger*.

CITIZENS' BUSINESS

BUREAU OF MUNICIPAL RESEARCH

ISSUED WEEKLY AT 805 FRANKLIN BANK BUILDING
PHILADELPHIA. ENTERED AS SECOND CLASS MATTER
JUNE 7, 1913 AT THE POST OFFICE AT PHILADELPHIA,
PA., UNDER THE ACT OF AUGUST 24TH, 1912—
SUBSCRIPTION FIFTY CENTS THE YEAR

A Lesson from the Fee Grab

No. 353   February 27, 1919

If Philadelphia city and county were one in *law* as they are in *fact*, there would have been no decision perpetuating the obnoxious fee system in our midst.

The Supreme Court's Verdict

The Supreme Court of Pennsylvania has spoken. Very reluctantly but none the less positively it has declared unconstitutional the law of 1913 which was designed to prevent an enormous flow of public funds, in the form of fees, into the private purse of the register of wills. Had this law been upheld, a moderate salary would have been substituted for the ancient method of payment by fees, and the public treasury would have been better off by approximately $200,000—an amount that would pay the mayor's salary for sixteen years. And that still does not take account of the future savings that would have been effected.

The Fiction of Separate County Government

It is not our present purpose to quarrel with the court; though that legal minds could come to different conclusions regarding this matter is shown by the dissenting opinion of one of the justices. We do wish to point out, however, that this decision might have been far otherwise had it not been for the absurd fiction of separate county government in Philadelphia.

The point that proved fatal to the law in question is that it ran counter to the constitutional provision against local or special legislation. Although general in its language, the law was, in fact, limited to Philadelphia county by the simple device of confining its application to counties containing a population of 1,500,000 and upwards. We are continually legislating for Philadelphia city by means of this device, but in the opinion of the court we cannot do so for the county. Had the register of wills been a "city" official the law would have been constitutional; since he is legally a "county" official the law has been held unconstitutional.

A Constitutional Obstacle to Home Rule

If the immediate item of community edification is the folly of this city-county fiction, the second item is the folly of having to regulate this kind of thing by state legislation at all.

Many of our citizens have long felt the need of greater home rule for Philadelphia. Government via Harrisburg has proved too round-about and generally unsatisfactory. Now, we are reminded that there are local affairs that even the legislature at Harrisburg has difficulty in regulating for us. In those departments of Philadelphia's government that happen to be "county" departments we are restrained from making adjustments, not merely by an uninterested state legislature, but by the constitution itself.

The Lesson

An important lesson to be drawn from all this is that we cannot have complete home rule in Philadelphia until our state constitution is amended. There is no good reason why a community in which city and county are coterminous should continue the fiction of two governments, but under the present state constitution these governments cannot be unified, nor can any changes in structure be made, even by the legislature, in the "county" government.

Let us therefore begin at the earliest possible moment to amend the constitution and get real home rule for Philadelphia.

I am a public employe and have been for a number of years, and I resent any statement made that I cannot be as efficient or as competent working for a municipality as I can for a private corporation.

—Ira W. Jayne, Superintendent of Detroit Recreation Commission, before the League of Michigan Municipalities.

BUREAU OF MUNICIPAL RESEARCH

ISSUED WEEKLY AT 805 FRANKLIN BANK BUILDING
PHILADELPHIA. ENTERED AS SECOND CLASS MATTER
JUNE 7, 1913 AT THE POST OFFICE AT PHILADELPHIA,
PA., UNDER THE ACT OF AUGUST 24TH, 1912 —
SUBSCRIPTION FIFTY CENTS THE YEAR

To Save Money—
But With Better Service

No. 354   March 6, 1919

This is not a brief for abolishing counties
everywhere. It is merely an attempt to utilize
for our city the benefits of certain experiences
in other communities.

Needless Complexity

Our dual system of city and county administration confuses the public mind, disorders the management of public affairs, and checks at the outset many improvements in local government. The worst part of it is that the distinction, from the standpoint of the citizen, is purely imaginary.

Counties Were Needed

County government, anyway, started as a unit of local government brought over from England in a day when all government was overwhelmingly rural; and the creation of counties in the United States ever since then has gone on that same assumption. Counties were organized to apply government to more or less sparsely settled regions where the chief business of government was to act as the state's local agent in performing state functions.

Conditions Changed

As urban areas grew up, city governments were formed to handle the special needs of the congested districts. But the scheme of county government was left unaltered.

So long as a city remained but a small part of its county the confusion was not serious. But when a city spreads over almost an entire county, and contains the majority of the population, problems and difficulties accumulate.

When—as in the case of Philadelphia—city and county are coterminous, and the county has lost its rural administrative characteristics and taken on many functions of ordinary municipal government and when the separate county organization is no longer founded on anything but legal phrases and political expediency, then the need of city and county consolidation, in both law and fact, becomes self-evident and essential.

Not Philadelphia Alone

The confusion is not confined to Philadelphia. It has come up elsewhere—Denver, St. Louis, Baltimore, San Francisco—and has been met and solved. And now comes news of a proposed constitutional amendment for our neighboring state of Ohio.

The proposal will, if adopted, free the entire state from the plaster of inflexible uniform county government, and will, in addition, permit the voters in counties of 200,000 and over to abolish any or all existing local governments within the county and substitute a single unified city-county government.

If Good for the "Sixth City," Why Not for the Third?

In Cleveland and Cuyahoga County, where the chief consolidation project is to be effected, the Civic League of Cleveland describes the issue thus:

To be substituted for:

$$\left.\begin{array}{rl} 1 & \text{county} \\ 3 & \text{cities} \\ 32 & \text{villages} \\ 16 & \text{townships} \\ 41 & \text{school districts} \end{array}\right\} 1 \text{ city-county.}$$

Beside an estimated saving of 20% in cost of administration (an estimate based on Denver's actual experience), Cleveland expects to avoid confusion of authority, to secure definiteness of responsibility and to promote administrative cooperation throughout the whole urban area.

Why are *we* so lax? When shall we hear the good news of a constitutional amendment in Pennsylvania, under which Philadelphia city and county can really be made one organization, free from the enormity that now stands in the way of effective government; free from the absurdity of duties of *city* administration performed by officials who are not city officials; free from civil-service dodging; free from conditions under which a discharged city employe can change his desk in City Hall and appear, when the smoke blows away, as an employe of the "county" of Philadelphia.

"Not only is eternal vigilance the price of liberty, eternal struggle is the price of liberty."—*Elihu Root.*

CITIZENS' BUSINESS

BUREAU OF MUNICIPAL RESEARCH

ISSUED WEEKLY AT 805 FRANKLIN BANK BUILDING
PHILADELPHIA, ENTERED AS SECOND CLASS MATTER.
JUNE 7,1913 AT THE POST OFFICE AT PHILADELPHIA,
PA.,UNDER THE ACT OF AUGUST 24TH,1912—
SUBSCRIPTION FIFTY CENTS THE YEAR.

1919 Charter Series: No. 1

'erfecting the Merit System

No. 355   March 13, 1919

If civil service is good for the city of
Philadelphia, why isn't it good for the
county of Philadelphia?

O NE of the important features of the new charter measure now before the state legislature is the proposal to strengthen and to extend the scope of the merit system in Philadelphia. In obtaining a clear understanding of this feature of the new charter, the following brief statement may be helpful:

1. The Merit System Extended to County Departments

The present law regulating the civil service of Philadelphia applies only to the departments directly under the mayor and to the office of the city solicitor. The one other "city" department—the receiver of taxes—was exempted from civil service by special legislation. The present law does not apply to any of the county departments; nor does it apply to departments in the twilight zone between county status and mayoral jurisdiction, such as the Fairmount Park commission.

If the proposals of the Charter Revision committee are adopted, all city and county departments, including those in the twilight zone, are brought under civil service. In order to avoid constitutional difficulties, the county civil service is provided for in a separate bill.

2. A Single Commissioner Chosen by the City Council

The present civil service law is administered by a commission of three members appointed by the mayor for overlapping terms of five years and removable at the pleasure of the mayor.

The proposed law will be administered by a

single commissioner, chosen for a term of four years by a two-thirds vote of all the members elected to the city council. Under the provisions of the county civil service bill, he will serve as ex-officio county civil service commissioner.

3. "Thumbs Down" on Juggling

The present law requires the civil service commission to submit the names of four eligible persons for a single vacancy. This permits of wider choice by the appointing officer than experience has shown to be necessary and it opens the way to favoritism.

Under the proposed law only two names will be submitted for a single vacancy.

4. Extension of the Trial-Board Idea

At the present time no policeman or fireman may be dismissed from the service without a right to be heard before a court of trial, composed of members of his department, of equal or superior rank. No such protection, however, is accorded other city or county employes.

Under the proposed law, not only policemen and firemen, but all employes who come within the scope of civil service provisions will have the right to be heard before a trial board designated by the civil service commissioner. The decision of this board, when approved by the commissioner, is binding upon the appointing officer. In case of a decision of dismissal, however, the accused employe may, within ten days, appeal to the Court of Common Pleas for a new hearing in this court.

The Shern act makes it unlawful for city employes to take active part in politics and provides that in case any employe violates this act he shall be dismissed either by the mayor or by his superior officer. Since political activity on the part of city employees is usually in response to the desire of their superior officers it has proved an ineffective method to leave the enforcement of the law entirely in the hands of these officers.

Under the proposed law a violation of the provisions against political activity is punishable, not only by dismissal, but also by fine and imprisonment; and the enforcement of the law is strengthened by giving any taxpayer the right to go into court and by writ of mandamus to compel dismissal.

Standardization of Salaries and Grades

The proposed civil service law also provides for a standardization of salaries and grades in the city and county service. This is in line with the general trend throughout the country to create more equitable conditions of employment in the public service.

"The budget provides a means through which citizens may assure themselves that their effort which has been diverted to community ends, is not used for private gain, is not misused nor frittered away.

"Above and beyond its relation to economy and efficiency in public affairs the budget may be made one of the most potent instruments of democracy."—*A. R. Hatton.*

BUREAU OF MUNICIPAL RESEARCH

ISSUED WEEKLY AT 805 FRANKLIN BANK BUILDING
PHILADELPHIA. ENTERED AS SECOND CLASS MATTER
JUNE 7, 1913 AT THE POST OFFICE AT PHILADELPHIA,
PA. UNDER THE ACT OF AUGUST 24TH, 1912—
SUBSCRIPTION FIFTY CENTS A YEAR

1919 Charter Series: No. 2

Bringing the Bullitt Bill Down to Date

| 356 | March 20, 1919 |

The best executive machinery that can be devised is not too good for Philadelphia.

CHANGES

in the Executive Structure of
PHILADELPHIA'S GOVERNMENT
proposed by the Charter Revision Bill

---

1. A purchasing agent supersedes the department of supplies.

2. A city architect is established.

3. A department of public welfare is created.

4. The bureau of health becomes a department.

5. The city solicitor is to be appointed by the mayor.

6. The city treasurer is to be the receiver of taxes.

7. The city controller is given entire charge of the city's bookkeeping system.

A MONG the most interesting and important of the changes proposed by the charter revision bill are those dealing with the structure of the executive departments. Although these changes are comparatively few, they cover nearly all the points where improvements can be effected in the absence of constitutional revision and go a long way toward bringing the framework of our city government into line with modern municipal practice. Let us consider them briefly.

Purchasing Put in Its Proper Place

The bill abolishes the department of supplies and vests its functions in a purchasing agent appointed by the mayor under civil service rules. The present department of supplies is a misfit. Created to do the city's purchasing, an important but after all not a major job, it nevertheless was placed on an equality with the other departments. The inconsistency of classing the head of the purchasing service with the heads of such departments as public safety and public works is apparent and is removed by the new bill. A supplementary bill extends the unified purchasing system to the "county" departments by making the city purchasing agent ex officio purchasing agent for the "county." The distinction is rendered necessary by constitutional restrictions.

A City Architect

A city architect is established by the bill. Like the purchasing agent he is to be appointed by the mayor under civil service rules. He is to take over all the routine architectural work of the city. The more important architectural jobs may, however, be handled by outside architects specially chosen by the city architect with the approval of the mayor. Besides coordinating a highly specialized part of the city's work now widely scattered among the departments, this arrangement will undoubtedly effect a considerable saving in money.

Welfare Activities Centralized

At present the more distinctly social welfare activities of the city are scattered among various departments and boards. The bureau of correction in the department of public safety has control of the house of correction at Holmesburg. The bureau of charities, of the department of public health and charities, manages the general hospital and almshouse. The board of recreation has charge of playgrounds and other recreational activities. Under the plan proposed by the charter bill all of these activities are to be placed under a department of public welfare. This department may be authorized by council to take over other welfare activities also. The creation of this department is in line with modern practice in many cities, notably Kansas City and Dayton. In all of these cities very beneficial results have followed the establishment of welfare departments.

Bureau of Health Becomes a Department `

The creation of the department of public welfare leaves the bureau of health as the only bureau in the present department of public health and charities. The bureau is a very large one, containing several divisions—medical inspection, housing and sanitation, dispensaries, vital statistics, child hygiene, food inspection laboratories, and contagious disease hospitals—and is of sufficient importance to be a separate department. The bill accomplishes this, at the same time abolishing the present department of public health and charities.

An Appointive City Solicitor

About election time there is always a great

deal of criticism of our blanket ballot and the great number of offices our voters are called on to fill. To help remedy this generally admitted evil the charter bill provides that the city solicitor, heretofore an elected officer, shall be appointed by the mayor, subject to confirmation by council. In addition to shortening the ballot this change makes for closer cooperátion between the city solicitor and the mayor, whose confidential legal adviser he is. The separate election of the city sòlicitor might easily prevent an effective administration of the city's business, by making it possible to have a city solicitor not in harmony with the mayor, or perhaps even politically opposed to him.

City Treasurer to be Receiver of Taxes

A study of the office of the receiver of taxes makes it clear that there is no real need for its existence as a separate department. It has no discretionary or custodial responsibilities and serves merely as a sort of conduit through which the money received flows daily to the city treasury. And a great deal of money (in 1917 over $8,000,000 exclusive of loan funds) does not go to the receiver of taxes at all but is paid directly to the city treasurer. Under the charter bill the city treasurer, after the expiration of the term of the present receiver of taxes, takes over the functions of the receiver of taxes, and is charged with the receipt as well as with the custody of all city funds. This consolidation is doubly advantageous, for, in addition to effecting an obvious saving of time and money, it helps to shorten the ballot.

City Controller to Have Charge of all City Bookkeeping

The charter bill gives the city controller entire charge of the accounts of all city departments. All city employes engaged in keeping these accounts are to be under his supervision and control. This provision makes it possible for the city to have a really unified accounting system under the control of the chief accounting officer, and will eliminate considerable duplication and make possible real progress in city accounting methods and further saving to the city.

This is but extending to our city government—which, after all, is a huge and complex business undertaking—the same kind of simplification and supervision of accounting and financial records that has proved invaluable in private business.

"A plural council is as valuable a guarantee of salvation in Philadelphia as a plural marriage in Utah."

—Zueblin.

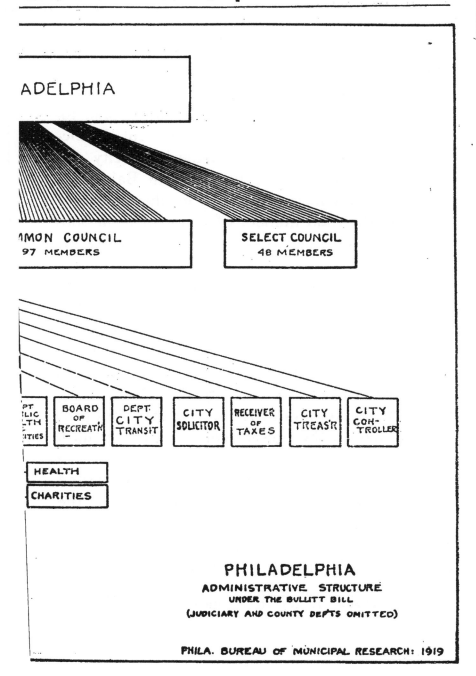

ADELPHIA

MON COUNCIL
97 MEMBERS

SELECT COUNCIL
48 MEMBERS

PT
LIC
TH
TIES

BOARD
OF
RECREATN

DEPT.
CITY
TRANSIT

CITY
SOLICITOR

RECEIVER
OF
TAXES

CITY
TREAS'R

CITY
CON-
TROLLER

HEALTH

CHARITIES

PHILADELPHIA
ADMINISTRATIVE STRUCTURE
UNDER THE BULLITT BILL
(JUDICIARY AND COUNTY DEP'TS OMITTED)

PHILA. BUREAU OF MUNICIPAL RESEARCH: 1919

"COUNCILS"

PROGRESS in Philadelphia for many years has been retarded by the city's unwieldy two-chambered system of councils. Philadelphia to-day shares with Baltimore the doubtful distinction of being the only large American* city still clinging to that system, and even in Baltimore, where the system is prescribed by the state constitution, the total number of councilmen in both branches is only 37 as compared with Philadelphia's 145.

Acting often as a check and obstruction to meritorious measures but never preventing the passage of iniquities such as the gas steal of 1905, the two-chambered system has long since demonstrated its absolute uselessness as far as municipal affairs are concerned. Recognizing this fact, the authors of the new charter bill propose to abolish the present councils and set up a single city legislative body with a greatly reduced membership. The new council is to be elected from the existing state senatorial districts on the basis of one councilman for every 20,000 assessed voters in each district. Based on 1918 figures this will give us a council of 21 members.

*To the best of our knowledge, the two-chambered city council is unknown in any other nation of the world.

We believe that there is a danger in making a city council too small to be really representative. This danger, however, has been avoided by the charter revisionists. Whether the system of election from senatorial districts, or from any other territorial districts, will prove satisfactory or not remains to be seen. It may be that further changes in the method of electing councilmen will become necessary. But, taken by and large, the councilmanic proposals of the charter revision bill are a great step in advance and will prove very beneficial to the city. One feature alone, the abolition of the two-chambered "councils," is indispensable to further municipal progress in Philadelphia.

Why not try a model 1919 council? At present we are using a model of 1796!

* * *

Think!

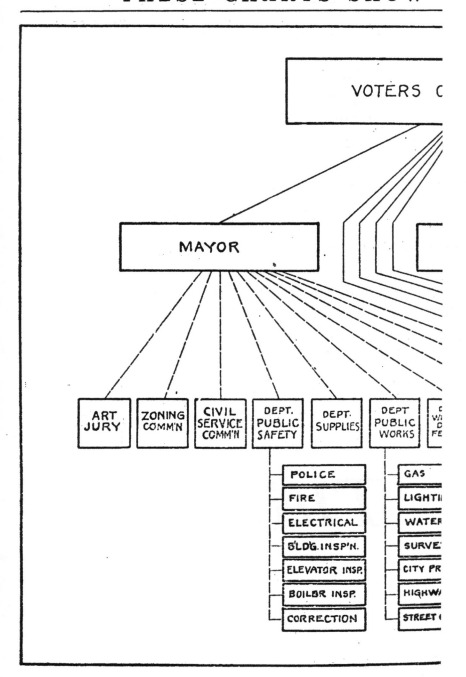

VOTERS

MAYOR

ART JURY

ZONING COMM'N

CIVIL SERVICE COMM'N

DEPT. PUBLIC SAFETY

DEPT. SUPPLIES

DEPT PUBLIC WORKS

POLICE

FIRE

ELECTRICAL

BLDG. INSP'N.

ELEVATOR INSP.

BOILER INSP.

CORRECTION

GAS

LIGHTI

WATER

SURVE

CITY PR

HIGHW

STREET

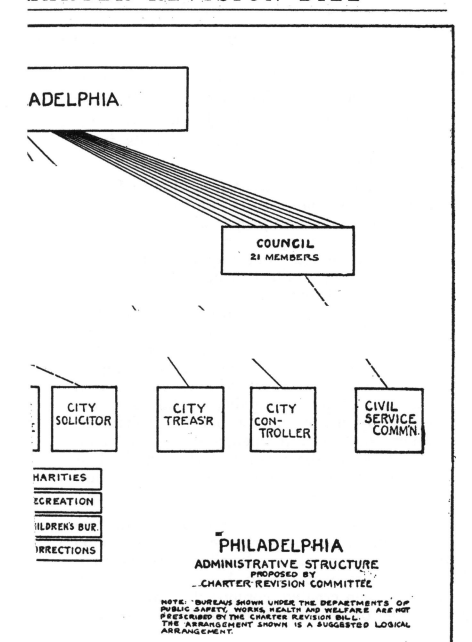

ADELPHIA.

COUNCIL
21 MEMBERS

CITY
SOLICITOR

CITY
TREAS'R

CITY
CON-
TROLLER

CIVIL
SERVICE
COMM'N.

HARITIES

ECREATION

HILDREN'S BUR.

ORRECTIONS

PHILADELPHIA
ADMINISTRATIVE STRUCTURE
PROPOSED BY
CHARTER REVISION COMMITTEE

NOTE: BUREAUS SHOWN UNDER THE DEPARTMENTS OF
PUBLIC SAFETY, WORKS, HEALTH AND WELFARE ARE NOT
PRESCRIBED BY THE CHARTER REVISION BILL.
THE ARRANGEMENT SHOWN IS A SUGGESTED LOGICAL
ARRANGEMENT.

PHILA. BUREAU OF MUNICIPAL RESEARCH: 1919

DAYTON'S DEPARTMEN

THE city of Dayton has established a Department of Public Welfare under its city manager. In the new charter of January 1, 1914, the Department issues a statement of its functions, in which it says:

> This charter was written by those who believe that human nature, under proper environment and with proper direction and encouragement is capable of far greater efficiency and service and happiness than has ever yet been attained in human experience. It is believed that it is the duty of a municipality to concern itself with the special problems of human life and community efficiency and betterment, just as well as with questions of safety, transportation facilities, good streets, etc. The result of such an effort on the part of a municipality, if honestly and efficiently made, cannot but be fruitful of much good to all the people of the city, both in respect to the raising of the standard of human efficiency, and the increase of community patriotism.

. . . The Division of Recreation administers the playgrounds in the parks and by cooperation with other organizations distributes playground facilities where needed. An Advisory Recreation Board has been created, composed of fifteen representatives of the Department of Public Welfare,

⸢ PUBLIC WELFARE

the Public Schools, and the Dayton Playgrounds and Gardens Association. In 1914 the public schools maintained eight playgrounds in their school yards; the city maintained six playgrounds; and the Playgrounds and Gardens Association twelve, each organization paying the supervisor of its playgrounds. The attendance for ten weeks was 200,000. The division also provided two life-savers, one beach guard, and one swimming instructor at the bathing beach on Island Park. The other park functions are in charge of the Division of Parks.

The Division of Corrections has established a municipal lodging house for men and its equivalent in the "Door of Hope" for women. It has transformed the workhouse, eliminating contract work and employing men on public works, including work on parks, levees, streets, municipal buildings, and workhouse gardens. The entire installation of the municipal lodging house was done by workhouse inmates. The food of the police station is prepared by them. It is self-supporting. There are also Divisions of Poor Relief and Municipal Employment. The Public Welfare Department has followed the example of Kansas City in organizing a Division of Legal Aid, which takes care of seventy-two cases a month. In 1914 of those aided 535 were white Americans, 96 negroes, and 93 foreign born.

—Charles Zueblin in *American Municipal Progress*. Published by Macmillan Co.

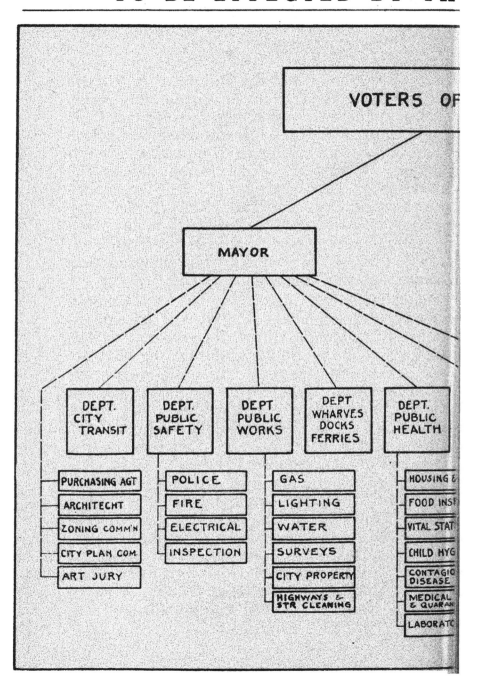

ᴄITIZENS' BUSINESS

BUREAU OF MUNICIPAL RESEARCH

ISSUED WEEKLY AT 805 FRANKLIN BANK BUILDING
PHILADELPHIA—ENTERED AS SECOND CLASS MATTER.
JUNE 7, 1913 AT THE POST OFFICE AT PHILADELPHIA,
PA., UNDER THE ACT OF AUGUST 24TH, 1912—
SUBSCRIPTION FIFTY CENTS THE YEAR·

1919 Charter Series: No. 3

Tin-Box Financing

ɔ. 357   March 27, 1919

The remedy: Metropolitan purse-strings for Father Penn

NO ORGANIZATION that requires money for its support can remain successful unless it keeps its expenses within its income.

The householder who does not do this, eats up his resources or goes into debt. The commercial enterprise that does not do it, courts failure. The lodge, or church, or city government, that does not do it, imposes unnecessary burdens on its members, and loses its power to render the service to which they are entitled.

It would seem that the very first thing to be accomplished in adjusting Father Penn's purse strings would be to enable him to keep track of his revenue and expense, and correlate them so that he can keep his expense within his revenue— seeing to it, of course, that his revenue is sufficient to meet the cost of the service which he wants to render.

Yet the financial legislation under which he has operated since 1879 does not set up a standard of revenue and expense. It sets up a standard of *receipts* and *disbursements*—that is, cash received and cash paid out.

Finance Deals with More than Cash

Now, cash has no fixed relation whatever to a person's, or a city's, financial position. A man can have thousands of dollars in the bank and still be a subject for the bankruptcy court. On the other hand, we have heard of a millionaire being put off a street car because he did not have a nickel with him.

So it has come to pass that Philadelphia, while operating on the cash receipts and disbursements basis set up by the Act of 1879, has year after year failed to live within its income. As a result, it has borrowed, on bonds, millions of dollars for policemen's and firemen's salaries, pens, pencils, soap, coal, junkets, and almost every conceivable kind of current expense, for which we of the present have no value. So long as cash is on hand to meet bills that fall due, the requirements of the present system are met: it makes no difference whether the cash represents revenue or borrowed money, or whether all the year's bills are "in" or not.

Earmarking "Funds"

By reason of this scheme of financing, a second expensive evil is present: namely, the splitting up of the city's cash into thousands of parts, and the actual setting aside or earmarking of these parts, or funds. If $500,000 has been set aside for certain work that some bureau plans to undertake toward the end of the year, and if, meanwhile, some other bureau needs an extra $500,000 for an emergency, and no funds remain unappropriated, the

3

$500,000 that is temporarily idle cannot be drawn upon. The city must either divert this cash permanently from its original purpose; or go out and borrow money, paying nearly twice as much interest as it receives on its idle deposit. Did you ever hear of a householder scouring the neighborhood for a quarter for his gas meter just because the quarter he had in the house had been ''set aside'' for next week's newspapers? Especially if his neighbor charges interest for lending him the quarter?

Unless the privilege of living in Philadelphia is to become a financial burden, these two expensive evils must be corrected: the annual budget must be made up on the basis of revenue and expense instead of the basis of cash; and the city's cash, instead of being set aside in separate funds like children's pennies in so many toy banks, must be mobilized as a great reserve unit, any available part of which may be sent into any sector where cash is needed.

These evils are corrected by the Budget Article of the Charter Revision Bill.

The Remedy in the Charter Revision Bill

The Article provides that, on the basis of information and suggestions from all the various department heads, the Mayor, as chief executive of the city, responsible for the city's executive program, shall submit to the City Council, by October 15, a budget, including his statement of the revenue and expense of the current and preceding years, the assets, liabilities and net worth of the city, a suggested program of work for the coming year, his estimates of the revenue and expense of the coming year, and his plan for financing his program.

At the same time, he must submit his budget to the City Controller in order that his figures may be audited, and that the financial experience of the city's chief fiscal officer may be at the disposal of Council, as that is the body to determine upon the adoption of the Mayor's program.

As for Council, that body is free to take whatever action it believes desirable. It may accept the Mayor's suggestions as they stand; it may increase or decrease any item; it may strike out any item or add any additional one; it may, if it chooses, take the Mayor's recommendations merely as a point of departure; for Council is the policy-determining body of the city, and is to have the right to determine finally the city's program of work and finance for each year.

Wherein the Buck Cannot be Passed

But the Article requires Council, in the course of its deliberations on the budget, to hold open public hearings. It requires, also, that by December 1, Council shall fix the tax rates for the ensuing year;

that the rates shall produce enough revenue, together with the revenue from all other sources, to cover the estimated expense of the coming year and the deficit (if any) of the current year. The ordinance that fixes the tax rates must show how those rates were arrived at. This is accomplished by setting forth, among other things, the deficit (if any) of the preceding year, the revenue and expense and surplus or deficit of the current year, the estimated expense of the coming year, and the estimated revenue from taxation and other sources to meet that expense.

Common Sense about "Appropriations"

The Article finds a way out of a difficulty under which cities have labored from time immemorial, namely, the practical impossibility of trying to settle in advance upon all the details of a year's financial program, or to foresee all the needs of each of the departments during a coming year. "Appropriation" ordinances therefore have worked great inequalities by giving some departments too much and others too little for their actual needs. The charter revision bill makes it unnecessary for Council, so long as it has adopted a general program for the year, immediately to settle all details. The authorizations to the several departments to incur the liability incident to the carrying on of their work may be made from time to time and for whatever

6

ength of time it seems desirable. The expectation is that Council will keep within the program it has adopted. If it fails to keep expenses within revenues, a deficit results, and the bill provides that the amount of the deficit shall be set forth in cold figures in the next year's budget estimates and shall have priority over the next year's expenses. Deficits are therefore prevented from accumulating and the public is enabled to judge each deficit on its merits, and to know definitely to what year and what Administration a deficit is chargeable.

It is also made possible to begin a piece of work or enter into a long term contract, without having to provide for the whole cost in the first year's tax levy; and it is made possible for the fiscal officer of the city to pay, when they fall due, any bills that have been legally incurred, with any money that is then available, without any special transfer by ordinance, thereby opening the way to the cutting down of unnecessary interest charges and the elimination of the expensive process of buying against hoped-for future appropriations. Frequently now, when a department's appropriation for a given purpose is exhausted, the only way an article can be obtained is by asking the dealer to deliver it at his own price, in the hope of getting his money in the future—a species of "government by donation" that costs Philadelphia considerably.

Getting Somewhere in City Finance

This Article, if enacted into law, will force the city to live up to a strict "pay-as-you-go" policy. It will require each year's provisions to be made on the basis of real income and expense. It will effectually eliminate borrowing for current expenses. It will make it impossible for deficits to be overlooked, hidden or accumulated, because they must be stated and each one must be met at the beginning of the following year. It will greatly curtail the mandamus evil. It will link the city's finances up with its accounting system and thus make it possible to derive from that system the kind of benefit for which accounting exists, and which a similar and equally costly system in a private business would be required to furnish.

It will put a final quietus on tin-box financing, and put the city of Philadelphia on the only basis on which a "going concern"—whether a common-sense corner merchant or a Bell Telephone Company—can remain financially sound.

Said Gladstone:

"Budgets are not merely affairs of arithmetic, but in a thousand ways go to the root of prosperity of individuals, the relation of classes and the strength of nations."

CITIZENS' BUSINESS

BUREAU OF MUNICIPAL RESEARCH

ISSUED WEEKLY AT 805 FRANKLIN BANK BUILDING
PHILADELPHIA. ENTERED AS SECOND CLASS MATTER.
JUNE 7,1913 AT THE POST OFFICE AT PHILADELPHIA,
PA.,UNDER THE ACT OF AUGUST 24TH,1912 —
SUBSCRIPTION FIFTY CENTS THE YEAR.

1919 Charter Series: No. 4

'ending to Our Own Business

No. 358   **April 3, 1919**

Greater home rule is one of the main ends sought in the proposed new charter.

The article on contracts retains the home rule principle. At the same time its effect, if enacted, would undoubtedly be to establish municipal street-cleaning and waste disposal in lieu of the contract system.

A GREAT many thoughtful people oppose the doctrine of government ownership or operation. They believe that as little as possible should be done by the city or other governmental unit and as much as possible by private endeavor. And there are undoubtedly many weighty and convincing arguments to support this position.

There are a number of activities, however, which every public-spirited citizen will readily agree should be carried on directly by the city. Take the prevention of crime, for example. We venture to state that there is not a citizen of Philadelphia who would not agree that the policing of the city should be done by government.

Fire protection is another matter that is generally conceded to be a proper function of the government of the city, and even the supplying of water, which on its face appears to be an ordinary public utility, has, largely because of its intimate relation to public health, almost universally been taken over as a municipal function.

So also with many other activities. Everywhere the tendency has been to "municipalize" all activities which directly and vitally affect the safety and health of all the citizens.

Philadelphia is not a laggard in this respect. Our city has kept abreast of others in taking over functions which vitally affect the people.

In one thing, however, Philadelphia is far behind the rest. The city stands out conspicuously as almost the only large city in the country that does not clean its own streets or remove its own ashes, rubbish and garbage. We in Philadelphia still cling to the old method of having this work done by contract, a method discarded by most of the other large cities of the country, including New York, Chicago, Boston, Cleveland, Baltimore, Detroit and Washington.

There is a reason why these cities have abandoned the contract system. It lies in the fact, which is coming to be realized more and more, that the cleanliness of a city bears a most vital relation to the health of its citizens—that clean streets are just as important as pure water. People everywhere are coming to feel that the city's cleanliness should be the city's direct concern and that it should not be left to private business undertakings whose primary care is, naturally, to make all the money they can out of their work.

But even if street cleaning did not so vitally affect the citizens there is still ample reason for its being done by the city rather than by contract. Street cleaning and kindred work differ from other kinds of public operations in that they must be done over and over again, for the effect of a single job disappears very quickly. The streets may be perfectly clean today and tomorrow be as dirty as ever. The very nature of street cleaning makes it difficult properly to inspect the work of the contractors. The only way the city can hope to do so is to have a city inspector with every street cleaning gang. Under this plan the city is entirely dependent upon the honesty and capacity of the inspectors, for, because of the ephemeral nature of the results of street cleaning, there is no way of checking up the inspectors' work adequately.

The result, as almost every city in the country has found, is that the inspectors, being human and often poorly paid, time and again yield to the influence of the contractors and permit them to slight their work and to increase their profits at the city's expense.

There has been quite enough said in the newspapers and elsewhere about the manifestations of this condition in Philadelphia. It is not the purpose of this bulletin to deal in allegations (if that's all they amount to) nor to cover ground usually reserved for the partisan propagandist.

The query naturally arises: what has all this to do with charter revision? The answer is that Philadelphia under existing laws *does not have the power to do its own street cleaning* even though it may want to do so. The charter revision bill *gives it that power* and in addition *requires* it to do street cleaning and kindred work unless three-fourths of council, with the approval of the mayor, authorize the contract system. The city should certainly have the right to decide for itself this important matter.

STATEMENT OF THE OWNERSHIP, MANAGEMENT, CIRCULATION, ETC., REQUIRED BY THE ACT OF CONGRESS OF AUGUST 24, 1912.

Of *CITIZENS' BUSINESS,* published *weekly* at *Philadelphia, Pennsylvania,* for April 1, 1919.

County of *Philadelphia* } ss.
State of *Pennsylvania* }

Before me, a *Notary Public* in and for the State and county aforesaid, personally appeared *Frederick P. Gruenberg,* who, having been duly affirmed according to law, deposes and says that he is the *editor* of *CITIZENS' BUSINESS* and that the following is, to the best of his knowledge and belief, a true statement of the ownership, management, etc., of the aforesaid publication for the date shown in the above caption, required by the Act of August 24, 1912, embodied in section 443, Postal Laws and Regulations, to wit:

1. That the names and addresses of the publisher, editor, managing editor, and business managers are:

Publisher, *Bureau of Municipal Research, Philadelphia.*
Editor, *Frederick P. Gruenberg.*
Managing Editor, *None.*
Business Managers, *None.*

2. That the owners are:
Bureau of Municipal Research. No capital stock.

3. That the known bondholders, mortgagees, and other security holders owning or holding 1 per cent or more of total amount of bonds, mortgages, or other securities are:
None.

(Signed) *Frederick P. Gruenberg.*

Affirmed to and subscribed before me this 20th day of March, 1919.

(Signed) *Martha H. Quinn.*

[SEAL] (My Commission expires January 16, 1923.)

BUSINESS

IPAL RESEARCH

FRANKLIN BANK BUILDING
AS SECOND CLASS MATTER
OFFICE AT PHILADELPHIA,
AUGUST 24TH, 1912 —
CENTS THE YEAR

e Registration
ws

zens are so busy earning
gether overlook their po-
ation bill now before the
sier for such busy men to

all they amount to) ńor
reserved for the partisan

The query naturally a
to do with charter revis
Philadelphia under existi
power to do its own stre
may want to do so. The
`it that power` and in addit
cleaning and kindred wo:
council, with the approve
the contract system. The
the right to decide for it:

STATEMENT OF THE OWNI
CULATION, ETC., REQI
CONGRESS OF *l*

Of *CITIZENS' BUSINESS*, p
Pennsylvania, for April 1, 19.

County of *Philadelphia* } ss.
State of *Pennsylvania* }

Before me, a *Notary Public*
aforesaid, personally appeared
having been duly affirmed acc(
that he is the *editor* of *CITI2*
following is, to the best of hi
statement of the ownership, n
said publication for the date
required by the Act of Augusl
443, Postal Laws and Regula

1. That the names and add
managing editor, and business

Publisher, *Bureau of Municipe*
Editor, *Frederick P. Gruenber*
Managing Editor, *None.*
Business Managers, *None.*

2. That the owners are:
Bureau of Municipal Resear

3. That the known bondholc
curity holders owning or holdi
amount of bonds, mortgages, o
None.

(Sig

Affirmed to and subscribed
March, 1919.
(

[SEAL]   (My Commissio·

_ ⊂ i

CITIZENS' BUSINESS

BUREAU OF MUNICIPAL RESEARCH

ISSUED WEEKLY AT 805 FRANKLIN BANK BUILDING
PHILADELPHIA. ENTERED AS SECOND CLASS MATTER.
JUNE 7, 1913 AT THE POST OFFICE AT PHILADELPHIA,
PA., UNDER THE ACT OF AUGUST 24TH, 1912—
SUBSCRIPTION FIFTY CENTS THE YEAR

Liberalizing the Registration Laws

No. 360   April 17, 1919

Thousands of our citizens are so busy earning
their living that they altogether overlook their political duties. The registration bill now before the
Legislature will make it easier for such busy men to
register, and so to vote.

A BILL (H. R. No. 718) has been introduced into the legislature, the purpose of which is thoroughly to revise Philadelphia's registration laws. Because of the fact that this bill removes the present registration commissioners from office, it has been attacked as a factional measure. It will, however, be unfortunate if this prevents its enactment, for the bill proposes some far-reaching and much needed reforms in our city's registration laws.

An Extension of Grace

Perhaps the most important of the provisions of the bill and the only one that space will permit us to discuss here is that contained in Section 9. This section provides that the board of registration commissioners shall sit daily in City Hall after the regular registration days and up to and including the second Saturday preceding the November election for the purpose of personally registering citizens, "who on account of illness, absence from the city, *business* or *personal* reasons *did not find it convenient* to appear at their polling places" and register on the regular registration days.

The practical effect of this section is to give the citizen, who for any reason has failed to register on the regular days, another chance to get his name on the voters' list. This is a change in the law that is very much worth while.

Catching the Crest of the Wave

At present, unless a citizen is ill or absent from the city on all three registration days, he must register on one of those days and cannot register later, and the registration days come so far ahead of the election—always more than a month and in municipal election years nearly two months—that popular interest in the election seldom arises until registration is over.

It happens that many thousands of good citizens, engrossed in their daily duties, do not realize that election time is coming on until weeks after the registration days are past, and then when they do become interested they find their suffrage rights foreclosed—they are not registered.

Making Duty Easier

The way to help this situation is not merely to chide our fellow citizens for failing to do their duty, but to make the doing of it easier and more convenient. This the new registration bill will do.

The Short Ballot Bulletin for February says of Philadelphia:

"A volunteer charter revision committee of leading citizens is planning some charter changes. Philadelphia still has a two-house municipal legislature—there are only a dozen other such fumble-foot devices left in America and they are small places in New England. . . . Philadelphia also has that quaint device, ineligibility for re-election, which any Pennsylvanian will solemnly tell you, gives independence of spirit to officeholders.

"But the new plan is all good as far as it goes.

"It proposes a single small council of large powers, and a budget system. Plank 8 of the platform reads: 'Fewer elective officers, eliminating those whose duties are chiefly administrative or clerical.'

"Constitutional barriers prevent any sweeping Short Ballot changes in the county and judicial offices, but the City Solicitor and Receiver of Taxes are slated for abolition as elective offices. The city government would then consist of a Mayor, Controller, Treasurer and a new small council elected singly from the eight senatorial districts—a score of officers in place of 200 in the whole municipality for the citizens and the press to keep tabs upon.

"The strength of the reform movement rests largely on the fact that Penrose has graciously deigned to smile upon it. Its weakness is the fact that the Vares frown upon it. Philadelphia awaits the results of the conflict of its autocrats. . . ."

The Forty-sixth conference of social work will be held in Atlantic City, June 1-8. An interesting and important program is planned.

CITIZENS' BUSINESS

BUREAU OF MUNICIPAL RESEARCH

ISSUED WEEKLY AT 805 FRANKLIN BANK BUILDING
PHILADELPHIA, ENTERED AS SECOND CLASS MATTER
JUNE 7, 1913 AT THE POST OFFICE AT PHILADELPHIA,
PA., UNDER THE ACT OF AUGUST 24TH, 1912—
SUBSCRIPTION FIFTY CENTS THE YEAR

It is Coming—But When?

No. 361   April 24, 1919

Five years ago the local demand for standardization of public employments was like a voice crying in the wilderness; today we hear many voices from many quarters—but now let us have some action.

Which Way the Wind is Blowing

Again we hear talk of standardizing salaries and grades in the public service. In Washington, D. C., a special commission has been appointed to investigate the salaries of federal government employes and to recommend a plan of standardization. In Harrisburg a bill has been introduced creating a state salary board "to fix, grade and equalize the salaries and compensation of employes of the executive branch of the state government." It is reported, also, that our state legislature will be asked to provide a salary-fixing board for Philadelphia.

Equal Pay for Equal Work

Regrettable as it is that the present city administration should have neglected its opportunity to inaugurate a standardization program in Philadelphia, it is not at all strange that the subject should be revived at this time. Our public payrolls are so full of inequalities and so much in need of overhauling that action of some sort is imperative. *The obvious need is for a standardization of work and pay so that employes doing equal work will receive equal pay.*

The New Charter and Standardization

In this connection it should be remembered that the new charter bill now before the legislature provides specifically for standardization of salaries and grades throughout the city and county services. The administrative body charged with this duty is the civil service commission It is not authorized to fix new rates of compensation, but as the employment agency of the city government it is required to classify and grad all positions according to duties and to recommend to the mayor and the council proper minimum and maximum rates of pay for the various grades.

The State Salary Board Bill

A different administrative arrangement is proposed for the state. There being no state civil service commission, the work of standardization is assigned to a board composed of the governor, the auditor general, the state treasurer and the attorney general. This board also is given final authority to fix salaries and wages. Under the circumstances the proposed arrangement is perhaps as good as can be devised, but the circumstances are a trifle unfortunate. In trying to standardize state employments before bringing them under civil service rules, we are putting the cart before the horse; we are reaching for a refinement of the merit system before laying its ground-work; we are hastening to equalize pay for similar jobs before taking care that the jobs are held by competent men. It would be more sensible first to enact a state civil service law, creating a state civil service commission, and then to require this commission to standardize employments in harmony with merit principles of appointment and promotion as well as in harmony with the principle of equal pay for equal work. The city of Philadelphia, fortunately, is already under civil service and the new charter will bring the county of Philadelphia under civil service also, thus clearing the decks for a real standardization measure.

Our Job at Home

This does not mean, however, that Philadelphia is predestined to salvation. Unless the civil service commission takes hold of the standardization problem in an intelligent manner, it will do us little good merely to have the proper legislation. The present commission might have proceeded with standardization under existing laws and without specific legislative mandate; but it failed to do so. The slight effort it did make about two years ago contributed nothing permanent, because it overlooked the fact that before you can standardize pay you must standardize work, and that standardization of work calls for job specifications. How much more scientific this effort would have been under direct legislative command than it was under mere legislative permission is, of course, beyond our knowledge.

Not Mere Hope, but Action

The past, however, cannot be undone; let us look toward the future. And let us not do so merely with hopeful expectancy, but with determination that the past shall not be repeated. In fairness to the thousands of city employes who are entitled to more equitable conditions of employment, and in fairness to that much larger body of citizens and taxpayers of Philadelphia who are entit'~d to more and better service at the hands of t eir government, the adoption of a real standardization program should be hastened with all possible speed.

I believe that a man should be proud of the city in which he lives; and that he should so live that his city will be proud he lives in it.—Abraham Lincoln.

Pol, Sci,

CITIZENS' BUSINESS

BUREAU OF MUNICIPAL RESEARCH

ISSUED WEEKLY AT 805 FRANKLIN BANK BUILDING
PHILADELPHIA. ENTERED AS SECOND CLASS MATTER
JUNE 7, 1913 AT THE POST OFFICE AT PHILADELPHIA,
PA. UNDER THE ACT OF AUGUST 24TH, 1912 —
SUBSCRIPTION FIFTY CENTS THE YEAR

BY ALL MEANS

et's take the Police out of Politics

No. 362   May 1, 1919

BUT—Let's *not*
1. Take them out of *city* politics only to put them into *state* politics.
2. Further eliminate home rule of home affairs.
3. Risk further abuse of the mandamus evil.
4. Decrease interest of citizens in municipal affairs by decreasing the importance of municipal affairs.

No Novelty

Dissatisfaction with the police department is neither a new phenomenon nor is it local to Philadelphia.

From the time that the regular police force became a recognized city institution in America there have been periods in almost every community during which the local department was under fire, and it is not difficult to understand why this should be the case. The nature of the duties of the police department, and its enormous importance in serving safety and welfare, make it peculiarly subject to temptation, on the one hand and to the fire of criticism on the other.

The attempt to correct the real or alleged fault of police departments by state action is also no new thing in political history. With our national naïveté we have placed faith for generations in legislation as a reform panacea, and in city after city, the evils of inefficient, corrupt or partisan police have resulted in removing them from municipal to state jurisdiction.

The Tests

The tests of this experiment are the simpl formulas: *Has it Worked? Will it Work*

In reply to the first question it will intere Philadelphians to know that at some time other since the Civil War, New York, Chicag

Brooklyn, St. Louis, Boston, Cleveland, Balti-more, Cincinnati, Detroit—as well as a number of smaller cities—had their local control of police taken away and state control substituted. In all but *three* of the nine large cities mentioned above, the local control was restored by the respective legislatures after periods of varying lengths. In only *one* case of the nine [Boston] is the plan of state control generally regarded as successful, and in that case everyone but the merest tyro knows that the fact that Boston is the state capital as well as the metropolis makes the whole situation entirely different.

Will It Work ?

Philadelphians are asked to acquiesce in a plan to turn over to the state the control of our police. There is no doubt that many of those who favor this plan honestly believe that it is the best, if not the only way to take the force out of politics, but these citizens have failed to examine the proposal critically. Will some future governor of the objectionably political type [and it is rumored that there have been such in Pennsylvania] make for our city a less partisan appointment as police head, than an equally "political" mayor? Has our experience in the past given us any ground for assuming that state politics in the future will be any purer or give us any higher standards of efficiency than municipal politics?

The Real Objection

The real objection is not "academic"—it is *intensely practical.* Today we have the phenomenon of constitutional officers and statutory salaries that limit our power to govern our local affairs—and all agree that these conditions usually make for costliness, for irresponsibility, for inefficiency. It is now proposed to turn our most important municipal function over to the *head of the state.* In other words, Philadelphia, already suffering from too many curtailments of its right to home rule in local affairs, is asked to forego control of its largest, most important and costliest municipal unit.

Presumably, the *expense* of conducting our police force will still be borne by Philadelphia's taxpayers. But the *control* will be vested in the head of the *state* government only one-fifth of whose taxpayers are directly concerned with the police affairs of our city.

And is the new state-appointed commissioner to have the power of the mandamus for salaries and other items as do the county officials?

Look before you leap, Philadelphians!

"Municipal institutions constitute the strength of free nations. A nation may establish a system of free government, but without municipal institutions it cannot have the spirit of liberty."—de Tocqueville.

CITIZENS' BUSINESS

BUREAU OF MUNICIPAL RESEARCH

ISSUED WEEKLY AT 805 FRANKLIN BANK BUILDING
PHILADELPHIA—ENTERED AS SECOND CLASS MATTER
JUNE 7, 1913 AT THE POST OFFICE AT PHILADELPHIA,
PA., UNDER THE ACT OF AUGUST 24TH, 1912—
SUBSCRIPTION FIFTY CENTS THE YEAR-

On, Philadelphia!

No. 363   May 8, 1919

> " It is time that we pay a decent reverence to our
> ancestors, not by doing what they under other cir-
> cumstances did, but by doing what they under our
> circumstances would have done."—*Lord Macaulay.*

The New Day

A new day is upon us. A new vision has opened to our minds; a new spirit is stirring our consciences; new problems clamor for solution; and new duties have devolved upon our citizens. This is true for the world and it is true for Philadelphia.

At the same time we still have affection for the old. The treasures of the past we still cherish. In the achievements of yesterday we still glory. The homes of our fathers are still dear to us; and Old Philadelphia we still love.

Our affection for the old is not incompatible with our vision of the new. From the good in the old we draw inspiration to achieve the new. Philadelphia occupies its proud place in the history of our country because it was here that the men and women of old did new things; and if Philadelphia is to retain its place in history it must continue to do new things and to live up to the new vision of the new day.

The Philadelphia of Tomorrow

In this new vision nothing looms more important than the part that government will play in our common life. More and more the things we want to do must be accomplished by co-operative effort and in government we have the most effective instrument of community co-operation. Whether we shall forge ahead or lag behind in the race for better things, will depend very largely upon the adaptation of our government to the new tasks it will be called upon to perform. The Philadelphia of tomorrow will be no better than its city government

2

More Light, not Heat

The Bureau of Municipal Research is dedicated to the cause of better government in Philadelphia. For ten years past it has devoted itself entirely to this cause. Its method has not been the political one, but rather that of careful scientific inquiry. It has proceeded upon the theory that first of all we must know the facts about our government, and then we are ready to make changes that are truly for the better. In the phrase of a noted American, the Bureau has sought at every turn to bring more "light, not heat" to bear upon the problems of our city government. It has rested its faith upon the potent power of truth.

* * * * * *

The Bureau of Municipal Research is not itself a part of the city government. It is a citizens' agency, brought into being by forward-looking Philadelphians and maintained entirely by their voluntary contributions. It has a staff of accountants, statisticians, civil service specialists, engineers and lawyers. Back of the staff is a board of twenty-five public spirited men and women. In its policy the Bureau of Municipal Research is absolutely non-partisan and impersonal.

By Way of Retrospect

The ten years of the Bureau's history have been years of notable achievements. In the brief compass of this leaflet it is possible to enumerate only a few:

1. Study of the Bureau of Compulsory Education. This resulted in a thorough reorganiza-

3

tion of that bureau so that today it is almost a model of its kind.

2. Study of the local weights and measures situation. This resulted in legislation establishing our present Bureau of Weights and Measures in Philadelphia.

3. Digest of health laws. This has proved an invaluable aid to the health officials of the city government, making available to them for the first time in convenient form the many laws and ordinances pertaining to health that formerly were scattered through numerous volumes.

4. Survey of school medical inspection. This resulted in a complete reorganization of the Division of Medical Inspection of the Bureau of Health and had the almost immediate effect of increasing by fifty per cent the treatment obtained for children with physical defects.

5. Inquiry into City Hall janitorial service. This resulted in an immediate reorganization of the service and a substantial annual saving.

6. Survey of the Domestic Relations Division of the Municipal Court. This resulted in the installation of a complete system of mechanical tabulation of the social data of domestic relations cases, and was instrumental in the adoption of various procedural improvements.

7. Studies in city finances. As a result of almost continuous attention to various phases of our city finances, including the budget, accounting methods, borrowing policy, and kindred topics, great improvements have been effected in the financial administration of the city. At the same time a sound basis has been evolved for the important fiscal legislation included in the new charter bill.

Expanding Horizon

So much for the past. What of the present and of the future?

At this time of general transition from the old to the new, the Bureau of Municipal Research, too, finds its activities entering upon a new phase. The field of its endeavors is rapidly broadening and its work is becoming more and more fundamental. Ten years of intimate contact with the operation of our local government have revealed to us many of the primal causes of governmental inefficiency, and it is to the eradication of these deeper causes that we are now bending our major energies.

The New City Charter

For a long time the Bureau of Municipal Research had been impressed with the need for a revision of our city charter. It had been urging many concrete changes. It therefore seized with alacrity the opportunity to join forces with a movement that promised to sweep aside at a stroke a large number of the underlying obstacles to better government in Philadelphia. For months the Bureau devoted nearly all of its facilities to the cause of charter revision and did an immense amount of work for the Charter Committee incidental to preparing the needed legislation. Today the prospects are bright that the new charter will be adopted and that Philadelphia presently will have machinery of government more suited to our time than that which we now have.

5

The School Survey

Nothing is more fundamental than education. The public schools of Philadelphia are most vitally related to our common welfare. In them are reared and fashioned the citizens of tomorrow. Yet our whole system of public education in Philadelphia is now under the fire of criticism. It is charged by some that this system fails to meet the needs· of today, that it is not properly conducted, that the dominant element in the Board of Education lacks vision.

In view of this situation, the Bureau of Municipal Research has joined forces with other agencies in publicly demanding a complete survey of our schools. Philadelphians are entitled to know the truth in this matter. They ·are entitled to know the strength as well as the weakness of the present school system; and in no better way can the truth be ascertained than by means of a survey made by disinterested outside specialists in education.

Cost of Living

Good government is intensely human. It serves human needs and it serves through human beings. Those who perform the services of government must be treated with human consideration or the character of their services will deteriorate. Among other things, they are entitled to receive at least a living wage. Such a wage is dependent upon the cost of living, and in these days of changing price levels how can anyone know what a living wage really is?

In an endeavor to answer this question, the

Bureau of Municipal Research made a painstaking inquiry into the household budgets of 260 workingmen's families in Philadelphia. On the basis of the information thus obtained it devised a standard of living expressed not merely in terms of dollars and cents, but in terms of actual goods and services, so that the current cost of that standard can be ascertained at any time by simply revising the price figures of the commodities appearing in it. This study has been completed and copies will be available as soon as they can be obtained from the printers' hands.

Other Activities

Other activities of importance can have but brief mention here. A municipal yearbook for Philadelphia is now in course of preparation. Our financial studies are continuing. We are still pushing the proposal to standardize the salaries and conditions of employment of city employes. Every week *Citizens' Business* carries to the public in brief bulletin form some message relating to the affairs of our government, and daily our general information service responds to the inquiries of persons seeking information on community questions.

What Next?

What is next on our program?

Unlimited opportunities for further service in the interests of better government are immediately ahead. We should like, for instance, to inquire into the methods of taxation in Philadelphia with a view to arriving at a more equitable basis for taxation. We also should like to make a study of paving contracts. We should like not only to ascertain the truth about street cleaning contracts and their performance, but to conduct engineering experiments that will demonstrate how to keep Philadelphia's streets really clean. We should like to do constructive work on the problem of municipal food markets. But we cannot do everything at once. Above all, we cannot go beyond our physical and financial resources. We need greater support than we now have, both in the number of interested persons and in the total amount of money contributions.

*　　*　　*　　*　　*　　*

Do you believe in making democracy as efficient and serviceable—nay, *more* efficient and serviceable than an autocracy? If so, will you think seriously about aligning yourself with the most active agency that is striving toward that end?

"Salaries of teachers are so low that they offer neither incentive to professional preparation, nor encouragement t long tenure. Moreover, the new and more lucrative opportunities which the war has made available to teachers have made serious inroads on the profession. It can not now be expected that qualified persons will continue to teach, o that capable ones will prepare for teaching, unless radical an sweeping changes are forthcoming in the salary scale."—*United States Bureau of Education Bulletin*, 1919, No. 4, p. 5

P Sci

CITIZENS' BUSINESS

BUREAU OF MUNICIPAL RESEARCH

ISSUED WEEKLY AT 805 FRANKLIN BANK BUILDING
PHILADELPHIA. ENTERED AS SECOND CLASS MATTER
JUNE 7, 1913 AT THE POST OFFICE AT PHILADELPHIA,
PA., UNDER THE ACT OF AUGUST 24TH, 1912—
SUBSCRIPTION FIFTY CENTS THE YEAR·

The Municipal Curb Market

o. 364   May 15, 1919

A city function: To make it possible to provide good, cheap food for he citizens.

An Old Problem

Once more the municipal market is before the people of Philadelphia. Last week resolutions were introduced into both branches of Councils authorizing the establishment of nine curb markets in as many different sections of the city.

A Step in the Right Direction

The establishment of municipal markets is one of the best ways to secure better prices for both farmers and consumers. The greater part of our population spends from forty to fifty per cent of its income for food. It therefore should be one of the important functions of the city to provide the means whereby good food can be bought cheaply. This venture will not be successful, however, unless it provides at the same time an incentive to produce more and more food.

The Colored Gentleman in the Fuel Supply

The resolution just introduced provides for "a permit to be issued free of charge and to farmers or *other persons* who are equipped to offer *fruits and vegetables* for sale to the public only." The italics are our own. We understood that in the event the city established curb markets, regulations would be enforced which would make it necessary to establish the responsibility of the farmer before a license and stand would be granted to him. The "other persons" phrase in the above mentioned resolution, however, kills entirely any hope for a real "farmers' market" by granting the privilege of a stand to any *middleman* who desires to sell fruits and vegetables exclusive ly. If it is merely an extension of an existing evil, the curb market will do little to reduce the cost of food to the consumer and nothing to encourage increased production on the part of the farmer, which is the basic need to produce low prices. The chief cause for complaint has been that in almost all of the markets, both private and municipal, the number of farmers present is exceedingly small. This condition has been caused by the excessive rents charged for stalls and by the numerous restrictions which in fact protect the retailer and discourage the farmer.

The Result

The general result has been that few farmers attempt to sell directly to the consumer. The curbstone market, being free, should offer an inducement to the farmer. However, the farmers who must come in long distances on regular days cannot advantageously patronize them unless they can be assured a market for *all* the products of their farm. How would the small farmer dispose of his chickens, eggs, cottage cheese and the numerous other articles on which he must depend to make his trip into town successful? Even the truck farmer relies to a greater or lesser extent on the sale of articles other than "fruits and vegetables."

Unfair

At the present time there is nothing to prevent any retailer from taking a stall in any market, private or municipal, and representing himself as a "farmer" and asking high prices for "fresh" vegetables, eggs and similar commodities, thus putting the real farmer at a great disadvantage.

Killing Two Birds with One Stone

If, instead of discouraging him, steps were taken to encourage the farmer by making it advantageous for him to bring his produce to the city and dispose of it directly to the consumer, two ends would be attained—the farmer could demand higher prices for his products than he has at present any chance of getting and the consumer would at the same time be buying cheaper and fresher food. The farmer, by getting good prices for his articles, would be encouraged to speed up production which is the most necessary thing to be accomplished.

The Remedy

Philadelphia's machinery for the distribution of food supplies within the city is too antiquated to be patched up. It needs to be entirely overhauled and expanded. The job is a big one and requires the services of a big man.

Fifty years of talking is sufficient. The time has come to act.

"The creation of an efficient electorate is far more important than the mere efficient performance of a governmental function. For this reason it may be unsound to urge that a power of government should be taken from the city because it has been improperly used or that the state could do the work better. The same sort of reasoning would lead us to forbid the child to use the pen because, forsooth, he cannot at once write as well as his instructor and sometimes smears himself and the copy with ink. With this note of warning we may turn to a solution of the problem of the control of police."—*A. R. Hatton.*

CITIZENS' BUSINESS

BUREAU OF MUNICIPAL RESEARCH

ISSUED WEEKLY AT 805 FRANKLIN BANK BUILDING
PHILADELPHIA. ENTERED AS SECOND CLASS MATTER
JUNE 7, 1913 AT THE POST OFFICE AT PHILADELPHIA,
PA., UNDER THE ACT OF AUGUST 24TH, 1912 —
SUBSCRIPTION FIFTY CENTS THE YEAR.

Use Our Schools!

No. 365   May 22, 1919

Do you realize that our school buildings
are idle about 7300 hours out of the 8760
hours in a year?

Amusement for Playtime

In these days everyone, young and old alike, recognizes the necessity of play. Labor laws are made in most of our states to secure playtime for our workers; public and private agencies have been organized to give us the amusement we require. Our city does much toward providing recreation for us. We have parks, playgrounds, play streets, recreation centers and piers; we have public libraries, museums, free lectures and art galleries; we have parades and band concerts—all to keep us occupied during playtime. And yet, when we see children, youths and even adults in the streets seeking amusement, engaged often in activities of questionable character, then we realize how much still is to be done.

Schools Idle about Five-sixths of the Time

One of the possibilities that has largely escaped our notice is the use of school buildings for recreational purposes. Most of these buildings are open about seven hours a day, five days in the week, for forty weeks. They represent a large investment of public funds. How much greater would be the return on our investment if the schools were utilized for more hours of the day! Is it not an economic waste for them to remain idle for so much time?

In 1913 we began to make more use of our school buildings, but unfortunately, we cannot claim much progress. Last fall provision was made for the opening at night of seventeen public schools, to provide recreation for those living nearby. Lectures, gymnastics, games, concerts, community sings, dramatic performances, moving pictures and dances are among the entertainments offered. It is to be regretted that most of these schools are not used every night in the week, but merely at stated times—"one or two nights a week," it was advertised, "as the needs require." Think of it—seventeen schools in this whole city to be used, and yet they are open only one or two evenings a week!

What Other Cities Are Doing

This movement to use the schools as neighborhood centers is growing rapidly in many places. New York City, Buffalo, Rochester, Boston, Jersey City and Pittsburgh are among the eastern cities that are trying it out. In a few western cities, the school brings together all the cultural resources of the community, not only providing gymnastics and amusement but also controlling the libraries, museums and art galleries.

A Growing Demand for Neighborhood Meetings

It has been said that Philadelphia has one of the most autocratic governments of the cities in the United States; that we lack democratic atmosphere. This would be difficult indeed for Philadelphians to believe; but the absence of community meetings is certainly a usual manifestation of undemocratic atmosphere. Recently, however, the demand for neighborhood meetings has been growing, and with the increasing demand has come in many sections of the city the problem of finding a meeting place. To be sure there are schools, large, comfortable public buildings, but they are closed. In most cases it is impossible, even after going through with the usual amount of red tape, to have them opened; and

so the meeting has to go elsewhere, hire a hal
undergo an unnecessary expense and perhaps los
its enthusiasm.

The Solution of Many Community Prob
lems

Recently the House of Representatives at Har
risburg passed an amendment to the school law
of Pennsylvania (House Bill 1238) to rende
possible the wider use of school buildings fo
community center activities. This amendmen
now in the hands of the Senate Committee o
Education, not only permits the use of schoc
buildings and grounds at the discretion of th
school board of each district, but goes furthe
making it mandatory upon these boards to equi
the buildings and allow them to be used out c
school hours, under school board direction, if
sufficient number of citizens demand it. A pet
tion signed by a number of residents equal to one
fifth the number of pupils enrolled in the schoo
presented to the school board compels the boar
to open and equip the school for such purpose
as may be required. This amendment has bee
introduced in response to the interest in the de
velopment of the community center idea fostere
by the Commission on Living Conditions of th
U. S. Department of Labor. It would be a mear
of providing a substitute for the saloon, an
would solve other community problems as wel

Other cities are benefiting from such a systen
why not Philadelphia?

"Municipal reform will not be permanent ur
less municipal functions are of increasing impor
ance."—Zeublin, American Municipal Progres
p. 397.

Pol, Sci,

CITIZENS' BUSINESS

BUREAU OF MUNICIPAL RESEARCH

ISSUED WEEKLY AT 805 FRANKLIN BANK BUILDING
PHILADELPHIA. ENTERED AS SECOND CLASS MATTER
JUNE 7, 1913 AT THE POST OFFICE AT PHILADELPHIA,
PA., UNDER THE ACT OF AUGUST 24TH, 1912 —
SUBSCRIPTION FIFTY CENTS THE YEAR

The Cost of Cleanliness

No. 366   May 29, 1919

Of course, the average man believes in clean streets, but if they're "too clean," it might cost too much (?)

Let's examine some costs!

MUNICIPALITIES DOING OWN STREET CLEANING.

	Cost per 1000 square yards cleaned.	Total cost per year.	Per capita cost per year.
Chicago,	30.9c	$1,404,990.68	$ .56
Pittsburgh,	30.0c	Not available.	Not available.
Washington,	16.5c	$ 259,482.00	$ .71

UNDER CONTRACT SYSTEM.

Philadelphia,	59.0c	$1,934,662.00	$1.13

The above costs are copied directly or computed from official city reports for the year 1917. Per capita costs are computed on estimated populations July 1, 1917, U. S. Census reports. Differences of topography and character of paving, together with differences in the frequency of cleaning, must be considered, but Philadelphia pays too much for the service rendered.

There are two systems in use for getting streets cleaned in cities. One is the contract system. The other method is to have the municipality do its own work. Philadelphia is a conspicuous example of the few remaining cities using the contract system.

In addition to the cities mentioned above,

Buffalo, Cincinnati, Columbus, Denver, Los Angeles, Louisville, Milwaukee, New York, New Orleans, Newark, Niagara Falls, St. Louis, San Francisco, Seattle and sixteen other cities clean their streets by municipal forces.

A FRANK ADMISSION

While it cannot be denied that cost figures are sometimes misleading and frequently fail to tell the WHOLE STORY, they are, after all, the only measuring device—the only basis of comparison—that we have. True, the work may be "slicked over" or a low standard may prevail. True, the cost per capita is not an absolute index. Some cities demand very frequent cleaning. This reduces the yardage cost and increases the per capita cost.

After all, the thing that counts—especially with us ordinary citizens—is satisfaction with results.

FOR THE SAKE OF THE ARGUMENT

Let's assume that the citizens of Philadelphia are satisfied with street cleaning conditions—*mark you,* we are merely assuming. Then, if a way were found to do the same work more cheaply, wouldn't it appeal to the taxpayer? And we're all of us taxpayers!

When a municipality does its own cleaning, it employs a single force and does the job.

When a contractor does the job, the city must employ a force to supervise the carrying out of the contract and the contractor must employ a like force to see that his men don't lie down on the job. So the city pays for this supervision twice! In addition *the contractor must meet his own overhead expense and make a profit!*

Now you know why municipal street cleaning is cheaper than contract street cleaning. Let's have the present job done cheaper *or have a better job done at the same cost,* through municipal street cleaning.

THERE HAS BEEN TOO MUCH DUST RAISED IN STREET CLEANING DISCUSSIONS!

"No government can now expect to be permanent unless it guarantees progress as well as order; nor can it continue really to secure order unless it promotes progress."—John Stuart Mill, in *The French Revolution and Its Assailants.*

CITIZENS' BUSINESS

BUREAU OF MUNICIPAL RESEARCH

ISSUED WEEKLY AT 805 FRANKLIN BANK BUILDING
PHILADELPHIA, ENTERED AS SECOND CLASS MATTER
JUNE 7, 1913 AT THE POST OFFICE AT PHILADELPHIA,
PA., UNDER THE ACT OF AUGUST 24TH, 1912 —
SUBSCRIPTION FIFTY CENTS THE YEAR·

Almost a Century Without Progress

No. 367   June 5, 1919

Virtue may be its own reward but
you can't live on it.

1833

"In this country, the schoolmaster, as he is termed, does not enjoy that consideration which the services required of him and the talents necessary to perform these services ought to confer on him. The men who are intrusted to form the minds of the youth of this country, and to direct their expanding energies, should be classed as a profession of the highest order. Their labors are great, their services are valuable, and therefore their reward should be so liberal as to attract the best talents. It is a melancholy truth, that in most parts of the country, even in New England, the occupation of a schoolmaster yields less profit than that derived from the humblest mechanical. labor.* * * Can any rational man think that the talents and acquirements that ought to be imparted, can be obtained for such wages? If a system of education is to be established, let the scale of expenditure be liberal; let it form an important department of the Government; let every man connected with its administration, from the head of the department to the humblest teacher, be considered as a highly valuable public, servant, and as such enjoy a liberal reward. Let this be done, and though the public schools will yield no revenue, they will annually contribute to the republic something more valuable—a body of virtuous and enlightened citizens."—Report of

House Committee on Education, Pennsylvania Legislature, session of 1832-3.

1919

"Harrisburg, May 27.—The Woodruff House bill providing an increase in salary for public school teachers was reported to the Senate today with numerous amendments. As it now stands it provides for a 20 per cent increase, one-half to be provided by the state and the other half by the school district. This would require an appropriation of $4,500,000 a year from the state. The administration considers this rather high in view of the demands on the state for funds, and it is expected that the increase will be pared down so that $3,000,000 a year can cover it."—Public Ledger. May 28, 1919.

How Long, Oh Lord, How Long!

In 1833 the teacher's value was acknowledged and monetary reward was suggested. Many times since then the same principle has been *acknowledged* but the *reward* has not been forthcoming. Let *us* be the ones to show our appreciation in a substantial way.

The particular method to be employed in bringing relief to the underpaid teachers of the state is not the issue of greatest concern in the present juncture. The important consideration is that something be done to provide this relief and that it be done speedily. Delay is fraught with danger. Do we wish to jeopardize the system which was established for the purpose of giving us "a body of virtuous and enlightened citizens"?

Clean! Cleaner! Cleanest!

The week of May 5 was officially designated as "Clean-up Week". The householders were urged to clean from garret to cellar and back again from cellar to garret. At the end of the week, the 1919 housecleaning was heralded as the most successful campaign yet conducted.

Approximately three thousand extra loads of rubbish were removed and the citizens were congratulated upon the amount of rubbish and dirt that they could produce from their homes. But consider the homes before the rubbish was removed. The accumulations in the cellars and garrets must have been insanitary and disease-producing.

With cellars and attics all clean and in order after this strenuous effort, let all the city keep clean throughout the year. In 1920 let us be able to boast that, try as hard as they would, the householders could not produce thirty extra loads of dirt.

CITIZENS' BUSINESS

BUREAU OF MUNICIPAL RESEARCH

ISSUED WEEKLY AT 805 FRANKLIN BANK BUILDING
PHILADELPHIA. ENTERED AS SECOND CLASS MATTER.
JUNE 7, 1913 AT THE POST OFFICE AT PHILADELPHIA,
PA., UNDER THE ACT OF AUGUST 24TH, 1912—
SUBSCRIPTION FIFTY CENTS THE YEAR

More Comforts in Our City Home

No. 368   June 12, 1919

Do we want Philadelphia to be lacking in modern
    conveniences?
If not, then we should provide at once more public
    comfort stations.

A Flaw in Philadelphia's Hospitality

It is the duty of every municipality to look after the comfort of its people, and in that respect Philadelphia is open to criticism. This city is not a thoughtful host, in that it does not provide the required hospitality for its citizens and guests. We refer to the absence of public comfort stations.

Have you ever realized how inadequate are the facilities which are offered for the necessary comfort of the people, particularly those who are visiting the city for only a day at a time? Just recently, on the day when Philadelphia gave such a rousing welcome to the boys of the 28th Division, the lack of comfort stations was very noticeable. The department stores were closed and the railroad stations were open only to passengers, access to the waiting-room floors being denied unless transportation tickets were shown.

True, that was an exceptional day, but a somewhat similar condition exists every Sunday and holiday, when countless transients are in the city.

A Lesson from Our Neighbors, Abroad and At Home

This need is not one newly recognized. A great many European cities have realized the urgent necessity for providing comfort stations for their citizens, and they have met the situation by establishing these stations at frequent intervals throughout the congested areas. Recently the movement has spread in American cities and such cities report great satisfaction with the plan. Some of the European cities use the fee system, thus making the stations at least partially self-sustaining, but this plan has not usually been considered feasible in the American cities.

The Ideal Public Comfort Station

The ideal comfort station is one that is equipped with drinking fountains, toilets, telephone booths and rest rooms. Under proper supervision stations of this kind would be a real asset to a city. They should be placed at intersections of main streets, in city squares and parks, playgrounds, recreation piers, all public buildings, libraries, market-houses and entrances to subway and elevated railway stations; and their location should be indicated by some distinctive sign. Wherever possible the entrance to the comfort station should be separate from the entrance to the building in which it is located, in order to facilitate access from the street.

Blending Comfort with Beauty

To overcome the objection of stations being possibly too conspicuous in the congested sections, it might be found advisable to have them underground with entrances similar to those of the subway. In the less congested sections, parks, etc., the buildings could be of an attractive design that would add to the appearance of the vicinity.

What We Can Do Immediately

Philadelphia must face this problem promptly! It is so acute at the present time that immediate action ought to be taken; but when the saloons are permanently closed, and as a result over eighteen hundred private comfort stations are discontinued, the situation will be even worse.

It is true that something has already been done. In January, 1895, an ordinance was passed by councils providing for the installation of public lavatories "on the premises of Police, Patrol and Fire Stations that are hereafter to be erected," and we are informed that this provision is being carried out. This, however, is not sufficient and more public comfort stations should be erected at once. Steps should now be taken to have comfort stations placed in the entrances to the subway and elevated lines now under construction, instead of the present practice whereby one is compelled to pay a fare in order to reach the elevated waiting room or subway platform where a lavatory—often locked—is located. This would entail no great change in the present plans and would greatly relieve the situation.

May not the ultimate management and development of our system of public comfort stations be one of the important activities to be undertaken by the proposed new Department of Public Welfare?

MENDICANCY

Once again the streets are thronged with professional beggars. Doleful ditties are solemnly, slowly sung by blind vendors who receive a shock when someone accepts the wares exposed for sale. That old atrocity, the barrel organ, drones its hymns over and over again to the musical accompaniment of tinkling coins.

What's become of the law on this subject?

If it's inadequate let's get a better one.

CITIZENS' BUSINESS

BUREAU OF MUNICIPAL RESEARCH

ISSUED WEEKLY AT 805 FRANKLIN BANK BUILDING
PHILADELPHIA. ENTERED AS SECOND CLASS MATTER
JUNE 7,1913 AT THE POST ___ PHILADELPHIA,
PA.,UNDER THE ACT OF ___ AUGUST 24TH,1912 —
SUBSCRIPTION FIFTY ___ CENTS THE YEAR

A SLUMP?

No. 369   June 19, 1919

"Early and provident fear is the mother of safety."

— *Edmund Burke*

Out of the Past

Last year it was widely advertised that the number of accidents occurring as a result of the Fourth of July celebration showed a marked decrease over previous years. "The better sense of the community prevailed," so says the newspaper notice, and while there was more noise, more waste of gunpowder and more accidents than there should have been, still the Fourth of 1918 was an improvement. No credit in this matter can be taken by our city government, for the police order covering the sale of fireworks was rescinded at the last minute. To review the scandal connected with the rescinding of that order is not to the point here, but a glance at the newspapers of June 20 and 22 of 1918 will help to freshen the memory.

Great Expectations

This year, in view of the end of the war, the noisiest Fourth of July in history is prophesied. The fireworks dealers are fully stocked with explosives and are expecting large sales for the great celebration. And no official action toward restriction has been taken! Are we going backward? Are we going to increase our long list of casualties? Are we going to have more fires, more deaths, more little children in our hospitals?

If not, once again we must rely on the "better sense of the community". Before it is too late let us make provision for a sane celebration.

From Foreign Shores

On July 4, 1918, almost all countries of the world except our own celebrated in a sane manner our Independence Day. The Stars and Stripes were honored in all allied countries. The Belgian tribute, as Minister Whitlock reports it, is as follows:

"Most touching demonstrations were made on the Fourth of July by the Belgian government and Belgian citizens. A beautiful and affecting ceremony was held in the morning, when Belgian troops, commanded by Gen. Der Utte, saluted our flag with many spontaneous acclamations of the president and the navy. All the Belgian ministers, members of the diplomatic corps and the officers commanding the Belgian, French, British, Portuguese and American bases in Havre were present. I received an eloquent telegram from the minister of war, who is at the front. The president's portrait was displayed in all the schools and Lincoln's Gettysburg address was read to the school children. Addresses were presented at the legation by delegations representing refugees and several Belgian societies."

The Dear Old U. S. A.

This Belgian tribute sets us a high standard. Let us be guided by it in our celebrations. Our public squares and parks offer facilities for safe, sane, intelligent, patriotic celebrations. All clubs, social settlements and communities should arrange patriotic programs which would in some measure offset the desire for the dangerous type of celebration.

Our overseas casualties have been all too heavy. Why add to them the casualties of a hazardous Fourth?

Governmental Research Conference Meeting

The Governmental Research Conference will hold its annual meeting in Chicago, June 23-24.

CITIZENS' BUSINESS

BUREAU OF MUNICIPAL RESEARCH

ISSUED WEEKLY AT 805 FRANKLIN BANK BUILDING
PHILADELPHIA. ENTERED AS SECOND CLASS MATTER
JUNE 7, 1913 AT THE POST OFFICE AT PHILADELPHIA,
PA., UNDER THE ACT OF AUGUST 24TH, 1912—
SUBSCRIPTION FIFTY CENTS THE YEAR.

1919 Charter Series: No. 6

The Merit System Advanced

No. 370   **June 26, 1919**

It is proposed in the remaining numbers of the charter series to outline briefly the principal features of the new charter bill- which has just been signed by the Governor.

In CITIZENS' BUSINESS No. 355 a general outline was given of the civil service proposals of the new charter bill as it was first introduced into the state legislature. As the old saying goes, however, "there is many a slip betwixt the cup and the lip." Even so it was with the proposed new charter during its tempestuous course through the legislative mill—and the hands of the attorney general—to a place on the statute books of our commonwealth. Of the two articles of this bill that underwent the most drastic changes, the article on civil service is one. Nevertheless, it is gratifying to report that the net result of the legislature's action is an advance and not a retreat for the merit system in Philadelphia. Briefly stated, this result is as follows:

1. The Attempted Extension of the Merit System to County Departments Fails

The charter bill as first introduced provided for an extension of the civil service law to county departments and to the departments in the twilight zone between county status and mayoral jurisdiction, such as the Fairmount Park Commission, with all its park guards. The receiver of taxes, who enjoyed special exemption from civil service, was also to be included under the law.

This progressive proposal failed altogether. The new charter expressly limits the application of merit principles to the departments and bureaus that already were under civil service.

2. A Commission of Three to be Chosen by the City Council

The original charter bill proposed a single civil service commissioner instead of a commission of three, and the selection of this commissioner by a two-thirds vote of all the members elected to the city council instead of by appointment by the mayor.

The new charter law restores the commission of three, but retains the new method of having the commissioners chosen by the city council, although by a majority rather than by a two-thirds vote.

3. "Thumbs Down on Juggling" Wins

The provision of the original new charter bill to reduce from four to two the number of eligible persons that must be submitted to an appointing officer for a single vacancy, has been retained in the charter law. Thus another door to favoritism has been largely closed.

4. The Trial Board Idea Confined to Policemen and Firemen

The original new charter bill proposed an extension of the trial board idea, then in effect in the police and fire forces, to the entire city and county service.

Under the new charter there is no such extension of the trial board idea. Policemen and firemen will continue to be the only municipal employes who are accorded any substantial protection against unfair dismissal. The only change from past practice is that the trial board for policemen and firemen will be under the jurisdiction of the civil service commission instead of under that of the director of public safety and the mayor.

5. Political Activity Curbed

The charter bill as originally introduced made political activity on the part of any city or county employe punishable not only by dismissal, but also by fine and imprisonment; and the enforcement of this provision was strengthened by giving any taxpayer the right to go into court and by writ of mandamus to compel dismissal.

Under the new charter only policemen and firemen engaging in political activity are punishable by fine and imprisonment and may be dismissed by taxpayer's action. The sole punishment of other city employes is dismissal from the service which is not made enforceable by taxpayer's action.

6. Standardization of Salaries and Grades

The original charter bill provided for a standardization of salaries and grades in the city and county service.

This provision is retained in the new charter, but its application is limited to the city service alone.

What a Man Does for Himself
    Dies With Him;
What a Man Does for His Community ..
    Lives Forever

———

"What Have They Done?"—"Well, What Have You Done?"

—Anonymous.

CITIZENS' BUSINESS

BUREAU OF MUNICIPAL RESEARCH

ISSUED WEEKLY AT 805 FRANKLIN BANK BUILDING
PHILADELPHIA. ENTERED AS SECOND CLASS MATTER
JUNE 7, 1913 AT THE POST OFFICE AT PHILADELPHIA,
PA., UNDER THE ACT OF AUGUST 24TH, 1912 —
SUBSCRIPTION FIFTY CENTS THE YEAR.

A Fourth-of-July
of Our Own

No. 371   July 3, 1919

Thunder on!   Stride on!
Democracy . . . .
                    —Walt Whitman

EVER since the days of 1776, Philadelphia has had a peculiar claim on July Fourth.

To the rest of the country this is a day for the commemoration of a great national event, but to Philadelphia it is also a day for the commemoration of a great local event. When the Liberty Bell rang out its message of independence one hundred and forty-three years ago, it rang *for* all America and it rang *to* all the world, but it rang *in* Philadelphia.

This year Philadelphia has still another reason for celebrating Independence Day. With the adoption of the new charter, this city has just leaped forward toward a more self-respecting, a more dignified, a more independent community life.

Not all that we hoped for has been achieved; complete home rule has not been won, nor could it be under our present constitution; but a noble beginning has been made. Enlarged powers over our own affairs have been secured from the state legislature, and the trammels of antiquated organization in the frame of our local government have been in part removed.

These are substantial gains that in themselves are cause for celebration. At this juncture, however, the mere fact that they were won overshadows in importance the things that have been won. The cynic who said that nothing could be done in Philadelphia and in Pennsylvania to improve civic conditions has been given his answer. On the other hand, the forces that have been battling, in season and out of season, for civic progress have been heartened by victory and filled with a new zeal for further advance. The community at large has been aroused to a new interest in local public questions and has been inspired with a deeper faith in the cause of better government. The spirit of progress and the spirit of reaction have had their test of strength, and the test has proven that progress *is* possible; that things *can* be done.

This victory, however, can have its greater significance only if we follow it up. Let us not forget that while we have won much, we have not won all. Because of constitutional limitations, charter revision has been able to go only part way to its goal. The state constitution itself must be revised to secure for us that degree of home rule for which we have been striving. In a sense, our battle has only begun; the first line trenches only have been taken; complete victory is a goal still separated from us by much hard effort. We must continue the fight; we cannot stop now.

It would be equally fatal to rest on our laurels after mere legislative victory. Philadelphia now has a better charter, but this new charter needs to be put into effect. If citizens are not alert, the fruits won in legislation may be lost in poor administration. There may even be sabotage from within to discredit the new charter. No, this is not the time to slacken our efforts, but rather to redouble them.

As a national holiday, July Fourth is not only a day of commemoration, but also a day of re-dedication. Let it be as much to us in a local sense as it is in a broader national sense. Let it be a day of rededication to our local task of achieving real democratic government, as well as of rededication to the national task laid down for us by our revolutionary forefathers in the days of 1776.

"It should be recognized that laws, constitutions or charters alone do not insure either virtuous people or good government. These simply control the *form* of government. The essential element in good government must come from the spirit in which the laws are administered. . . ."

—DIRECTOR WILLIAM S. TWINING
before the Business Science Club of Philadelphia.

CITIZENS' BUSINESS

BUREAU OF MUNICIPAL RESEARCH

ISSUED WEEKLY AT 805 FRANKLIN BANK BUILDING
PHILADELPHIA. ENTERED AS SECOND CLASS MATTER
JUNE 7, 1913 AT THE POST OFFICE AT PHILADELPHIA,
PA. UNDER THE ACT OF AUGUST 24TH, 1912 —
SUBSCRIPTION FIFTY CENTS THE YEAR

1919 Charter Series: No. 7

Modern Municipal Machinery for Philadelphia

No. 372   July 10, 1919

Some Accomplishments of the New Charter:

1. *A Purchasing Agent*
2. *A City Architect*
3. *A Department of Public Welfare*
4. *An Appointive City Solicitor*
5. *A Unified Accounting System*
6. *A Small Single Chambered Council*

OF the structural changes proposed in the original charter bill the reorganization of Councils was the only one that provoked widespread public discussion during the period of legislative deliberation. It was not, however, the only important structural change embodied in the bill, nor was it the only important structural change that finally became law. The fact is that a number of important changes of this character appeared in the original bill and nearly all of them with but slight modifications have since become a part of our city charter. They are summarized briefly as follows:

1. A Purchasing Agent Supersedes the Department of Supplies.

The original charter bill would have substituted for the old department of supplies a purchasing agent to be appointed by the mayor under civil service rules. The charter act retains this provision but provides that instead of being appointed under civil service rules the purchasing agent shall be appointed by the mayor subject to confirmation by the city council. A supplementary bill making the city purchasing agent ex officio county purchasing agent died in committee.

2. A City Architect Established.

The provisions of the original bill relating to the new office of city architect are retained in the charter act with the modification that the city architect is not to be appointed under civil service rules, but, like the purchasing agent, appointed by the mayor subject to confirmation by the city council.

3. Department of Public Welfare Assured.

The original bill proposed to center the activities of the bureau of correction, the bureau of charities and the board of recreation in a new department of public welfare. This proposal with a slight modification is carried out by the charter act. During the passage of the bill it was so amended that no hospitals will come under the department of public welfare, but all city hospitals will be brought under the department of public health.

4. Bureau of Health Becomes a Department.

Following the provisions of the original bill the charter act raises the bureau of health to the rank of a department to be called the department of public health.

5. An Appointive City Solicitor.

The new act provides that the city solicitor shall be appointed by the mayor subject to confirmation by the city council instead of being elected as heretofore. This was a proposal of the charter committee which went through without change.

6. Receiver of Taxes Remains Elective.

The original bill proposed that the city treasurer should take over the functions of the receiver of taxes and that the latter office be abolished. This change was bitterly opposed by the present receiver of taxes and at his instance the attorney general had it stricken from the bill.

The result is that the act as passed does not change the law as to these offices.

7. City Bookkeeping System Centralized.

The charter act provides for a completely unified accounting system for the city, to be under the jurisdiction of the city controller. All employes of the city engaged in keeping the accounts are to be under the controller's supervision. This provision was one of the original proposals of the charter committee and was passed without change.

8. Reorganization of Councils.

Despite a great deal of heated discussion, the original proposal of the charter committee substituting a small single chambered council for the present large two chambered body was finally adopted without change. Members of the new council will be chosen by state senatorial districts instead of by wards as in the past. Each district will be entitled to one councilman for every 20,000 assessed voters or major fraction thereof. On the basis of 1918 figures this will give us a council of 21 members, as compared with our present legislative body of 145 members.

"The most important event in American municipal history since the adoption of the present frame of government for New York City is the new charter of Philadelphia."—*New York Evening Post,* June 25, 1919.

Pol. Sci.

CITIZENS' BUSINESS

BUREAU OF MUNICIPAL RESEARCH

ISSUED WEEKLY AT 805 FRANKLIN BANK BUILDING
PHILADELPHIA. ENTERED AS SECOND CLASS MATTER
JUNE 7, 1913 AT THE POST OFFICE AT PHILADELPHIA,
PA., UNDER THE ACT OF AUGUST 24TH, 1912 —
SUBSCRIPTION FIFTY CENTS THE YEAR

1919 Charter Series: No. 8

Municipal Street Cleaning Now Has Right of Way

No. 373   July 17, 1919

The charter committee's proposals regarding contracts were the ones, apparently, that gave the
charter's opponents the greatest disquiet.

Yet in the last analysis neither the original bill
nor the act as finally passed provides anything un-
reasonable or factional.

The Main Bone of Contention

No item in the entire program of the Charter Committee precipitated so lively a debate as the one requiring the city to do its own street cleaning and kindred work of an "unspecifiable" character.

The arguments and the proposals of the charter committee were set forth in CITIZENS' BUSINESS 358 of April 3rd—No. 4 of this Charter Series. Briefly, the original charter bill contained a provision that Philadelphia *must* do its own street cleaning and repairing, as well as the collection of ashes, waste, rubbish and garbage, after December 31, 1919. A proviso permitted doing this work by contract if three-fourths of the council and the mayor so decided.

The Amendments

The governor held—and we think not entirely without reason—that changed conditions in the future might make this rigid three-fourths provision seem unduly irksome. He thought that so mandatory a stipulation by the legislature was an invasion of the principle of home rule, and in deference to his wishes "a majority" was substituted for "three-fourths" in the proviso. Moreover, in deference to the opinion of the city solicitor and other public officials, the date for making it the city's duty to clean its own streets and remove waste was advanced one year—to December 31, 1920.

The Purpose Achieved

In the long view of history these amendments to the original charter proposals will be regarded as trifling—one year is as but a day in the life of a great city, and municipal (instead of contract) street cleaning will be so much a matter of course in the future that the famous proviso will have no importance.

The principles sought have been attained. The city is kindly "permitted" to do by itself what every modern city has been doing for years, and the fact that it ought so to do is written into the law, although an execption is made possible if the peoples' representatives so vote.

Long Term Contracts Now Permitted

An excellent feature of the charter article on contracts—one also subjected to considerable discussion and amendment—is the section that permits the city to enter into contracts for longer than one year, which is the present maximum period. The advantages of freedom to enter upon long-term contracts for certain purposes are so obvious as to need no comment.

The city's interest is protected by a stipulation that whenever the term of a contract exceeds four years, there shall be inserted in the contract a clause reserving to the city the right to cancel such contract at any time after four years, without liability by the city to the contractor.

"In reorganizing the Civil Service system, means must be found to eliminate the lazy and inefficient. The best way to do this is to make Government employment more attractive for the industrious and efficient."

—*Hon. Edward Keating*
in the Searchlight for July, 1919.

CITIZENS' BUSINESS

BUREAU OF MUNICIPAL RESEARCH

ISSUED WEEKLY AT 805 FRANKLIN BANK BUILDING
PHILADELPHIA. ENTERED AS SECOND CLASS MATTER
JUNE 7, 1913 AT THE POST OFFICE AT PHILADELPHIA,
PA., UNDER THE ACT OF AUGUST 24TH, 1912—
SUBSCRIPTION FIFTY CENTS THE YEAR

1919 Charter Series: No. 9

Philadelphia's Changed Budget Procedure

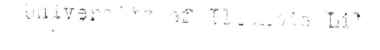

No. 374   July 24, 1919

A brief statement of the principal changes effected by the new charter in the city's budget procedure.

OF the numerous changes wrought by the city's new charter, those relating to the budget are by no means the least beneficial and significant.

Mayoral Budget Provided

Perhaps the most noticeable budgetary change is that which places upon the mayor the responsibility of initiating an annual work-and-financial program and submitting it directly to the council.

No longer will the council receive from the city controller a mere compilation of departmental requests, which in form and detail are unsuited to its needs. Instead, it will receive from the mayor a co-ordinated, inclusive program, setting forth his estimates of the departmental needs, and framed in such form and detail as the council prescribes.

The City Controller's Part

Except for the preparation of an estimate of receipts and an estimate of fixed liabilities, which estimates the mayor must include in his program, and which the council is required to follow, the city controller is relieved of all duties now performed by him in connection with the annual budget.

The Council Acts

Upon receipt of the mayor's program the council is to begin consideration of it in open public sessions. After this program has been duly considered the council decides the amount of taxes needed for the ensuing year, levies those taxes, provides for the fixed liabilities estimated by the city controller, and then appropriates the rest of the city controller's estimate of receipts for the other needs of the city. These needs are determined solely by the council, which is not in any degree limited or bound by the mayor's estimates or recommendations.

Real versus Fictitious Estimates

The inflexible, fictitious formula by which receipts have been "estimated" for the last forty years, has at last been scrapped. From now on, the estimates of receipts can be very close approximations of real estimates, as changed factors are to be fully taken into account.

Borrowing for Current Expenses Prohibited

The long-lived custom of borrowing money for current expenses is prohibited. Except for the borrowing of money in anticipation of the collection of revenue, or of the issuance of bonds already authorized, and except for the creation of purely emergency loans not exceeding two million dollars at any one time, money may be borrowed only for purposes which the city controller certifies to be capital expenditures.

Unexpected Receipts Immediately Available

Unexpected receipts may, upon certification by the city controller, be appropriated during the year in which received,

4

instead of lying idle until the succeeding year, thus, among other things, reducing the need for emergency and other loans.

Making City Money Work

The wasteful practice of borrowing money before the city actually needs it is made unnecessary, for the new charter specifically provides for the advancing, without restriction, of money between the loan fund and the general fund. This, in effect, consolidates the only two really important funds of the city, places their money, as it were, in one pot, and thus abolishes the anomaly of borrowing millions of dollars for one fund when the other fund has millions which it does not need at the time—perhaps will not need for months.

Certain Contracts Require Only Partial Appropriations

The prohibition against entering into a contract unless an appropriation for the full amount of the contract has previously been made, is modified so as to permit certain long-term contracts to be entered into without the necessity of making appropriation for more than the first year's share of the amount of the contract. Each succeeding year's share of the contract must, however, be provided for by appropriations.

Moral Claims to be Brought into the Limelight

"Moral claims" against the city can no longer be sandwiched in with regular appropriations or otherwise taken care of in concealment. They must now be provided for in ordinances which deal exclusively with moral claims. Furthermore, the name of each claimant and the amount he is to receive are to be specifically set forth, and the ordinance must obtain a two-thirds vote of the council and also the approval of the mayor.

An Interesting Study

A comparison of the budgetary provisions of the new charter with those of the charter bill at the time it was introduced into the legislature will prove interesting.

The most notable difference between them is the basis adopted. The charter revision committee sought to have the city financed on a basis substantially similar to that of well-managed private enterprise. It set up a minimum "pay-as-you-go" standard in revenue and expense accounting terms. This would have made it unnecessary to impose various inflexible, complicated and costly limitations and qualifications, such as those required by the cash receipts and disbursements basis in order to obtain the same desirable results.

For reasons that will not be gone into at this time, the Attorney General insisted upon a continuance of the cash receipts and disbursements basis that has obtained for years past. As a result, the budgetary provisions of the new charter are framed along those less satisfactory lines.

An Evaluation

Viewed from the popular standpoint, the charter revision committee succeeded in getting practically all that it sought in the way of budgetary reform. Viewed from the standpoint of the specialist in public finance and accounting, or of the man who sees the numerous possibilities of the charter committee's original budgetary standard, the charter revisionists were forced to sacrifice some of their finest proposals, but obtained about sixty per cent. of what they set out to secure in budget matters.

It Was Ever Thus!

Every man will own that an author, as such, ought to be tried by the merit of his productions only; but pride, party, and prejudice at this time run so very high that experience shows we form our notions of a piece by the character of the author. Nay, there are some very humble politicians in and about this city who will ask on which side the writer is before they presume to give their opinion of the thing written.— Benjamin Franklin, in *Digging for Hidden Treasure*.

CITIZENS' BUSINESS

BUREAU OF MUNICIPAL RESEARCH

ISSUED WEEKLY AT 805 FRANKLIN BANK BUILDING
PHILADELPHIA. ENTERED AS SECOND CLASS MATTER
JUNE 7, 1913 AT THE POST OFFICE AT PHILADELPHIA,
PA., UNDER THE ACT OF AUGUST 24TH, 1912—
SUBSCRIPTION FIFTY CENTS THE YEAR

A Violation of the Spirit if not of the Letter

No. 375   July 31, 1919

Article III, section 7 of the Constitution of Pennsylvania contains the words:

> "The General Assembly shall not pass any local or special law . . . . . Regulating the affairs of counties, cities, townships, wards, boroughs, or school districts:"

Of Course They Celebrated

There was a party in the department of the Recorder of Deeds when the news came that the governor had signed the bill increasing every salary in the office—save only that of the recorder of deeds himself. Naturally, a large body of men—for the most part poorly paid—felt elated to know that the legislature had relieved their financial plights to a certain extent.

But the Method is Wrong

It makes us smile a little whimsically to read this new law—House Bill No. 1160—after we had just been congratulating ourselves on the greater measure of home rule secured through the charter legislation. In the charter, *not a single mandatory salary is set up*—except, very properly, that of the councilmen—whereas the bill under discussion mentions each position in the office by title, and sets up a salary.

The absurd rigidity of this new law can best be understood by citing some of the positions for which salaries are fixed. These include:

"one cashier and assistant bookkeeper $1500
two chief deed index clerks   2100
one miscellaneous clerk   1500
six miscellaneous clerks   1500
one chief compare clerk mortgages   1600
two assistant custodians of records   1200
three assistant custodians of records   1200"
etc., etc., etc.

No, gentle reader, the legislature did not say:

"Bill Smith $2000
Tom Brown   1800
Ike Jones   1500"
etc., etc., etc.

Nor did it even establish salaries for:

"The short fat blond from the 27th
ward $2500
The lanky, cross-eyed boy from the
6th   1800
The faithful door bell puller of the
X division of the Y ward   1200"

but one is tempted to guess that the bill-drafter had as his guide a roster of Philadelphia's department—*not the constitutional provision against special legislation.*

Too Much State Dictation

The Bureau of Municipal Research need hardly take the trouble to explain that it is not opposed to more adequate salaries for public servants. Together with its demand for more efficient and competent service from public employes, it has stood consistently for a public policy of fair compensation.

This new law, however, is a fundamentally false way to get at the problem. In the first place, it takes care of one department of our city-county government, without reference to a square deal for other departments, in many of which there are also faithful and underpaid employes.

In the second place, it places beyond the jurisdiction of the local council, the control over local details of government which should without question be in the hands of the city's own authorities.

In the third place, it creates an inflexible organization with titles entirely too restrictive. Since this organization is a creature of the legislature, it will require legislative action even to modify it slightly.

A Look Ahead

Some day a new or amended state constitution will enable Philadelphia to discard forever the outworn and fictitious distinction between "city" and "county." At some not distant day, too, a real salary standardization program will be inaugurated in our city service.

When these happy events come to pass, the straightjacket law just signed will have to go, but in the meantime it is just one more incubus—just one more premium on inefficiency, complexity, unfairness.

In connection with the very special kindness extended to one particular department of our local government, it is pertinent to quote these words of Herbert Spencer:

"No one can be perfectly free till all are free; no one can be perfectly moral till all are moral; no one can be perfectly happy till all are happy."

CITIZENS' BUSINESS

BUREAU OF MUNICIPAL RESEARCH

ISSUED WEEKLY AT 805 FRANKLIN BANK BUILDING
PHILADELPHIA, ENTERED AS SECOND CLASS MATTER
JUNE 7, 1913 AT THE POST OFFICE AT PHILADELPHIA,
PA., UNDER THE ACT OF AUGUST 24TH, 1912.—
SUBSCRIPTION FIFTY CENTS THE YEAR.

1919 Charter Series: No. 10

The New Charter and Loans

No. 376   **August 7, 1919**

What does the new charter say about loans?
**What changes does it make in the city's
loan and sinking fund transactions?**
Are the changes in the right direction?

Couldn't Be Ignored

The new charter simply had to deal with loans. No act worthy of the name "charter" could ignore this very important and far-reaching subject. Furthermore, if the new charter was to give Philadelphia a new and improved fiscal system—as was repeatedly promised by the governor and by the charter revision committee—it had to take hold of the loan question, and *make some marked changes.*

When the charter bill left the hands of the charter revision committee it provided for a fiscal system that was really new, inclusive, harmonious, and practical.

All in One Place

Except for very brief and incidental references to loans in the article on the budget, all the charter provisions relating to loans and sinking funds were assembled in an article entitled "indebtedness." All of these provisions were drawn with extreme care and were in complete harmony with the revenue and expense budget procedure which the bill made mandatory.

With the forced elimination of the revenue and expense budget procedure and the substitution in its place of the cash receipts and appropriation basis, it became necessary to insert several new provisions relating to loans, in order to accomplish the same results that would have been accomplished *automatically* by the revenue and expense basis originally provided. These provisions, instead of being grouped with the others relating to loans and sink-

2

ing funds, were placed in the article which was substituted for the original budget provisions.

Indebtedness Provisions Unscathed

The indebtedness article became law exactly as introduced in the legislature, except for the elimination of six words that related to temporary loans in anticipation of the collection of revenue, which temporary loans it became necessary to treat at greater length under the substitute plan.

Space does not permit a discussion of the philosophy of loans and sinking funds, nor does it allow a further comparison between the bill as introduced and the bill as enacted into law. We shall, therefore, have to be content with a brief statement of the principal provisions relating to loans and sinking funds contained in the charter.

Simplified Law

For purposes of simplification and clarification practically all statutory law relating to loans and sinking funds was expressly repealed so far as Philadelphia was concerned. Purely technical reasons account for the two or three laws that were not so repealed.

As a result of the express repeal of the numerous laws that applied in whole or in part to Philadelphia, and the setting up in the charter of an almost inclusive loan procedure—certain details were not set up for constitutional reasons—we have only the state constitution, the charter, and two or three other laws (instead of a large number) to

3

look to for the law regarding Philadelphia's loans and sinking funds.

In Accord with Changed Council

Inasmuch as our large, unwieldy, time-consuming, two-chambered council, to which a large part of the loan procedure had been specially adapted, is to be succeeded on January 5, 1920 by a small single-chambered council, the entire loan procedure has been adapted to the new local legislative body.

Makes Constitutional Amendments Self-Executory

In order to eliminate the necessity of awaiting action by the legislature before certain future constitutional changes relating to indebtedness can be put into effect, the indebtedness article is worded so as to make these particular changes effective as soon as they become part of the constitution.

Encourages Serial Bonds

As a means of compelling the issuance of serial bonds instead of long-term bonds in cases where long-term bonds are not to the best interest of the city, and also as a means of taking certain mysteries and certain possibilities of "high finance" out of Philadelphia's sinking funds, the charter provides that all money required by the constitution or otherwise to be applied to the eventual payment of bonds or other indebtedness shall be applied at as early a date as possible to the purchase and actual cancelation of the indebtedness to which it eventually is to be applied.

4

Cuts Red Tape

In the case of indebtedness for which the constitution requires the approval of the electors before it can be incurred, the new charter provides a vastly simpler and speedier procedure than that which it repeals. Formerly councils passed an ordinance signifying the desire of the city to increase its indebtedness and also setting a time for an election by the people on the question of whether or not the indebtedness shall be increased; and then passed another ordinance after the electors had given their consent to the increase, authorizing the incurrence of the indebtedness. Under the new charter provisions, the council merely passes one ordinance authorizing the incurrence of the indebtedness, subject to the consent of the electors.

Four Kinds of Debt

The charter recognizes four distinct classes of indebtedness:

1. Temporary loans in anticipation of the collection of revenue.
2. Temporary loans in anticipation of the issuance of bonds or other evidences of indebtedness previously authorized.
3. Emergency loans.
4. Other indebtedness.

With the exception of temporary loans in anticipation of the collection of revenue, all indebtedness must receive the affirmative votes of two-thirds of all the members of the council before it may be incurred.

5

Temporary Financing

In the case of temporary loans in anticipation of the collection of revenue, the mayor, the city controller, and the city solicitor, or any two of these, may negotiate such loans, provided that the total amount outstanding after their negotiation does not exceed ten per cent of the estimated revenue receipts of the year. These loans are required to be represented by notes maturing the same year in which they are issued, and provision must be made for redeeming them during that year.

Temporary loans in anticipation of the issuance of bonds or other evidences of indebtedness previously authorized may be issued without any limit other than the amount of the bonds or other evidences of indebtedness in anticipation of which they are issued. These loans must mature within one year from the time they are issued. By the judicious use of these loans the city can arrange to carry a very much smaller cash balance than in the past, thus saving large sums in interest charges; can postpone the flotation of bonds until market conditions are favorable, and thus float bonds at a lower rate of interest than otherwise would be possible; can carry a fair amount of its debt at a lower rate of interest than it would have to pay on the same debt if in the form of long-term bonds; can save the four mill state tax that it would have to pay on the same debt were it represented by bonds; and can do several other things highly advantageous to itself.

Provision for Emergencies

Emergency loans may be created by the council, provided the aggregate amount of emergency loans outstanding after their creation does not exceed two million dollars. These loans differ from the other temporary loans in that they are not issued

6

in anticipation of cash to be received later, but are issued for the purpose of securing cash that will be free for additional appropriation. Unless paid within the year in which they are issued, emergency loans must be provided for out of the revenues of the succeeding year before any of those revenues may be appropriated for general purposes.

The temporary loans of the past are done away with. The $1,200,000 limitation formerly existing is replaced by the limits mentioned in connection with the three foregoing kinds of loans.

Long-Term Financing

The fourth class of indebtedness may be issued up to the amount of the constitutional limitations and may be issued for any length of time up to fifty years. Ordinances authorizing such indebtedness must provide for the collection of a tax sufficient to pay the interest thereon and the principal thereof as required by the constitution.

This indebtedness may be authorized only "for the purpose of acquiring property, erecting buildings, bridges, or other structures (but not for the repair of the same), paving streets (but not re-paving or repairing the same), or for any other permanent improvements or capital outlay of any kind, provided that all of such proposed expenditures are certified to the council by the city controller to be capital expenditures as distinguished from current expenses, prior to the authorization of such debt." However, if during the preceding year current funds were used for capital expenditures, the current funds may be reimbursed from loan moneys borrowed for that purpose.

More Light for the Voter

In the case of such of this indebtedness as must receive the consent of the electors before it can be incurred, the new charter requires the advertising of a certificate of the city controller concerning the city's indebtedness. This certificate is far more informative and more suitable as a guide to the electors than has ever before been presented to them.

The council is given the right to purchase any of the city's debt at any time it is able to do so, but any debt so purchased is required to be canceled. This affords opportunities for advantageous refunding or reducing of the city's indebtedness at any time.

Improvements, Without Rigidity

In drafting the indebtedness article great care was exercised to provide for a number of desirable possibilities and to avoid too narrow a path for the city to follow. Although serial bonds were considered most advantageous to the city as a general proposition, they were not made absolutely compulsory. Care was taken, for example, so to word the article that there would not be the slightest question about the city having the right, should it some day so desire, to acquire an indispensable public plant or utility, or any other property which it might have the right to purchase, on an instalment or deferred purchase plan if within the constitutional limitations as to amount and maximum period of debt.

USUALLY we manage to treat the topic of our weekly bulletin in the brief space of five or six hundred words. We wish to keep CITIZENS' BUSINESS, above all, *brief*. There is so little accurate information available to citizens, however, on certain aspects of local government—notably on finances—that we feel that it is necessary occasionally to sacrifice mere brevity for accuracy.

Pol. Sci.

CITIZENS' BUSINESS

BUREAU OF MUNICIPAL RESEARCH

ISSUED WEEKLY AT 805 FRANKLIN BANK BUILDING
PHILADELPHIA, ENTERED AS SECOND CLASS MATTER
JUNE 7, 1913 AT THE POST OFFICE AT PHILADELPHIA,
PA., UNDER THE ACT OF AUGUST 24TH, 1912 —
SUBSCRIPTION FIFTY CENTS A YEAR

AUG 19 1919

We're for *Preventing* Difficulties
Are You?

No. 377   August 14, 1919

If you were running a large business, could you
have a salary policy based on partiality, guesswork,
indifference, inequity—and get away with it?

A Sensitive Topic

A large part of the tax-dollar goes for salaries. And salaries are a touchier point than ever in these days of rising living costs. Hence it is not surprising that a great number of bills affecting salaries are ground through the state legislature and the local councils nowadays.

Patchwork

But it ought to astonish us that no one points out the futility and the unfairness of piecemeal salary raises. The merest tyro in administration ought to be able to see that isolated salary raises merely afford some measure of relief to the individuals concerned. They do not afford general relief; they often work general hardship; and they do nothing toward the promised standardization of salaries and grades of employment.

Are the sporadic increases adequate? Are they too large for the respective positions? Do they increase the relative injustice to the other employes, who did not benefit by special legislation? Is it, or is it not, time to stop dabbling with the subject? Does it not call for comprehensive treatment *immediately?*

We Told You So

Had the mayor and his civil service commission, kept their promise to the public to carry through a comprehensive program of standardizing salaries and grades, there would now be abundant data available on which a scheme could be predicated to alleviate the present acute salary situation in the city's service.

However—spilled milk.

Absurd

We now have a spectacle of curious inconsistencies. The governor approves a bill raising practically every salary in one department (see CITIZENS' BUSINESS No. 375, July 31) while he vetoes another measure (allotting a fixed percentage of the local tax levy to the police pension fund) because the matter is one that should properly be the concern of the local councils.

And, our mayor reduces the amount of an ordinance to raise the salary of the head of the Bureau of Charities on the ground that the bureau chief's salary should not be greater than that of his superior officer, the assistant director of the department. Was His Honor aware, we wonder, that of the sixteen bureau chiefs in the city's service, *ten* now get *more* than the $4000 salary paid to each assistant director (taking perquisites into consideration), three get *the same*, and that only three get *less* than the assistant director?

Fetishes and Facts

An examination of the salaries of the chiefs—ranging from $2000 to $10,000—discloses no special scheme or plan. At the same time there are no obvious incongruities, considering the wide divergence in the character of the positions. In any revision of these salaries based on qualifications, duties and responsibilities, the changes, if any, would probably be moderate increases in a few cases. There seems to us to be no administrative nor equitable reason why a bureau chief should necessarily get less salary than the assistant director of his department. If there are such reasons, the whole salary scheme calls loudly for revision on that score alone.

But there *are* inequities; there *are* salary maladjustments that injure the employes' morale and that affect adversely the quality of public service. These should be corrected—and speedily.

The Double Command to Action

In this connection it is pertinent to remark that whereas formerly there was no *legal obstacle* in the way of standardizing the municipal service, since the adoption of the new city charter it has become the *legal duty* of the civil service commission to standardize the service.

More compelling, however, than the legal mandate is simply the existing state of affairs. There are certain necessary city employes—a good many of them—whose work is indispensable to the daily living of 2,000,000 Philadelphians. If their work is to continue, they must be able to have the necessaries of life and to pay their bills. It would seem to be a matter of common sense, where resources are limited, as they are when they consist of money raised by taxation, to abolish sinecure jobs and pay necessary workers adequately. That is one of the things that standardization is intended to accomplish. Anything else is injustice. Long continued injustice breeds discontent, and discontent is not to be regarded lightly. Chicago's nonchalant treatment of municipal employes has led to some em-embarrassing strikes.

It would seem to be an excellent time for Philadelphia's administration to begin keeping this particular promise.

Philadelphia *City* had $18,000 on deposit in the North Penn Bank as of December 31, 1918. According to the newspaper reports this balance remained at the time of the crash.

It is a little item of interest to citizens to know that this deposit is unsecured and may be wiped out. Had the Philadelphia *School District* had a similar deposit, the taxpayers' money would have been protected, as required by law, either by a surety bond or by a deposit of approved securities.

Why shouldn't the *city* take equally good care of its taxpayers? The banks pay the same rate of interest on both kinds of deposits.

The Double Command to Action

In this connection it is pertinent to remark that whereas formerly there was no *legal obstacle* in the way of standardizing the municipal service, since the adoption of the new city charter it has become the *legal duty* of the civil service commission to standardize the service.

More compelling, however, than the legal mandate is simply the existing state of affairs. There are certain necessary city employes—a good many of them—whose work is indispensable to the daily living of 2,000,000 Philadelphians. If their work is to continue, they must be able to have the necessaries of life and to pay their bills. It would seem to be a matter of common sense, where resources are limited, as they are when they consist of money raised by taxation, to abolish sinecure jobs and pay necessary workers adequately. That is one of the things that standardization is intended to accomplish. Anything else is injustice. Long continued injustice breeds discontent, and discontent is not to be regarded lightly. Chicago's nonchalant treatment of municipal employes has led to some emembarrassing strikes.

It would seem to be an excellent time for Philadelphia's administration to begin keeping this particular promise.

Philadelphia *City* had $18,000 on deposit in the North Penn Bank as of December 31, 1918. According to the newspaper reports this balance remained at the time of the crash.

It is a little item of interest to citizens to know that this deposit is unsecured and may be wiped out. Had the Philadelphia *School District* had a similar deposit, the taxpayers' money would have been protected, as required by law, either by a surety bond or by a deposit of approved securities.

Why shouldn't the *city* take equally good care of its taxpayers? The banks pay the same rate of interest on both kinds of deposits.

CITIZENS' BUSINESS

BUREAU OF MUNICIPAL RESEARCH

ISSUED WEEKLY AT 805 FRANKLIN BANK BUILDING
PHILADELPHIA. ENTERED AS SECOND CLASS MATTER
JUNE 7, 1913 AT THE POST OFFICE AT PHILADELPHIA.
PA., UNDER THE ACTS OF AUGUST 24TH, 1912—
SUBSCRIPTION FIFTY CENTS A YEAR

1919 Charter Series: No. 11

Philadelphia Stirreth

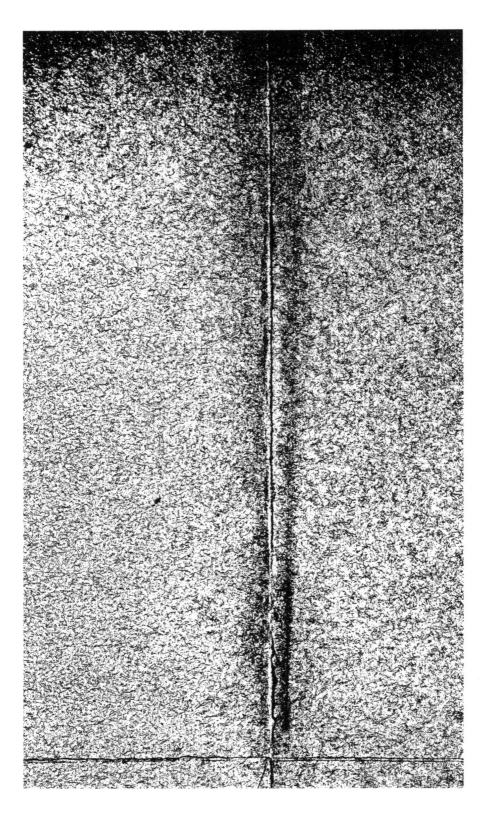

ORPTION in what was transpiring
rsailles did not prevent Phila-
a from applying the self-criti-
and constructive impulse of the
to its own local government.
t as "reconstruction" is used as
boleth in every community to
every needed (or other) program
nomic or social action, so has
ocracy" become the watchword
litical action. In Philadelphia
had long been a feeling of discon-
ith the antiquated framework of
ipal government, and two years
number of civic bodies attempted
ure from the legislature the en-
nt of some twenty measures
ed to patch up the defects of the
led city charter.

enthusiasm of the legislature's
se can readily be measured by
ct that all of the bills died
mmittee. A quickened sense
litical responsibility, however,
ht about the organization of a
ovement for the legislative ses-
ust ended, and it is gratifying to
le to report that a genuine ad-
has been secured in the direc-
f more efficient and more demo-
city government.
Philadelphia situation prior to
w charter is by no means easy to
ehend, despite the fact that to
litical scientists its organization
and scheme of government would
r relatively simple—compared,

for instance, with Chicago's. Th
plicating factors in Philadelphia's
ter problems are historical and "
ical," *i.e.*, partisan.

HISTORICAL BACKGROUND

The historical complications
offer no special difficulties had
Philadelphians been willing to
nize frankly that changed com
conditions call for changed mac
—that tradition is of itself not a
worthy guide to action. It is
esting to note that in this hi
tradition-bound city there is le
herence to "things as they are'
was formerly the case. Perha
war explains the change. Ho
there still remained a large meas
fondness for the old, and this fo
had been consistently utilize
politicians to continue the statu
To illustrate—when the presen
was welded together out of t
city proper and diverse town
villages, in 1854, compromises
deemed necessary in order to
opposition from Germantown and
outlying districts. Accordingly
citizens of Germantown contin
this day to elect their town cler
they and five other sections of th
also elect their poor district o
who levy separate poor taxes f
respective "townships," which
dition, by the way, it seems the c

417

unty are physically coterminous
heir finances as well as many
governmental features were par-
unified in the consolidation act.
1873 Pennsylvania adopted a
constitution, and, in common
all other state constitutions of
eriod, a considerable amount of
ory matter was written into its
asic law. Among other things,
ew constitution continued the
:e of election by the people of
ber of county officers, so that a
elphia voter at a municipal
n is supposed to exercise his
ion in the choice of a long list of
s of widely varying functions
sponsibilities.

only important amendment to
harter" of 1854 was the Bullitt
1885 which was a great advance
direction of simplified, responsi-
vernment. This bill drew its
tion from the charter of the city
oklyn and its primary purpose.
emphasize the separation of the
ive and legislative branches of
ment, and to concentrate power
sponsibility in the mayor. Be-
of constitutional difficulties, the
ade no changes in the county
ment, nor did it disturb either
cameral council or the six poor
ts. The council continued to
elect and common branches, and
years went by the aggregate
ership grew to the imposing
r of 145—the largest municipal
ture in the United States. It is
because of this obsolete and

The local judges (aggregating 29
common pleas, orphans' and mu
courts, and 28 magistrates) are e
by the people. Under the ex
arrangement the mayor, the he
two city and nine "county" d
ments are also elected. There
number of boards and officials c
by the common pleas judges, an
heads of the remaining city d
ments are chosen by the mayor.

The public schools are not und
city government, but are under a
of public education, appointed b
common pleas judges, which bo
empowered by law to levy taxes a
conduct the school system en
independently of the city govern
The school code of 1911 which cr
this independent status has, o
whole, worked well, but there are
demands for improvements in
school management. These den
found expression in movements
pendent of that for charter revisi
the details will not be discussed

The legislative body, which
been unchanged in general form
1796, was patterned after the
parliamentary model of an uppe
a lower house. The select c
consists of one councilman from
of 48 wards, while the common c
seats one from each ward for
4,000 names on the list of ass
voters for that ward, except that
ward has at least one common co
man.

The old ward lines have unde
but few changes, despite the

largest ward has
and only five com-
r a population of
,000. The forty-
a wide variety of
ns between these

ove-described per-
r was resented by
elieves in equitable
as there is no con-
in favor of the
as doomed to even-

L COMPLEX

t for a long time
sideration of the
strictly on their
between the two
lican organization
his strife has, to a
ent, spread to the

nent is under the
h of the organiza-
Senator Edwin H.
hich is the faction
a's senior United
es Penrose. The
ijority of the state
ally believed to be
rose faction.
the latter group,
have allied them-

and pleading with the legislature and the governor not to disturb the beautiful symmetry of the venerable system.

In the meantime the self-constituted citizens' charter committee had begun to crystallize the existing sentiment in the city in favor of a better charter, and all the newspapers aided the cause. When this sentiment became discernible, the Vare faction skilfully altered their tactics and declared that there was undoubted need for certain changes in the framework of the city's government, but that the charter committee's bills were unsatisfactory. Thereupon they introduced a measure described as one that would "take the police out of politics" and another ostensibly for the purpose of reforming the city's financing. A careful perusal of each of these measures disclosed nothing but perfect red herrings. As a means of confusing the legislature and as a means of complicating the problem of charter revision these measures were well conceived, but no impartial critic could find in them any contribution to the strengthening or bettering of the municipal machinery.

While the proposals of the charter committee were declared, by their Vare critics, to be "tarred with the Penrose stick," the measures were really by no means partisan in character and were drafted by students and specialists after man

avoided this issue, admittedly
ley offend their political allies.

merits or faults of the charter
must be conceded, did not deter-
its passage nearly so much as
e political situation. The Pen-
and the handful of Democrats
rted the independents and so
e bill through, but not until
nor Sproul and his attorney-
l had dictated a number of
tant amendments—some as sops
Vare followers, some of no signi-
e at all, and some that they no
honestly believed to be im-
ments. The amended bill passed
June, just before the adjourn-
and it received the governor's
ure on June 25. It had been
uced by Senator George Wood-
(described as an independent,
with Penrose support) on
3, nearly four months of sus-
legislative inaction, lobbying,
achination thus intervening.

HANGES PROPOSED, AND THOSE
SECURED

charter bill was a compromise
re, as are most legislative proof its character. It provided,
er, an inclusive frame of gov-
nt to the extent that the state
tution and our limited political
tion permit at this time. Be-
of limitations of space we shall
ttempt to go into great detail
ing each proposal nor even as to
final amendment of the city's

20,000 assessed voters. Propos
secure some representation at la
well as a splendid effort to intr
some rational system of propor
representation, were defeated i
charter committee. After viole
bate and various attempted a
ments in the legislature the cou
the new charter is as originall
posed by the charter committee,
us a council of 21 to begin with.

The powers of the mayor are
what modified in the new act.
are some structural improveme
the departments under his juris
such as the separation of healt
charities (now under one depart
and the creation of a new depar
of welfare to cover the charity
rections and recreational fun
but more especially to work
modern social lines. The effo
shorten the ballot were restrict
constitutional provisions, but
in this direction was taken i
proposals that the city's chie
officer, now elective, be appoint
the mayor, and that the posit
receiver of taxes, a purely orna
elective office, be abolished.
act finally passed, the charter
mittee and the reactionaries d
honors—the city solicitor be
appointive, but the status o
receiver of taxes remains unch

The civil service and corrupt
tises laws, which were passed i
famous "penitential" legislativ
sion of 1906, are somewhat str
ened and improved. In lieu of

nd firemen, to all civil servants,
 the course of the legislative
ing the size, of the commission
stored to three chosen .by the
l, however, instead of by the
. The proposal to extend the
oard privilege to others than
nen and firemen was eliminated.
ious political activity of po-
n and firemen is effectively
d and the too-wide choice of
ligibles for a single vacancy is
d to two. In a supplementary
attempt was made by the revi-
s to extend the merit system to
ty" as well as to all "city"
ments, but this bill never got
the senate committee.

charter bill set up fundamental
s in the fiscal procedure of the
y requiring a mayoral budget
t, however, restricting the free-
f the council in its action on it.
rticle of the charter required
ng on a revenue and expense
ting basis instead of on a basis
of cash receipts and cash dis-
ents as the existing law pro-
The initiation by the mayor,
e untrammeled freedom of ulti-
action by the council, survived
gislature, but the accounting
s were ripped out because the
or's attorney-general insisted
ley were "too technical."

powers of the city controller
larged to give him jurisdiction
ll the city's bookkeeping, thus
it possible to have a centralized

Philadelphia is one of the last
the sole remaining large city i
civilized world that has its
cleaning and waste removal do
private contract. In recent
there has been growing disc
with the inefficiency of these se
and studies of the methods em
elsewhere revealed the fact that
functions are usually perform
the municipalities themselves.
cordingly, the new charter requir
city to do its own street cleanin
waste removal after Decembe
1920. In deference to the hom
principle, and with the thoug
providing for some unforseeable
tion, it is stipulated that work
character may be done by cont
the council, by a majority vote
the approval of the mayor, so d
The original proposal of the c
committee was to make the exc
only if three quarters of the c
and the mayor consented to d
kind of work by contract, and a
this point was waged the most
contested fight in the charter cam
the governor finally ordering "r
ity" substituted for "three quar
The charter act also makes it p
for the city to enter into contra
periods longer than one year, a
not allowed under the present sta
By this means it is hoped to m
possible to secure genuine comp
in bidding on municipal contra
result not obtainable under th
year limit. The reason for the

however, to touch upon the ial features of the program and nal act and to make clear the changes and the objects sought attained. By this new charter—

but no less by the civic educatio its advocates and opponents fur —old Philadelphia has taken a stride forward into the ranks o gressive American municipalitie

CITIZENS' BUSINESS

BUREAU OF MUNICIPAL RESEARCH

ISSUED WEEKLY AT 805 FRANKLIN BANK BUILDING
PHILADELPHIA. ENTERED AS SECOND CLASS MATTER
JUNE 7, 1913, AT THE POST OFFICE AT PHILADELPHIA,
PA., UNDER THE ACT OF AUGUST 24TH, 1912 —
SUBSCRIPTION FIFTY CENTS THE YEAR·

No. 379 August 28, 1919

The new charter has not muddled the city's finances. The
finance provisions are not unconstitutional. There is no need
of an extra session of the legislature. But it is noteworthy
that the section under attack was written in, over protest, by
certain opponents of the charter.

the   but no less by the civic education that
and   its advocates and opponents furnished
—old Philadelphia has taken a giant
forward into the ranks of pro-
rican municipalities.

CITIZENS' BUSINESS

BUREAU OF MUNICIPAL RESEARCH

ISSUED WEEKLY AT 805 FRANKLIN BANK BUILDING
PHILADELPHIA. ENTERED AS SECOND CLASS MATTER
JUNE 7,1913 AT THE POST OFFICE AT PHILADELPHIA,
PA.,UNDER THE ACT OF AUGUST 24TH,1912—
SUBSCRIPTION FIFTY CENTS THE YEAR·

A Bit of Inside History

No. 379   August 28, 1919

> The new charter has not muddled the city's finances. The finance provisions are not unconstitutional. There is no need of an extra session of the legislature. But it is noteworthy that the section under attack was written in, over protest, by certain opponents of the charter.

The Boomerang Returns

Now is the time to place some blame where it properly belongs.

A suit is pending to test the validity of $90,070,000 of unissued city loans. In connection with it, sensational predictions have been spread broadcast, having as one of their results—if, indeed, not as their prime object—the blaming of the framers and sponsors of the new city charter for the so-called "loan muddle" into which the city is alleged to have fallen.

No better service could be rendered the citizens of Philadelphia at this time than by stating emphatically that the framers and sponsors of the new city charter are in no wise to blame for the present litigation, but that *certain enemies of charter revision* who hold high offices in the city government are wholly responsible for the section of the new law out of which the suit arises. A brief statement of facts will make this clear.

The History Begins

One of the major results which the charter committee sought to obtain for Philadelphia, and which the governor repeatedly promised, was a new and modern fiscal system. In keeping with the magnitude of the task and the intricate and important

2

problems involved, the charter committee devoted a very large part of its energy to a detailed study of the city's financial system. The services of lawyers, accountants, specialists in governmental problems, and a specially engaged professional bill drafter were used for several months. As a result of the joint work of the charter committee and of these consultants, the charter bill, as introduced in the senate on March 3, 1919 contained a fiscal system for Philadelphia that was new, inclusive, harmonious, workable, and calculated to produce highly beneficent results.

In Two Separate Articles

Except for very minor details, the charter committee's fiscal system was divided into two successive articles—one devoted to indebtedness, and the other to budget, revenues, expenses, tax rates, and other related matters.

As introduced by the charter revisionists, all details relating to indebtedness, including an entirely new and simplified procedure for authorizing loans and for administering the city's sinking funds, were placed together in the one article. This article was all-sufficient, in view of the automatic or self-executing character of the revenue and expense standard of financing which the budget article compelled the city to follow. It was not necessary under this standard to put any restrictions on the purposes for which loans could be issued. The city was required to raise enough revenue to meet its expenses—or, what amounts to the same thing, keep its expenses, including depreciation, within its income. Through simple accounting means it would be clearly demonstrated that so long as the city complied with this requirement it was not borrowing money for current expenses. Under this plan all money borrowed by the city and all other debts of the city would be fully represented and offset by increases in the city's property or assets.

Time Elapses

Although the charter bill was introduced early in the session of the legislature, and although both the city solicitor and the city controller had announced in unmistakable terms that they were opposed to any changes in the city's financial system, it was not until the eleventh hour that any public criticism was made in Harrisburg against the financial provisions of the charter bill.

When the criticism did come, it was only after the foes of charter revision had succeeded in having the attorney general demand that the charter committee's budget article be withdrawn from the charter bill, and that a budgetary and financial standard based on cash receipts and disbursements

CITIZENS' BUSINESS

BUREAU OF MUNICIPAL RESEARCH

ISSUED WEEKLY AT 805 FRANKLIN BANK BUILDING
PHILADELPHIA. ENTERED AS SECOND CLASS MATTER.
JUNE 7, 1913 AT THE POST OFFICE AT PHILADELPHIA,
PA., UNDER THE ACT OF AUGUST 24TH, 1912—
SUBSCRIPTION FIFTY CENTS THE YEAR

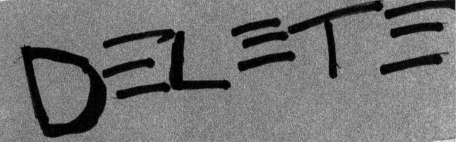

No. 380   September 4, 1919

> Morale is an all important factor in efficiency.
> We must not sacrifice it by permitting favoritism
> to determine promotions in the city service.

The Boomerang Returns

Now is the time to place some blame where it properly belongs.

A suit is pending to test the validity of $90,070,000 of unissued city loans. In connection with it, sensational predictions have been spread broadcast, having as one of their results—if, indeed, not as their prime object—the blaming of the framers and sponsors of the new city charter for the so-called "loan muddle" into which the city is alleged to have fallen.

No better service could be rendered the citizens of Philadelphia at this time than by stating emphatically that the fram...

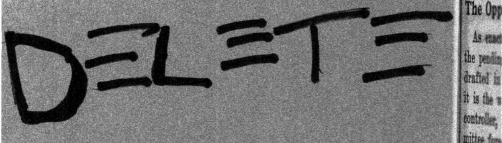

One of the major results which the charter committee sought to obtain for Philadelphia, and which the governor repeatedly promised, was a new and modern fiscal system. In keeping with the magnitude of the task and the intricate and important

be substituted. The attorney general's instructions also required that a representative of the revisionists sit down with the opposition and come to an agreement with them on the substitute article.

The Unavoidable

In compliance with the attorney general's behest a series of conferences was held with the charter's opponents, at all of which the opponents insisted on using drafts prepared in the city solicitor's office as the basis for discussion. The few changes that the charter committee's representative succeeded in effecting in the city solicitor's drafts were obtained only at great cost of time and energy. Conditions were such that the substitute article had to go in without even the minimum study and polishing that the charter committee wished to give it.

The Opponents' Wording

As enacted into law the article under attack in the pending taxpayer's suit is virtually the article drafted in the city solicitor's office. In essence, it is the wording which the city solicitor, the city controller, and the chairman of the finance committee forced into the charter against the protests of the charter revisionists. The responsibility is on the shoulders of these three officials and the attorney general. The wording is as different from that of the charter committee as night is from day. The opponents of the charter were unreceptive to suggestions—even those made simply to clarify their own draft.

A Vital Suggestion Turned Down

At one point in the conferences the suggestion was made on the part of the revisionists that words be added to the draft to indicate whether or not the prohibition against borrowing money for current expenses was to apply to all loans to be *issued* after the effective date of the article, or only to loans *authorized* after that date.

This suggestion was disposed of by the charter opponents on the ground that they did not want the prohibition to apply to loans authorized prior to the effective date, and that without specific wording to that effect the courts would unquestionably take the stand that only loans authorized after that date were restricted to purposes other than current expenses.

It is precisely the lack of this specific wording that has given rise to the litigation in question and to all the sensational assertions and predictions unjustifiably based thereon.

What Is and What Isn't

The charter committee's article on indebtedness (article XVIII), except for the elimination of six words made necessary by the article substituted for the original budget article, was enacted into law exactly as introduced in the legislature. That article is in no way involved in the pending suit. The only part of the new charter that is involved is section 8 of article XVII, which, as above stated, is not the work of the charter committee.

6

CITIZENS' BUSINESS

BUREAU OF MUNICIPAL RESEARCH

ISSUED WEEKLY AT 805 FRANKLIN BANK BUILDING
PHILADELPHIA. ENTERED AS SECOND CLASS MATTER
JUNE 7, 1913 AT THE POST OFFICE AT PHILADELPHIA,
PA., UNDER THE ACT OF   AUGUST 24TH, 1912—
SUBSCRIPTION FIFTY CENTS THE YEAR-

Merit or Favoritism
—Which?

No. 380   September 4, 1919

Morale is an all important factor in efficiency.
We must not sacrifice it by permitting favoritism
to determine promotions in the city service.

Shall Merit Determine Promotions?

The recent public hearing of the civil service commission on the proposed changes in the civil service rules was the first of its kind to be held under the new charter. In fact, it was the first of its kind ever held by a civil service commission in Philadelphia.

One of the important questions that evoked considerable discussion at the hearing was whether department heads should be given entire freedom in selecting men from lists of eligibles for promotion, or whether they should be required to appoint men in the order of their standing on the list. Under the existing rule department heads can promote anybody who has passed the promotion examination no matter where he may rank on the list of eligibles.

Spokesmen at Public Hearing Say, Yes

In the discussion of this question the sentiment appeared to be almost unanimous in favor of requiring that appointments from promotion eligible lists be made in the order of merit as determined by the promotion examination. No one insisted on restricting choice absolutely, but the consensus of opinion was that only a limited number of names, possibly two or three, ought to be submitted to the appointing officer for a single vacancy. The members of the civil service commission, particularly the president of the commission, took an opposite view, but the question was taken under advisement by them with the assurance that the views expressed by those who attended the hearing would be given careful consideration.

Civic Workers and City Employes Agree

It is noteworthy that the representatives of the city employes' organizations who were present and the representatives of such civic agencies as the Pennsylvania Civil Service Reform Association were in substantial agreement on this question. Both groups preferred promotion in the order of demonstrated merit. This circumstance is suggestive of the possibility of uniting the forces of the civil service reform movement and the movement toward the organizing of public employes for the improvement of civil service methods and the advancement of the merit system.

The Commission's Objection Not Valid

The objection of the civil service commission to a rule requiring the appointing officer to promote men in the order of their standing on the promotion eligible list does not seem valid. The president of the commission maintained that civil service examinations were not infallible tests of the relative fitness of different candidates for promotion and therefore it would be bad public policy to insist that precedence in promotion be given to the eligibles highest on the list. In answer to this objection it is pertinent to ask whether the provision of the civil service law requiring the selection of one person from the two standing highest on an original entrance list is not also a mistake. The underlying principle is the same in both cases, namely, that the fallibility of the civil service examination is far less to be feared than the constant wire pulling, the personal and political favoritism, and the disinclination of self-respecting workers to take meaningless civil service examinations, which are the inevitable result of permitting appointments from any place on the list.

The Practice of Other Cities and States

It is, moreover, a general practice in other cities and states where promotion examinations are used to require the appointment of eligibles on promotion lists in the order of their standing, a limited choice usually being allowed as in the case of original entrance. For example, in the cities of New York, Chicago, Buffalo, San Francisco and Cleveland; and in the states of Ohio, New Jersey, California and New York the appointing officer may promote any one of the three eligibles having the highest rank; but he is not permitted, if he so desires, to choose the last man on the list, no matter how long the list may be, as he may in Philadelphia under existing rule.

Up to the Commission

The decision of this question rests with the civil service commission. Despite the fact that the present officials are responsible for the existing loose promotion rule, it is to be hoped that after due deliberation they will take the same view of the matter that other cities and states have taken and that has received the endorsement of the friends of better government everywhere, including the city employes themselves.

BY THE WAY

A little over two weeks ago we asked the secretary of the civil service commission to state publicly "what particular professions, trades or vocational groups" constitute the seventy-five per cent of the city service which he claimed the commission had standardized. As yet no statement has been forthcoming.

CITIZENS' BUSINESS

BUREAU OF MUNICIPAL RESEARCH

ISSUED WEEKLY AT 805 FRANKLIN BANK BUILDING
PHILADELPHIA. ENTERED AS SECOND CLASS MATTER
JUNE 7, 1913 AT THE POST OFFICE AT PHILADELPHIA,
PA., UNDER THE ACT OF AUGUST 24TH, 1912 —
SUBSCRIPTION FIFTY CENTS THE YEAR-

The Lot of the Public Official

No. 381   September 11, 1919

Government by discussion is the essence of democracy, and there can be no effective discussion that excludes criticism. Hence a public official should take criticism as a matter of course.

ONE of our public officials recently deplored the fact that men in public life were subjected to so much criticism. According to his statement, as quoted in the press, the new Council is going to be composed of mediocre timber, simply because persons of standing will not seek office and submit to the suspicions cast upon men in public life.

A Path Not Strewn With Roses

Perhaps this note of discouragement is excusable for the moment. No one will contend that the path of the public official is ever strewn with roses, for it is not. So long as the will of the community is not unanimous, but has its internal conflicts, it is inevitable that he who is chosen to carry out that will should meet with criticism. It is inevitable, also, that some of this criticism should be unfair.

The Law of Compensation

There is no reason, however, why any public official who is honestly trying to do his duty as he sees it, should give up in despair. After all, the drawbacks to public office have their compensations. If censure meted out publicly is more than ordinarily stinging, so also is praise publicly bestowed more than ordinarily gratifying. If responsibility in public office is greater than in private life, so also is the opportunity for service in public office greater than in private life. If no one meets with such overwhelming reproach as the public official who fails, neither is anyone so highly honored as the public official who succeeds.

Two Kinds of Criticism

There are two kinds of criticism to which men in public office are subjected. The one arises out of mere personal antagonism and is directed against the person of the official; the other grows out of differences of opinion on public questions and is directed against the conduct of the official. The first kind of criticism may properly be resented by any man in public life, for it contributes nothing to the better administration of public affairs; but the second kind should never be resented. If any man has an idea which he sincerely believes to be for the public good, he should be left entirely free to express it publicly, even if in so doing the conduct or policy of some public official must be censured. This kind of criticism, in fact, should be welcomed, for it may point the way to progress.

The Way of Democracy

In an autocracy criticism may be silenced by resort to arbitrary power, by suppression of freedom of speech, freedom of the press and freedom of assemblage; but in a democracy criticism can be met only by removing the cause or by demonstrating in open discussion that the critic is wrong.

SINKING FUND "MYSTERIES"

In an editorial under the above heading, the *Bond Buyer*, a publication devoted to government, state and municipal bonds, in its issue of August 16, 1919, after referring to the reprint in the same issue of CITIZENS' BUSINESS, No. 376, entitled, "The New Charter and Loans," comments as follows:

One cannot help but recall that there are also mysteries as yet unexplained, surrounding certain other public sinking funds which are being piled up for the purpose of retiring many millions of dollars worth of long term Highway, Canal and other bonds.

Is not Philadelphia's new plan, whereby funds appropriated to sinking funds will be used at as early a date as possible to the actual purchase and cancellation of the city's own bonds, better than the New York State system whereby a political office-holder has at his disposal each year a fund of something like ten million dollars to be invested, at his discretion, in a choice of dozens of different classes of bonds at prices he deems right? New York State has built up sinking funds amounting to almost fifty million dollars and yet the State's total of outstanding State bonds has not been reduced and will not decrease until the maturity date of her exceedingly long term bonds comes around. Meanwhile, the taxpayer contributes something like thirteen millions annually for debt service, a neat sum for a politician to play with. In the fiscal year ended June 30, 1918, the State Comptroller purchased investments for the sinking funds aggregating no less than $9,547,485.41. The interest he collected on the cash and investments of these unwieldly, graft-breeding accumulations amounted to the respectable sum of $2,946,088 and the cash balance on hand often exceeds $5,000,000.

If there is any one who believes that such sums of money are handled to the best advantage when placed in the public treasury, he need only study the records of New York State's Sinking Fund transactions for a few years.

Pol Sci.

CITIZENS' BUSINESS

BUREAU OF MUNICIPAL RESEARCH

ISSUED WEEKLY AT 805 FRANKLIN BANK BUILDING
PHILADELPHIA—ENTERED AS SECOND CLASS MATTER
JUNE 7, 1913 AT THE POST OFFICE AT PHILADELPHIA,
PA., UNDER THE ACT OF AUGUST 24TH, 1912—
SUBSCRIPTION FIFTY CENTS THE YEAR.

School Problems—Are You Solving Them?

No. 382   September 18, 1919

"Time is short, your obligations
are infinite."
—*Massillon*

Our Opportunity

September is here once again. School bells are ringing and thousands of children are entering the buildings all over the city. Another school year has begun; another opportunity is being given to us, the citizens of Philadelphia, to solve the many school problems that were not solved last year. It is an opportunity that we cannot afford to miss. We are busy today trying to make Philadelphia a better, cleaner city, but the people make the city. These children in our schools, our children and our neighbor's children, are the future citizens of Philadelphia. They will carry out the work that we begin, they will develop our plans, they will fulfill our ideals.

But will they? Unless the ideals implanted in them during school days measure up to our own highest ideals, they hardly will. Are we assuring to these children the very best that we can give them? How anxious are we that they shall become good, true citizens of Philadelphia?

What "We have Left Undone"

Let us look at the conditions here as the school doors open. When school closed last term 20,000 children in the city were on "part time". As school resumes this fall 20,000 children, or maybe more, are still on "part time" and there are no new structures to relieve the situation. How much of this is a confession of indifference and inefficiency? The responsibility, it is true, lies primarily with the board of education. Yes, but we shall have to go farther than the board of education. We keep the present school board; we allow their inaction; the blame is ours.

Not only are thousands of children on "part time" and thousands more so packed together that teachers cannot do their best work, but still other thousands are spending five hours a day in charge of poorly equipped teachers. Are you satisfied to have your child one of the fifty-five or sixty-five whom one young teacher endeavors to interest, to discipline, and to teach at the same time? Teachers have been urged during the past few years to stick at their posts and have been reminded that it was their patriotic duty to stay at their work but many, even if they so desired, have not been able to afford to be patriotic in this way and hundreds of teachers have left the force to earn a living wage. Many have left the profession for all time. They have made good in their new work and their employers are anxious to retain them. In a great number of cases they are working under better conditions, receiving better salaries, and are relieved of the great responsibility attached to teaching. Philadelphia now offers her teachers an increase in salary, an increase all too inadequate for their needs, but an increase nevertheless. It remains a fact, however, that valuable material has been lost. Once again who is to blame?

Action for the New School Year

The difficulties all reflect on us. We are apathetic, lukewarm, careless. We are shirking the responsibility that really rests on us. Why do we not begin by demanding that the much-talked of and long-lost school survey to show us the conditions existing in our school system actually be made? Why do we not demand a more alive board of education, one composed of younger men who will keep abreast of the times? Why do we not demand the money to pay teachers a salary that will command the best that the market has to offer? The best are none too good for our children, and Philadelphia and Pennsylvania are wealthy enough to give us the best. Then, when we have done our part, but not before, our schools will be veritable factories of democracy and our children will learn the privileges and obligations of intelligent citizenship.

SAVING OUR FEELINGS

When we have a difficult problem to solve it is always wise to begin by ascertaining all the pertinent facts. This procedure often saves us an extravagant expenditure of "feeling". Recent employment difficulties in other cities have aroused no end of feeling, but justice will not be done until feeling is adjourned long enough to permit of a dispassionate examination of the facts. The city government of Philadelphia, too, has its employment problems. Important salary and wage adjustments will have to be made in the very near future. Let us begin by ascertaining the facts and we shall be spared much useless waste of feeling.

CITIZENS' BUSINESS

BUREAU OF MUNICIPAL RESEARCH

ISSUED WEEKLY AT 805 FRANKLIN BANK BUILDING
PHILADELPHIA. ENTERED AS SECOND CLASS MATTER
JUNE 7, 1913 AT THE POST OFFICE AT PHILADELPHIA,
PA., UNDER THE ACT OF AUGUST 24TH, 1912 —
SUBSCRIPTION FIFTY CENTS THE YEAR.

Grounds for Hope

No. 383   September 25, 1919

Both of the men that have any ghost of a chance
of being the next mayor have spoken on the matter
of the welfare department.
  Both speak fair words of promise.
  Much is at stake.

Promises

Recently a group of representative social workers addressed a letter to each of the two leading mayoralty candidates at the primary, calling attention to the new Department of Public Welfare and urging the appointment as director of it of a man or woman on a basis of qualifications and viewpoint alone.

Each of the candidates replied in a highly satisfactory manner, assuring the social workers of his interest in the new department and of his determination to select a director without reference to political considerations and with an eye single to the purposes for which the department was created.

Reasons for Encouragement

The cynic will say at once, of course, that a candidate for office will promise anything—and goodness knows campaign promises in the past have often enough justified the cynicism. But a perusal of the two letters from the would-be mayors shows that the matter must have been taken seriously, for we find not merely pleasant words but in both cases a rather clearly thought out understanding of what the welfare department signifies.

The process of taking the older municipal departments out of politics is bound to be long drawn out. Slowly the public conscience gets around to the realization that schools, then police, then health perhaps are functions too sacred and important to be jeopardized by partisan or factional selfishness, and progress is made bit by bit toward the idea that *all* government is an instrument of service—not merely a provider of perquisites.

The Welfare Department, however, is new in Philadelphia. This fact alone encourages the hope that this department may be spared from the very beginning the demoralizing consequences of "political" administration. Whoever is to be our next mayor has an unprecedented opportunity to start the tradition right by his choice of a director.

Home Rule? Rather!

The new charter gives control over charities, corrections and recreation to this new department. But it does vastly more. It gives the Council virtually unlimited power in assigning new welfare functions to this department in these words:

"It [the department of public welfare] shall

also have jurisdiction over such other matters affecting the public welfare as may be provided by ordinance."

Here, at least, no one can complain of state interference. Here we have substantially complete home rule. But home rule is no automatic device. If it is to be of benefit at all *it must be utilized by the local authorities.*

Make or Break

Upon the new mayor's choice of a director, then, for the formulation of programs and policies, and upon the new council for wise action on such programs and policies will depend the degree of success or failure of this new venture.

Whether the Department of Public Welfare is to stand in the future of Philadelphia as one of the great and important parts of our municipal government, or as a relatively routine matter, is likely to be determined for all time before snow flies.

We cannot Americanize the foreigner until we Americanize the conditions under which he works and lives.—*J. L. Bowles, Jr.*

CITIZENS' BUSINESS

BUREAU OF MUNICIPAL RESEARCH

ISSUED WEEKLY AT 805 FRANKLIN BANK BUILDING
PHILADELPHIA. ENTERED AS SECOND CLASS MATTER
JUNE 7, 1913 AT THE POST OFFICE AT PHILADELPHIA,
PA., UNDER THE ACT OF AUGUST 24TH, 1912 —
SUBSCRIPTION FIFTY CENTS THE YEAR

The Mayor as Budget Maker

No. 384   October 2, 1919

One of the first sections of the new charter to become operative is the one relating to the budget. To what extent the city of Philadelphia will reap immediate advantages under this section will depend upon the degree of intelligence and sympathy with the new provisions that the present officials will bring to their task.

The New Charter Produces

One of the earliest results of Philadelphia's new charter is now familiar to all of us who have been reading the daily newspapers of the last few weeks.

The mayor is preparing the city's budget for next year! He is doing something that heretofore has not been required of Philadelphia's mayor. For the first time, he is definitely assuming the initiative and leadership in financial affairs that rightly belongs to the city's chief executive.

A Comparison

Were it not for certain provisions of the new charter Philadelphia would not have a mayoral budget for next year—in fact, would have no budget at all. But, thanks to the charter, instead of a mere compilation of departmental requests prepared by the chairman of the finance committee and another mere compilation of departmental requests prepared by the city controller, both mutually irreconcilable and the latter practically useless from the standpoint of the needs of the city's legislative body, councils will receive a real budget, although it may not be perfect.

Councils will have before them for consideration, and as a guide for making the annual appropriations and fixing next year's tax rate, what amounts to a single, coordinated request for all of the departments and other units of the city government. Instead of having to consider twenty-seven or more unrelated and, for the most part, highly inflated requests it will have the benefit of the mayor's previous consideration and determination of the propriety of the numerous departmental requests.

Opportunities that Knock

Despite the fact that the charter revisionists were unsuccessful in getting all of their budgetary and financial reforms through the legislature, and despite the fact that the city's hands are somewhat awkwardly tied in budgetary matters, there is great opportunity for both the mayor and councils to make changes and improvements of one kind or another that will go far toward enlightening the citizens as to the city's finances, toward speeding up the city's business, toward getting 100 cents of value for every dollar spent, and toward making the city government the service-rendering enterprise it is supposed to be.

STATEMENT OF THE OWNERSHIP, MANAGEMENT, CIRCULATION, ETC., REQUIRED BY THE ACT OF CONGRESS OF AUGUST 24, 1912.

Of *CITIZENS' BUSINESS*, published *weekly at Philadelphia, Pennsylvania,* for October 1, 1919.

County of *Philadelphia* } ss.
State of *Pennsylvania* }

Before me, a *Notary Public* in and for the State and county aforesaid, personally appeared *Frederick P. Gruenberg*, who, having been duly affirmed according to law, deposes and says that he is the *editor* of *CITIZENS' BUSINESS* and that the following is, to the best of his knowledge and belief, a true statement of the ownership, management, etc., of the aforesaid publication for the date shown in the above caption, required by the Act of August 24, 1912, embodied in section 443, Postal Laws and Regulations, to wit:

1. That the names and addresses of the publisher, editor, managing editor, and business managers are:
Publisher, *Bureau of Municipal Research, Philadelphia.*
Editor, *Frederick P. Gruenberg.*
Managing Editor, *None.*
Business Managers, *None.*

2. That the owners are:
Bureau of Municipal Research.   No capital stock.

3. That the known bondholders, mortgagees, and other security holders owning or holding 1 per cent or more of total amount of bonds, mortgages, or other securities are:
None.

             (Signed) *Frederick P. Gruenberg.*

Affirmed to and subscribed before me this 19th day of September, 1919.
             (Signed) *Martha H. Quinn.*

[SEAL]   (My Commission expires January 16, 1923.)

BUSINESS

IPAL RESEARCH
FRANKLIN BANK BUILDING
AS SECOND CLASS MATTER
OFFICE AT PHILADELPHIA,
AUGUST 26TH, 1912 —
CENTS THE YEAR—

s for Modern
sks

October 23, 1919

is indispensable to good
lent becomes more com-
nes increasingly necessary
to exercise this watchful-
it civic agencies equipped

other that will go far 1

citizens as to the city's

ing up the city's busin

cents of value for eve

ward making the city

rendering enterprise it

STATEMENT OF THE OWNE
CULATION, ETC., REQU
CONGRESS OF A

Of *CITIZENS' BUSINESS*, pu
Pennsylvania, for October 1, 1:

County of *Philadelphia* } ss.
State of *Pennsylvania* }

Before me, a *Notary Public* 1
aforesaid, personally appeared
having been duly affirmed acco
that he is the *editor* of *CITIZ*
following is, to the best of hi
statement of the ownership, n
said publication for the date
required by the Act of August
443, Postal Laws and Regulat

1. That the names and add:
managing editor, and business
Publisher, *Bureau of Municipa*
Editor, *Frederick P. Gruenberg*
Managing Editor, *None*.
Business Managers, *None*.

2. That the owners are:
Bureau of Municipal Resear

3. That the known bondhold
curity holders owning or holdi
amount of bonds, mortgages, c
None.

(Sign

Affirmed to and subscribed
September, 1919.

[SEAL]   (My Commissi

CITIZENS' BUSINESS

BUREAU OF MUNICIPAL RESEARCH

ISSUED WEEKLY AT 805 FRANKLIN BANK BUILDING
PHILADELPHIA. ENTERED AS SECOND CLASS MATTER
JUNE 7, 1913 AT THE POST OFFICE AT PHILADELPHIA,
PA., UNDER THE ACT OF AUGUST 24TH, 1912 —
SUBSCRIPTION FIFTY CENTS THE YEAR

Modern Tools for Modern Tasks

No. 387   October 23, 1919

Citizen watchfulness is indispensable to good government. As government becomes more complex and technical it becomes increasingly necessary for the individual citizen to exercise this watchfulness through independent civic agencies equipped for the purpose.

ONE of the strangest things about civic progress is its matter-of-fact character. As a rule there is nothing at all miraculous in even the most decided forward steps in government once all the facts of the situation are fully known. It is only to the distant observer who is unable to know these facts that the change comes like a stroke of lightning out of a blue sky.

The Demand for Better Service

Most advances in government are made not so much in an effort to attain certain theoretical ideals as in response to the prosaic demand for better service. Philadelphia's streets were dirty and the citizens wanted to have them cleaner than they were kept under the contract system of street cleaning. Hence the change in our charter enabling the city to do its own street cleaning. The abstract theorist may call this a victory for the principle of government operation of public utilities—for city streets are public utilities—and he may wonder how such a group of hard-headed men of affairs as the members of the charter committee ever succumbed to the acceptance of so debatable a principle; but to the ordinary citizen the change to municipal street cleaning is simply an effort to get cleaner streets.

How the Welfare Department Came to Be

So also is the creation of the new department of public welfare but a response to the demand for better service. Curiously enough, the greatest enthusiasts for this new department were the social welfare workers in private agencies who it might be supposed would resent the invasion of their field by the city government. As a matter of fact their only thought was to have certain needs met that could not be met adequately in any other way. They no more than the members of the charter committee had any interest either in opposing or in favoring the extension of governmental activity *per se*.

Looking Backward—and Forward

If we should trace the growth of Philadelphia's city government from its small beginnings to its present huge organization with upwards of twelve thousand employes and a yearly budget of more than forty millions of dollars, we should find the explanation of that growth, not in any preconceived theory of political science, but in this same demand for better service.

It is reasonable to suppose that this demand will continue in the future as in the past and that in response to this demand our city government will undertake many functions that as yet are left to private initiative or that are not performed at all. This means that the machinery

of our government will become increasingly complex and increasingly technical. At the same
time the citizen's duty to watch the workings of
his government will become correspondingly
more difficult and more exacting.

The Independent Audit

If this is to be the trend of development in the
future, then it is obvious that independent citizens' agencies such as the ones in the United
Civic Campaign will be more imperative than
ever. It is through them that the private citizen
is enabled to exercise that scrutiny which is indispensable to honest and efficient government.
It is only through such agencies that the citizen
stockholder is able to secure the "independent
audit" of the affairs of his government that business stockholders insist upon having of the
affairs of the business in which they have their
money invested.

Training for Probation Officers.

The Municipal Court of Philadelphia has recently
inaugurated a commendable plan of training for probation officers in its service. Arrangements have been
made enabling these workers in the court to attend
lectures twice weekly in the Pennsylvania School for
Social Service and thus to broaden their outlook as
well as to add to their equipment for the work in
which they are engaged. Thus far ten supervisors
and special workers have been detailed to attend these
lectures. In addition the court has begun a series of
addresses by leaders in the field of public service.
These addresses are given monthly and are open not
only to workers in the court but also to others who are
interested in social service.

Pol. Sci

CITIZENS' BUSINESS

BUREAU OF MUNICIPAL RESEARCH

ISSUED WEEKLY AT 805 FRANKLIN BANK BUILDING
PHILADELPHIA. ENTERED AS SECOND CLASS MATTER
JUNE 7, 1913 AT THE POST OFFICE AT PHILADELPHIA,
PA., UNDER THE ACT OF AUGUST 24TH, 1912 —
SUBSCRIPTION FIFTY CENTS THE YEAR

Comprehensive City Planning

No. 388   October 30, 1919

It is optional under the new charter for the council
to provide for a City Planning Commission. Shall
we avail ourselves of this opportunity by creating an
irresistible public demand for its creation?

History of Comprehensive Plans Movement

Exactly ten years ago public interest in city planning crystallized in a meeting of citizens at the Mayor's office. Various committees were appointed who made studies and recommendations that were endorsed at a citizens' meeting on February 24, 1911. Soon after, an ordinance was passed providing for a permanent committee with powers to carry out the provisions of the proposed plan, but this committee was subsequently declared an illegal body and abolished.

An ordinance approved February 17, 1912 created the existing permanent committee on comprehensive plans, a purely advisory body of ten citizens and seven public officials, which was empowered to cooperate with the director of the department of public works whose duty it became to develop comprehensive plans. The proper executive officials were charged with carrying out these suggestions only if deemed advisable and if legally authorized. While the committee was given $6,500 in 1912 for special services, such as employing experts, this amount was thereafter considerably reduced and was entirely discontinued after 1914. Being thus stripped of the funds necessary for carrying on much needed studies, the usefulness of the committee has greatly diminished. For over a year, in fact, the committee has been inactive.

Where Do We Stand Now?

Upon examining the facts of the situation, we find that although much effort has been expended in the past ten years, the existing agencies have failed to produce a comprehensive city plan. It is perfectly clear that a city plan comprises more than a mere street layout. It is certain that the future prosperity of our city is vitally dependent, among other things, upon the plans which we now adopt for the location and confinement of industrial, commercial and residential areas; for railroad and waterways, shipping facilities; for electrical railway transit; for an adequate system of streets to carry vehicular traffic; for parks, playgrounds and other recreational facilities; and for adequate sanitation of the city area. While our city has prospered to a great degree without such well planned provisions in the past, we realize that in order to meet the requirements of the present intensive industrial competition, we must provide those conveniences that will attract industries to Philadelphia, but above all we must make Philadelphia a good place to live in.

The Provisions of the Charter

Article II, Section 10, of the new charter provides that the city may create by ordinance a commission on city planning whose members shall be appointed by the mayor. This commission is expressly charged in making its recommendations to the council to give thorough consideration to the present and future needs and growth of the city, with reference to its means of intercommunication and transportation, and also with reference to the location of streets, public buildings and open spaces. Thus, comprehensive treatment of the problem is assured. In reporting directly to the council and not through any one department head, this commission will be able to secure equal cooperation from all city departments, and can work out a plan of development in which all of the various phases of city planning are properly correlated.

What Should Be Our Part?

Before a comprehensive city plan can be operative in Philadelphia, the following steps must be taken:

1. Provision by ordinance for a city planning commission as per Article II, Section 10 of the new charter.

2. Appointment of the commission by the mayor.

3. Preparation of a comprehensive plan by the commission.

4. Adoption of such city plan by the council with the necessary enabling ordinances.

5. Creation of an organization with power to carry out the provisions of the plan.

The road ahead is long and full of the possibilities of delay. Accordingly let us act now to accomplish the first step. The new charter makes a city planning commission optional with the council; the weight of public opinion must demand its creation. We should endeavor to inform ourselves more fully on questions of city planning. There is being held in our very midst at this time a meeting of the American Civic Association whose discussions are of interest to the public of Philadelphia. Every citizen should hear the prominent men who are scheduled to speak on city planning subjects.

Meeting of American Civic Association at Philadelphia, Oct. 29-31, 1919. Headquarters at the Bellevue Stratford Hotel.

List of meetings of particular interest in city planning:

Oct. 29, 10:30 A. M.—Subject: Civic Centers.
Oct. 30, 2:30 P. M.—Subject: Regional Planning.
Oct. 31, 9:30 A. M.—Subject: Urban and Suburban Zoning.

BUREAU OF MUNICIPAL RESEARCH

ISSUED WEEKLY AT 805 FRANKLIN BANK BUILDING
PHILADELPHIA. ENTERED AS SECOND CLASS MATTER
JUNE 7, 1913 AT THE POST OFFICE AT PHILADELPHIA,
PA., UNDER THE ACT OF AUGUST 24TH, 1912—
SUBSCRIPTION FIFTY CENTS THE YEAR—

A Suggestion to the Mayor-Elect

No. 389   November 6, 1919

Social welfare work has become, if not a distinct profession, at least a highly specialized vocation. It is as essential to the success of the new welfare department that its director be a person qualified by training and experience in social work as it is essential to the success of our law department that its head be a person qualified by training and experience in law.

In the Days Gone By

There was a time when almost anybody of general intelligence was thought to be qualified for public office. This was in the pioneer days of American life when the functions of government were few and simple. In those days the typical local community managed to get along with only a few public officials, such as an assessor, a treasurer, a justice of the peace, a constable, a recorder, and a small council or other legislative body. With the possible exception of a knowledge of law, no special training or experience was necessary to fit a man for any of these public offices.

It is Different Now

Today we have a very different situation. The functions of government are no longer few and simple. They have, in fact, become more complex in character than those of the most diversified private enterprise thus far developed anywhere. Our cities in particular have led the way in adding to the tasks of government. In response to the demand for better service on the part of city dwellers our municipal governments have taken on a multitude of new duties that our great-grandparents never even dreamed of. These new duties, moreover, have become constantly more technical. A layman in the olden days might have had little difficulty in discharging his duties as assessor or as justice of the peace, but how would he fare today as director of the department of public works or as chief of the bureau of health? In a score of other equally important official positions he would fare no better.

The Change in Public Sentiment

Not only do the tasks of modern government call

for more than lay qualifications in holders of public office, but public sentiment has become equally insistent. Can anyone conceive of a mayor of Philadelphia appointing a man as director of the department of public health who is not either a physician or a sanitary engineer and still retain public confidence? Would the community tolerate for a moment the appointment of a city solicitor who is not a lawyer, or the selection of a transit director who is not specially qualified for that post by training and experience? These and many other important positions under our city government are so obviously professional in character that citizens take it for granted that only professional men can fill them properly. The appointment of laymen to posts of this character is rightly regarded as a prelude to deteriorated service.

A New Department and a New Profession

The new charter has created under our city government a new department, that of public welfare. The functions of this department will be both old and new—they will include some functions that were formerly performed by other departments and probably other functions that have not heretofore been performed by any branch of the city government. The centralization of all welfare work in one department, however, is entirely new, and in effect gives definite recognition to an activity of government which in the past has had only incidental attention. At the same time it gives recognition to a field of endeavor that has become highly specialized and has many of the attributes of a profession, that of social welfare work.

The Public's Expectation

This new departure is not somebody's whim; it

is an effort to perform more adequately and more efficiently an important service that the community needs. It will meet the expectations of the people of Philadelphia only if it is put under intelligent and sympathetic direction so that all the possible advantages of having this work done publicly will accrue to the community. *In other words, the people of Philadelphia, particularly those who have taken the most active interest in social welfare work in this city in the past, expect the appointment of a person as director of the new department who is as well qualified by training and experience in social work as the city solicitor will be qualified by training and experience in law and the director of public works by training and experience in engineering.*

An Opportunity and a Danger

This is going to press before election day, but it will not appear until after the election has been held and we shall know beyond even the shadow of technicality who our next mayor is to be. It is comforting, however, that at least one of the candidates in the field has left no doubt in the minds of the citizens as to his intention in the matter of the appointment of a welfare director. If this good intention is carried out it will insure at once the confidence and the hearty cooperation of the whole profession of social welfare workers and their public-spirited supporters in this city and elsewhere, just as the appointment of a well qualified physician as director of public health will immediately inspire the confidence and secure the cooperation of the medical profession.

Without such confidence and cooperation no mayor can expect his administration *fully* to succeed.

CITIZENS' BUSINESS

BUREAU OF MUNICIPAL RESEARCH

ISSUED WEEKLY AT 805 FRANKLIN BANK BUILDING
PHILADELPHIA, ENTERED AS SECOND CLASS MATTER
JUNE 7, 1913 AT THE POST OFFICE AT PHILADELPHIA,
PA., UNDER THE ACT OF AUGUST 24TH, 1912 —
SUBSCRIPTION FIFTY CENTS THE YEAR

The Supreme Court Sustains the Charter

No. 390 November 13, 1919

The financial provisions of the new city charter, the constitutionality of which was questioned in the recent loan litigation, have been sustained by the supreme court of Pennsylvania.

Proper Financing Wins

The supreme court of Pennsylvania handed down a decision on November 5 that will be hailed with satisfaction throughout the United States, for it is in line with the movement for proper governmental financing that is rapidly gaining ground everywhere.

This decision is the outcome of the case of Kraus vs. Philadelphia, which questioned the right of the city to issue, after July 25, 1919, any portion of the $90,070,000 of unissued loans that had been authorized prior to that date. In the demurrer filed by the city, in answer to the "taxpayer's bill of complaint," section 8 of article 17 of the new city charter was strongly attacked.

The Supreme Court Differs with the City Solicitor

In this case the state supreme court unanimously decided against all of. the numerous interpretations and views advanced by the city solicitor, who sought to have section 8 of article 17 of the new city charter declared unconstitutional, in whole or in part, or at least to have it interpreted so as to leave some loopholes through which the city might continue its practice of borrowing money for current expenses. Fortunately, this section has been declared constitutional in its entirety and, if anything, it has been strengthened by the highest court having jurisdiction in the matter.

A Momentous Decision

The decision of the court is of momentous import to Philadelphia. Through it the charter revisionists have won a large part of the battle which they so valiantly fought. They have secured one of the major objects which they sought to achieve, even though the legal mechanism that had to be employed was less efficient than the one they originally proposed.

The Gist of the Decision

Of the many points that have been settled by the opinion of the court, the following are of particular interest at this time:

1. Section 8 of article 17 of the new city charter is *not* unconstitutional.

2. Inasmuch as the state constitution legislates for the city of Philadelphia by name, and as a class by itself, in connection with indebtedness, the legislature may do likewise.

3. Philadelphia cannot borrow money for current expenses, as distinguished from permanent improvements and other capital outlays, *except* in "emergency loans." ("Emergency loans" may be made for any municipal purpose, whether capital outlay or current expense, up to an aggregate of $2,000,000 outstanding at any one time; but they must be paid within the year in which created, or else out of the revenues of the succeeding year before ordinary appropriations are taken care of.)

4. Philadelphia cannot borrow money for permanent improvements or other capital outlays *unless* the city controller certifies to the council (or councils until January 5, 1920), prior to the authorization of the loan, that it is for capital outlays, or *unless* the borrowing is through emergency loans.

5. The city controller's certificate to the effect that

the expenditures to be made from the borrowed money are capital outlays is *final and conclusive.*

6. The unissued portions of all loans authorized prior to July 25, 1919 are invalidated.

7. Such of the invalidated loans as were for capital outlays may be re-enacted by council (or councils) *after* the city controller has certified that the purposes for which the new loans are to be issued are capital outlay purposes.

8. The authorizations given to councils by the electors in 1916 to increase the city's indebtedness by $67,100,000 and by $47,425,000 are not invalidated *except* to the extent that they cover current expenses; and such of the unissued loans based on these authorizations as the city controller certifies were for capital outlays may be re-enacted by council (or councils) *without* further assent of the electors.

9. Only loans authorized in full conformity with the provisions of the new city charter may be issued; *all others are invalid.*

City Planning and Zoning
Public Meeting at Witherspoon Hall
on Tuesday, November 18th at 8 P.M.
Admission Free—No Invitations Required

This meeting will be held under the auspices of the Conference on Comprehensive City Planning recently organized with the purpose of urging the creation of a City Planning and Zoning Commission under the provisions of article 2, sections 9 and 10 of the new charter. Over thirty civic agencies, including existing city departments and bureaus, have been represented by delegates to this conference to promote the common good of the citizens of Philadelphia.

The principal speaker will be Edward M. Bassett, of New York, counsel for the New York Zoning Commission. Local speakers will discuss various phases of the Philadelphia city planning problem, including the proposed zoning regulations now before councils.

CITIZENS' BUSINESS

BUREAU OF MUNICIPAL RESEARCH

ISSUED WEEKLY AT 805 ₩ FRANKLIN BANK BUILDING
PHILADELPHIA. ENTERED AS SECOND CLASS MATTER
JUNE 7, 1913 AT THE POST OFFICE AT PHILADELPHIA,
PA., UNDER THE ACT OF AUGUST 24TH, 1912 —
SUBSCRIPTION FIFTY CENTS THE YEAR

Who Crippled the Civil Service Trial Board?

No. 391   November 20, 1919

Had the recommendations of the charter committee become law, the present trial board would not be without the power to compel the attendance of witnesses.

An Unfortunate Omission

It is unfortunate that the trial board established under the civil service commission by the new charter lacks the power to subpoena witnesses. That this lack of power might prove embarrassing in the conduct of hearings before the trial board was easy to foresee, and the failure of witnesses to attend a recent trial fully justifies the fears that have been entertained on this score.

The omission of the power of subpoena from the civil service article of the new charter is wholly inexcusable. It was contained in the former civil service act and it was also possessed by the old police and fire courts of trial that were superseded by the present trial board under the civil service commission.

Who Is to Blame?

In view of these facts it will interest the public to know how this flaw crept into the new charter. It was not through any fault of the charter committee. Had the recommendations of this committee as set forth both in its report and in the charter bill as originally introduced in the state senate become law, the civil service commission, and any person or board appointed by the commission to make an investigation or to conduct a hearing, would have had the power of subpoena, and the present difficulty would never have arisen.

This recommendation of the charter committee, however, did not become law. When the bill was referred by the governor to the attorney-general for examination and revision, the latter insisted upon numerous changes and, among other things, *excluded that part of the civil service article that gave the power of subpoena to the civil service commission and its agents.* The responsibility, therefore, rests upon the governor and the attorney-general and not upon the charter committee.

Permanent and Temporary Remedies

What is the remedy for the difficulty that the trial board has encountered? There is only

one that will afford a permanent and satisfac_
tory solution, namely, to amend the present
civil service article of the new charter at the
earliest opportunity. In the meantime the civil
service commission is following a logical
course by requesting the city solicitor to peti_
tion the court of common pleas for permission
to subpoena and compel the appearance of wit_
nesses at the hearings of the trial board. The
commission might adopt the additional make-
shift of establishing a rule requiring all city
employes to respond to the requests of the commission to appear when needed as witnesses.

Hereafter let us think twice before we permit
a so-called "practical man" to brush aside in
a few minutes the measures that have been
worked out with great care by persons who
have given years of study to the particular
problems involved.

The most serious indictment against the American
municipal system is not its toleration of awkward
charters or incompetent officials, not its use of blank
ballots or party designations, not its faulty accounting
or evasion of civil service rules, but its failure to
interest and instruct the people in public affairs.—
W. B. Munro.

CITIZENS' BUSINESS

BUREAU OF MUNICIPAL RESEARCH

ISSUED WEEKLY AT 805 FRANKLIN BANK BUILDING
PHILADELPHIA. ENTERED AS SECOND CLASS MATTER
JUNE 7, 1913 AT THE POST OFFICE AT PHILADELPHIA,
PA., UNDER THE ACT OF AUGUST 24TH, 1912—
SUBSCRIPTION FIFTY CENTS THE YEAR

The Cost of a Workingmen's Standard of Living in Philadelphia at November 1919 Prices

No. 393   December 4, 1919

In this issue the figures contained in the Bureau's report just published by the Macmillan Company under the title "Workingmen's Standard of Living in Philadelphia" are brought down to date.

What the Dollar Will Buy

In these days of high living costs no one needs to be reminded that it isn't the *number of dollars* he receives on pay day, but *the things those dollars will buy* that tell the story of his prosperity or adversity. Yet we do not always realize that a dollar today will buy only as much as we could get for fifty-five cents in the days just before the outbreak of the world war. This, however, is a cold fact attested by the official index numbers of the federal bureau of labor statistics which give the increase in the cost of living in the shipbuilding centers of the United States, during the period from July 1914 to June 1919, as 80 per cent. In other words, a man who was getting a salary of $1,000 a year in 1914 would have to receive $1,800 at the present time to be able to maintain his pre-war standard of living.

It's the Standard of Living that Counts

The longer we wrestle with the problem of wage adjustment, especially in the public service, the more forcibly it is brought home to us that ultimately it is the standard of living that counts. When we, the people of Philadelphia, through our representatives in City Hall, determine upon a wage scale for the men and women employed by the city government, we are in effect determining for them their standard of living. Conversely, if we, as Philadelphians, have pride in the standard of living our chosen citizens are able to maintain, then it behooves us to see that the wage scale adopted by our measures up to our pride.

The Standard Expressed in Goods and Services

Obviously our first need is for a concrete description of such a standard of living. Without this we are talking in generalities that mean next to nothing. A little over two years ago the Bureau of Municipal Research of Philadelphia set itself to the task of outlining, in terms of actual goods and services, what it considered a fair minimum standard for a workingman's family, and the report just published by the Macmillan Company under the title "Workingmen's Standard of Living in Philadelphia" is the result.

What the Bureau's Report Contains

This report not only contains our suggested standard of living, but it presents an array of facts obtained from the household budgets of 260 workingmen's families in Philadelphia. Upon these facts this standard is largely based. The report also gives the annual cost of the standard at autumn 1918 prices, which was $1,636.79.

The Cost of the Standard Brought Down to Date

Since the autumn of 1918 the cost of living has continued to go up. It was necessary, therefore, to revise the prices appearing in the standard and bring them down to date. This was done during November of the current year with the result that the annual cost figure has been advanced to $1,803.14, an increase of slightly more than 10 per cent over the 1918 figure. Through the courtesy of the publishers by whom our report has been copyrighted we are reprinting in the following pages the suggested standard of living with the prices as of November 1919. Below is a summary of these pages:

Total		$1,803.14
Specified standard		$1,490.20
Housing ....$	300.00	
Fuel and light	84.23	
Food	674.30	
Clothing	346.63	
Carfare	35.40	
Cleaning supplies and service...	49.64	
Unspecified standard—21% of cost of specified standard		$ 312.94

The "unspecified standard", it should be explained, covers those classes of expenditure in the household budget that do not lend themselves readily to expression in terms of actual goods and services. They are health; furniture and furnishings; taxes, dues and contributions; recreation and amusements; education and reading; insurance; and miscellaneous expenditures. It has been found by investigation, however, that all these classes combined normally constitute about 18 per cent of the total household expenditures of workingmen's families or equal about 21 per cent of the expenditures included under the "specified standard". Hence the use of the method employed above in determining the amount for th

OF A FAIR STANDARD OF LIVING FOR A FAMILY OF FIVE, CONSISTING OF PARENTS, BOY OF 13, GIRL OF 10, AND BOY OF 6

TOTAL............................ $1,803.14

SPECIFIED STANDARD............................ $1,490.20

Housing—annual rent............................ $ 300.00
Two-story house, with six rooms, facing street; bathroom, including toilet, washstand, and tub; laundry; furnace; and facilities for cooking and lighting with gas.

Fuel and Light

	Unit	Price per unit	Annual quantity	Annual cost
Total.......	....	....	....	$ 84.23
Coal, pea.....	ton	$ 9.95	2½	$ 24.88
Coal, stove....	ton	12.30	2½	30.75
Gas..........	1000 cu. ft.	1.00	26	26.00
Matches......	box of 500	.05	52	2.60

Food

	Unit	Price per unit	Annual quantity	Annual cost
Total.......	....	....	....	$674.30
Bread and cereals	....	....	....	*$121.03*
Bread........	16 oz. loaf	$ .08	988	$ 79.04
Buns and rolls.	24 oz. doz.	.25	52	13.00
Cakes, misc....	lb.	.30	13	3.90
Cornmeal.....	lb.	.05	26	1.30
Cornstarch....	16 oz. pkg.	.10	13	1.30
Flour, wheat...	12 lb. bag	.86	13	11.18
Macaroni.....	12 oz. pkg.	.10	13	1.30
Oatmeal......	lb.	.08	52	4.16
Rice..........	lb.	.15	39	5.85
Meats and fish...	....	....	....	*$115.96*
Beef, equal parts of brisket, chuck and round........	lb.	$ .25	286	$ 71.50
Chicken.......	lb.	.42	26	10.92
Fish, fresh....	lb.	.15	78	11.70

	Unit	Price per unit	Annual quantity	Annual cost
bstitutes..	....	....	....	$166.27
s, dried...	lb.	$ .15	13	$ 1.95
se........	lb.	.40	26	10.40
....	doz.	.65	78	50.70
fresh....	qt.	.14	728	101.92
dried....	lb.	.10	13	1.30
ng......	....	....	....	$ 55.77
r........	lb.	$ .77	26	$ 20.02
....	lb.	.30	32.5	9.75
nargarine.	lb.	.40	65	26.00
getables...	....	....	....	$ 82.80
age......	2 lb. head	$ .10	39	$ 3.90
ts.......	2 lb. bunch	.08	39	3.12
....	doz. ears	.45	13	5.85
ce.......	4 oz. head	.10	13	1.30
ıs........	lb.	.07	91	6.37
oes, Irish	pk.	.54	78	42.12
oes, sweet	pk.	.72	1	.72
ch.......	pk.	.48	4	1.92
; beans...	pk.	.80	4	3.20
toes.....	pk.	1.10	13	14.30
vegetables	....	....	....	$ 14.69
....	19 oz. can	$ .18	13	$ 2.34
....	19 oz. can	.23	13	2.99
toes.....	19 oz. can	.18	52	9.36
uits......	....	....	....	$ 28.28
s........	pk.	$ .90	13	$ 11.70
es.......	doz.	.60	19.5	11.70
es.......	pk.	.75	6.5	4.88
uits......	....	....	....	$ 4.68
s........	lb.	$ .25	13	$ 3.25
ıs.......	15 oz. pkg.	.22	6.5	1.43
....	....	....	....	$ 30.42
ses......	18 oz. can	$ .18	26	$ 4.68
, gran....	lb.	.11	234	25.74
s........	....	....	....	.$ 30.55
....	8 oz. can	$ .22	13	$ 2.86
....	lb.	.42	52	21.84
....	lb.	.45	13	5.85

Total..............................	......		...... $346.63

Husband.............................. ...... | | ...... *$ 86.48*

Caps, wool and cotton mixture, 30% wool, lined or unlined.....................	$ 1.00	1	$ 1.00
Hats, soft or stiff felt, medium grade......	2.50	½	1.25
*Hats, cheapest straw, stiff brimmed.......	2.00	½	1.00
Sweaters, 60% wool....................	6.50	½	3.25
Overcoats, overcoating, 40% wool........	20.00	⅓	6.67
Suits, cheviot or cassimere, 50% wool....	20.00	1	20.00
Extra trousers, worsted face, cotton back.	4.50	1	4.50
Overalls, denim.......................	2.00	2	4.00
Working shirts, cotton flannel or flannelette................................	1.75	2	3.50
Working shirts, cotton shirting..........	1.50	2	3.00
Dress shirts, printed madras............	2.00	2	4.00
Collars, stiff or soft washable...........	.25	6	1.50
Ties, silk and cotton four-in-hand........	.75	3	2.25
Suspenders, cotton or lisle elastic web....	.50	1	.50
Belts, cheap leather....................	.65	½	.33
Handkerchiefs, cotton..................	.15	6	.90
Nightshirts (homemade), 5 yds. 36 inch muslin, thread, and buttons...........	1.54	1	1.54
Nightshirts (homemade), 5 yds. 27 inch outing flannel, thread, and buttons.....	1.79	1	1.79
Summer underwear, sets, Balbriggan......	1.00	3	3.00
Winter underwear, sets, 25% wool.......	2.00	1	2.00
Socks, common cotton..................	.20	12	2.40
Shoes, gun-metal welt..................	6.00	2	12.00
Shoe repairs, half-soled and heeled.......	2.00	2	4.00
Rubbers, storm.......................	1.00	1	1.00
Gloves, knitted yarn, 75% wool.........	.75	1	.75
Garters, cotton elastic web.............	.35	1	.35

*For this article the seasonal price was used.

Wife......			$ 80.28
Hats, plain velvet, little trimming........	$ 3.00	½	$ 1.50
*Hats, plain straw, little trimming........	2.00	1	2.00
Coats, Kersey cloth, pile fabric, cheviot, or mixtures....................	18.00	½	9.00
Wash dresses (homemade), 6 yds. 36 inch percale or gingham, thread, and buttons	2.13	2½	5.33
Suits, wool poplin or other material, 50% wool....................	25.00	½	12.50
Skirts, serge, panama cloth, or plaid mixtures....................	5.00	1	5.00
Shirtwaists (homemade), 2½ yds. cotton voile or lawn, thread, and buttons......	1.00	3	3.00
Shirtwaists (homemade), 2½ yds. 36 inch washable silk, thread, and buttons.....	5.25	½	2.63
Petticoats (homemade), 3¾ yds. 36 inch muslin, cambric, or sateen, thread and buttons....................	1.35	2	2.70
Corsets, standard make.................	2.00	1	2.00
Corset covers, cambric with narrow embroidered or lace edging.............	.40	2	.80
Summer underwear, cotton ribbed union suits....................	1.25	3	3.75
Winter underwear, winter weight cotton union suits....................	1.50	2	3.00
Nightgowns (homemade), 4 yds. 36 inch muslin, or outing flannel, thread, and buttons....................	1.34	2	2.68
Handkerchiefs, cotton.................	.10	6	.60
Gloves, cotton or chamoisette...........	.85	1	.85
Aprons (homemade), 5 yds. 36 inch figured percale or gingham, thread, and buttons	1.78	3	5.34
Stockings, plain cotton.................	.30	9	2.70
Shoes, gun-metal welt..................	6.00	2	12.00
Shoe repairs, half-soled and heeled.......	2.00	1	2.00
Rubbers, storm........................	.90	1	.90
Boy, age 13......................			$ 74.65
Caps, wool and cotton mixture, 30% wool, lined or unlined......................	$ 1.00	1½	$ 1.50
Hats, wool and cotton mixture..........	1.25	½	.63
Sweaters, 60% wool...................	3.25	½	1.63
Overcoats, overcoating, 30% wool.......	10.00	½	5.00
Suits, 60% wool, cassimere, union cheviot, or suiting......................	10.00	1½	15.00
Extra trousers, 35% wool, union cheviot..	1.75		1.75

*For this article the seasonal price was used.

Boy, age 13—Continued

*Extra trousers, cotton khaki...............	$ 1.50	2
Blouses (homemade), 2½ yds. 36 inch percale or gingham, thread, and buttons...	95	5
Collars, stiff or soft washable............	25	2
Ties, silk Windsor.......................	40	2
Belts, cheap leather.....................	40	½
Handerkchiefs, cotton...................	10	6
Nightshirts (homemade), 3½ yds. 36 inch muslin, thread, and buttons...........	1.08	1
Nightshirts (homemade), 3½ yds. 27 inch outing flannel, thread, and buttons.....	1.26	1
Summer underwear, sets, Balbriggan.....	.75	3
Winter underwear, sets, winter weight cotton, fleece-lined......................		2
Stockings, cotton ribbed.................	.30	18
Shoes, gun-metal welt...................	4.50	4
Shoe repairs, half-soled and heeled.......	1.75	4
Rubbers, storm.........................	.75	1
Gloves, fleece-lined, cotton back.........	.75	1
Garters (homemade), 1 yd. cotton elastic web.................................	.15	2

Girl, age 10...........................

*Hats, tailored straw....................	¢ 1 75	1		
Hats, velveteen or corduroy.............		1		
Sweaters, worsted face, cotton back......	3.50	1		
Coats, cheviot, 50% wool...............	7.00	½		
Wash dresses (homemade), 4½ yds. 32 inch gingham or chambray, thread, and buttons....................	1.70	8		
Petticoats (homemade), 2 yds. 36 inch muslin and 2½ yds. lace or edging, thread, and buttons.................	.88			
Petticoats (homemade), 2 yds. 27 inch outing flannel, thread, and buttons.....	.73			
Drawer waists, muslin...................	.45	5		
Drawers (homemade), 2 yds. 36 inch muslin, thread, and buttons.............	.63	6		3.7
Union suits, cotton, fleece-lined..........	1.25	2		2.5
Nightgowns (homemade), 3 yds. 36 inch muslin, and 1½ yds. lace or edging, thread.......................	1.00	1		1.0
Nightgowns (homemade), 3 yds. 27 inch outing flannel, thread...............	1.07	1		1.0
Handkerchiefs, cotton...................	.10	6		.6
Gloves, fleece-lined, cotton back.........	.75	1		.7

*For this article the seasonal price was used.

Girl, age 10—continued

Stockings, cotton ribbed..................	$ .30	12	$ 3.60
Shoes, gun-metal welt.....................	4.00	4	16.00
Shoe repairs, half-soled and heeled........	1.60	2	3.20
Rubbers, storm...........................	.75	1	.75
Garters (homemade), 1 yd. cotton elastic web...........................	.15	2	.30
Ribbons, 1 yd. 3 inch silk face............	.25	8	2.00

Boy, age 6..

			$ 40.81
Caps, wool and cotton mixture, 30% wool	$ 1.00	1½	$ 1.50
Sweaters, worsted face, cotton back......	3.00	1	3.00
Overcoats, overcoating or union cheviot, 30% wool............................	8.00	½	4.00
Wash suits (homemade), 2½ yds. 36 inch percale or gingham, thread, and buttons.	.95	6	5.70
Ties, silk Windsor......................	.40	1	.40
Handkerchiefs, cotton...................	.10	6	.60
Nightgowns (homemade), 3 yds. 36 inch muslin, thread, and buttons...........	.92	1	.92
Nightgowns (homemade), 3 yds. 27 inch outing flannel, thread, and buttons.....	1.07	1	1.07
Drawer waists, muslin...................	.45	3	1.35
Drawers (homemade), 1½ yds. 36 inch muslin, thread, and buttons...........	.48	4	1.92
Union suits, cotton, fleece-lined..........	1.00	2	2.00
Stockings, cotton ribbed.................	.30	18	5.40
Shoes, satin calf, machine sewed or nailed	2.65	3	7.95
Shoe repairs, half-soled.................	1.60	2	3.20
Rubbers, storm..........................	.75	1	.75
Gloves, fleece-lined, cotton back.........	.75	1	.75
Garters (homemade), 1 yd. cotton elastic web.................................	.15	2	.30

Carfare

	Unit	Price per unit	Annual quantity	Annual cost
Total......................	....	....	....	$35.40
Carfare of husband...........	ride	$.05	604	$30.20
Carfare of family............	ride	.05	104	5.20

Cleaning Supplies and Services

	Unit	Price per unit	Annual quantity	Annual cost
Total..........................	....	....	.......:	$49.64
Personal......................	....	....	.......:	*$19.14*
Toilet soap..................	small bar	$.10	70	$ 7.00
Toothbrush..................	brush	.25	5	1.25
Toothpaste or toothpowder....	tube or box	.10	12	1.20
Combs, hard rubber..........	comb	.25	1	.25
Hairbrushes, wooden back....	brush	.40	½	.20
Shoe polish..................	box	.12	12	1.44
Barber's services:				
Husband..................	shave and haircut	.50	10	5.00
Children..................	haircut	.35	8	2.80
Household......................	....	....	....	*$20.26*
Laundry soap...............	½ lb. bar	$.075	120	$ 9.00
Starch......................	lb.	.10	24	2.40
Bluing......................	pt.	.15	12	1.80
Clothesline..................	yd.	.025	5	.13
Clothespins.................	doz.	.03	1	.03
Stove polish.................	box	.05	26	1.30
Furniture polish.............	pt.	.42	2	.84
Cleanser....................	box	.06	36	2.16
Collars sent to laundry.......	collar	.05	52	2.60

Unspecified cleaning supplies and services—26% of cost of specified requirements.................................. *$10.24*

UNSPECIFIED STANDARD—21% of specified standard... $312.94

THIS issue of CITIZENS' BUSINESS is especially designed in size and style for insertion in *"Workingmen's Standard of Living in Philadelphia"* as a supplement to the latter.

CITIZENS' BUSINESS

BUREAU OF MUNICIPAL RESEARCH

ISSUED WEEKLY AT 805 FRANKLIN BANK BUILDING
PHILADELPHIA. ENTERED AS SECOND CLASS MATTER
JUNE 7, 1913 AT THE POST OFFICE AT PHILADELPHIA,
PA., UNDER THE ACT OF AUGUST 24TH, 1912 —
SUBSCRIPTION FIFTY CENTS THE YEAR-

The Possibilities in the School Lunch

No. 394   December 11, 1919

For the school term ended June 30, 1918, there were 605 pupils classified as "backward" who had been 20 months or more in grade. This represents an unproductive expenditure amounting to $39,325.00. Can we apply this money to a better use?

The Need for School Lunches

The school lunch in its primary conception is intended for the improvement and preservation of the health of the children in our public schools. No excuse has to be offered for its establishment for such a purpose, and that there is need for such service there can be no doubt.

According to authoritative statement, from three to eight per cent of the school population of the average city suffers from malnutrition, the percentage being higher since the necessities of the war period have so reduced the availability of food supplies.

Faulty nutrition may be due to lack of fresh air and sunshine rather than to lack of food; it may de due to lack of proper rest and recreation, or to lack of proper proportion of food values in the diet, or to improper preparation and hurried or irregular habits of taking food.

The fact that in many instances school lunches are provided through private agencies whose funds are limited necessarily curtails the extent of the service, and the value of the experiments undertaken cannot always be determined because of the difficulties under which the work is done.

The Educational Possibilities of the School Lunch

School lunches may serve the purpose not only of *health* but of *education* as well, and should, therefore, receive serious consideration as part of the educational program in any community.

Through the school lunch, controlled by the educational system, we may provide fundamental education in the science and art of nutrition and dietetics; and in this day in which we have come to realize more fully the physical defects of the youth of our nation, we are compelled not to neglect such an opportunity for health education.

Nutritious food substances may be popularized, methods of food preparation may be taught, the balanced ration and caloric requirements may be made understandable at the school lunch counter; while at the school lunch table proper habits of eating may be developed.

The Nutrition Class

For the group of children distinctly malnourished, that is seven per cent below weight for their height, the nutrition class, with its charts, tape line, scales, etc., in charge of the school physician and nurse or teacher, may become a living demonstration to the entire school of the progress from ill health to robustness through proper food, fresh air, sunshine, recreation and rest.

The Economic Considerations

Can a department of education afford to undertake such a comprehensive scheme of fundamental health education? To reverse the question, can it afford *not* to undertake such a program?

A malnourished child cannot "keep up" with his work in school; his anaemic under-nourished brain refuses to absorb the education which is offered. In consequence he is a drag upon the educational system and a dead weight of expense.

In the school system of Philadelphia there were in 1919 at each promotion period approximately 31,000 children who failed of advancement. In 1918 it cost the city $32.02 for the education of each child in the grade schools.

It is legitimate to assume that in this unpromoted group the average proportion of malnutrition obtains, which, if corrected, would insure the normal advancement of these pupils and an incidental saving of approximately $40,000 per year. As a by-product we should be able to establish a practical and popular method of instruction in the fundamental basis of health, *i. e.,* nutrition. The additional sums necessary to finance such an advance in education would be money well spent.

AN OPPORTUNITY

Time—December 29 to January 1.
Event—Convention of the Pennsylvania State Education Association.

Don't think that you are not interested. A glance at the comprehensive program of the convention will prove that everyone is concerned.
Here are a few topics of the program:

> How should the Schools in a Democracy Function in Citizenship
> Reconstruction in Education
> Americanization
> Economy of Time in Education
> Health Education and Child Hygiene
> The School as a Community Pivot
> Household Arts, Community Kitchens, etc.

We have a few copies of the preliminary program. Others may be secured from Dr. Oliver P. Cornman, Board of Public Education, 19th and Ludlow Sts. Take a few minutes and look it over.

CITIZENS' BUSINESS

BUREAU OF MUNICIPAL RESEARCH

ISSUED WEEKLY AT 805 FRANKLIN BANK BUILDING
PHILADELPHIA, ENTERED AS SECOND CLASS MATTER
JUNE 7, 1913 AT THE POST OFFICE AT PHILADELPHIA,
PA., UNDER THE ACT OF AUGUST 24TH, 1912 —
SUBSCRIPTION FIFTY CENTS THE YEAR

A Suggestion to the Commission on the Revision of the State Constitution

No. 395   December 18, 1919

> A way to make sure that cities, counties, boroughs, school districts and the other local governments conduct their finances properly.

A Truly Difficult Problem

Of the numerous problems that the commission on revision of the state constitution will face for solution, none is likely to be more urgently in need of correction, or more difficult of satisfactory settlement, than those relating to the finances of the more than five thousand local governments of the state. That this is so, is being increasingly recognized as the commission proceeds with its task of modernizing the fundamental law of the commonwealth.

A Solution Must be Found

But however baffling the problems of local finance may be, the commission simply must arrive at some solution for them, and must set up standards or limitations of one kind or another in the constitution itself. Where to draw the line between what should go in the constitution, and what may be determined from time to time by the legislature and other bodies or officials, is by no means an easy part of the commission's arduous duties.

What to Avoid

Were the commission to go into the subject of local finance exhaustively and to arrive at a thoroughgoing solution, it would find itself in possession of a somewhat lengthy document. Then would come the battle between those who believe in sewing things up by constitutional provisions, and those who believe in placing in the constitution only such provisions as will "stand the test of time nobly and satisfactorily".

The extremists of the first group would vote in favor of inserting in the constitution every detail of the necessarily elaborate plan evolved by the commission, whereas the extremists of the other group would oppose every effort to insert anything beyond the most fundamental and most permanent features of that plan.

Whatever is done, however, the constitutional provisions should not be ambiguous or susceptible of different interpretations, as so often has been the case; nor should they be so rigid or inflexible as to fail to take into account changing conditions or differences in needs; nor should they be too difficult or expensive to amend.

A Suggestion

It is suggested to the commission that it make as exhaustive a study of local finance, both in Pennsylvania and elsewhere, as its time and resources will permit, and that it give earnest consideration to the advisability of creating a permanent "Municipal Finance Commission", with power to regulate and supervise the finances of all cities, counties, boroughs, townships, school districts, and other local governments in the state.

Advantages of a Municipal Finance Commission

Such a commission could regulate and supervise the finances and accounts of the local governments in much the same manner as the Public Service Commission regulates and supervises the finances and accounts of the public utilities.

Such a commission could set up and enforce high standards of financing and accounting for the more than five thousand local governments under its jurisdiction; could adopt clear-cut, detailed regulations for the guidance and control of the local governments; could modify these regulations as frequently as conditions demanded; could advise and guide the local governments in matters of finance; could accomplish all that any amount of constitutional and statutory provisions could hope to accomplish; could put an end to the great mass of litigation that is constantly taking place in connection with local finance; in fact, could place Pennsylvania in the very front rank in all matters of local finance and accounts.

"The dogmas of the quiet past are inadequate to the stormy present. The occasion is piled high with difficulties and we must rise with the occasion. As our case is new so we must think anew and act anew."
—*Abraham Lincoln.*

CITIZENS' BUSINESS

BUREAU OF MUNICIPAL RESEARCH

ISSUED WEEKLY AT 805 FRANKLIN BANK BUILDING
PHILADELPHIA. ENTERED AS SECOND CLASS MATTER
JUNE 7, 1913 AT THE POST OFFICE AT PHILADELPHIA,
PA., UNDER THE ACT OF AUGUST 24TH, 1912 —
SUBSCRIPTION FIFTY CENTS THE YEAR

A Dilemma and One Way Out

No. 396	December 25, 1919

With the natural resistance of the taxpayer to higher taxes and the reasonable insistence of city employes upon a living wage, a third way out should be hailed with delight.

Our Standard of Living Considered Low.

As was to be expected, our suggested standard of living, described in "Workingmen's Standard of Living in Philadelphia", has provoked a great deal of editorial and other comment. It is noteworthy, however, that thus far no one whose criticism has come to our attention has found the standard unduly generous; on the contrary, practically every one has appeared a bit astonished at the meager provision that was made for the family's needs. With reference to all of these comments, it can only be stated that our suggested standard of living is not lower than the actual standards of self-supporting workingmen's families in Philadelphia as we found them in our investigation.

The Other Side of the Picture

There is, however, another side of the picture that should not be overlooked. It will be remembered that at current price levels the annual income necessary to enable a workingman's family of five persons to maintain this standard is $1800, which is roughly equivalent to a daily wage of $5.75 for 313 working days in the year. Let us see how the city payroll compares with these figures.

What the City Actually Pays

Unskilled laborers at the present time receive from $2.75 to $3.25 per day, plus a 10 per cent bonus, which brings their daily wages up to $3.02½ as a minimum and $3.57½ as a maximum rate. For next year it is proposed to increase the bonus to 20 per cent, so that unskilled laborers will receive a total daily income ranging from $3.30 to $3.90. Even skilled laborers often fall considerably below the figures required by the standard. There are, for example, blacksmiths, carpenters, painters, plumbers, steamfitters, electricians and stationary engineers who now receive a base rate of only $4.00 a day, which the 10 per cent bonus brings up to $4.40 and the proposed 20 per cent bonus will bring up to $4.80.

Policemen and firemen fare quite as badly. Including the proposed 20 per cent bonus, first year patrolmen will receive next year a daily wage of $3.60 and the other patrolmen will receive $4.20. Hosemen and laddermen will receive a sliding scale of pay ranging from a minimum of $1320 per year to a maximum of $1560. The vast majority, in fact, of city employes now receive less, and under the proposed arrangements, will continue next year to receive less than $1800 a year, which is the figure required to provide the admittedly modest standard of living set forth in our report.

The Dilemma

These facts bring the citizens of Philadelphia face to face with a serious situation. A further increase in salaries and wages, assuming that the number of employes remains the same, means a still higher tax rate. On the other hand, inadequate compensation of city employes has already resulted in depletion of the ranks of many of our most essential city bureaus and departments. Are we then caught between the two horns of an inexorable dilemma? Or is there a third way out?

The Third Way Out

While it is true that the third way out in this particular situation is not an easy one, yet there is such a way. It consists of the unromantic task of scrutinizing every item of expenditure in the city's budget and separating the essential from the non-essential.

In this connection, two pertinent suggestions are in order. The first one is merely a reminder that under the new charter the civil service commission is directed to standardize salaries and grades throughout the city service. This command of the new charter should be complied with as early as possible. In the process of standardizing salaries and grades the *superfluous jobs in City Hall will come to light* and corrective measures may be taken. Isn't it better to have an adequate group of adequately paid employes. than a superfluous group of inadequately paid employes?

The second suggestion relates to the sinking fund. The city appropriations for 1920 set aside, directly and indirectly, over $6,000,000 for sinking fund purposes. This is a large amount and should be examined with the greatest care. If the sinking fund does not actually need so large a sum to pay off city debt at maturity, the appropriation should be reduced accordingly and the money thus released might then be applied to needed increases in salaries and wages.

CITIZENS' BUSINESS

BUREAU OF MUNICIPAL RESEARCH

ISSUED WEEKLY AT 805 FRANKLIN BANK BUILDING
PHILADELPHIA ENTERED AS SECOND CLASS MATTER
JUNE 7, 1913 AT THE POST OFFICE AT PHILADELPHIA,
PA., UNDER THE ACT OF AUGUST 24TH, 1912 —
SUBSCRIPTION FIFTY CENTS THE YEAR—

What About Zoning?

No. 397   January 1, 1920

The proposed zoning ordinance was not passed
and the present zoning commission goes out of existence on January 5.   A new commission should
be appointed and provided with funds to continue
the work.

The Zoning Ordinance

On November 6, 1919, there was introduced into councils a zoning ordinance to regulate the location, size and use of buildings. This ordinance was referred to the survey committee which held a public hearing on December 2, and which then passed on the ordinance to the city solicitor for an opinion. This step, taken at the eleventh hour of the existence of the old councils, practically closed the door on zoning under the old administration.

Public Interest in Zoning

At the public hearing just referred to, as well as at the special hearings conducted by the zoning commission, there was manifested a keen interest in the subject of zoning, but it was quite clear that the public was not yet ready for so important a measure of legislation, and that its immediate passage would be inexpedient because it was not generally understood and there would not be public support for its enforcement. In this connection it is to be recalled with regret that mimeographed copies of the ordinance had not been widely distributed, and were not even available to all of the persons and organizations particularly interested in the contents of the ordinance, and that the maps which are an integral part of the ordinance were not available in adequate number.

How the Ordinance was Drafted

Under the authority of Act 175, P. L. 285 of May 11, 1915, and in accordance with resolution of councils of July 20, 1916, the mayor appointed the existing zoning commission which comprises seven public officials and five citizens who represent certain business and civic organizations. This commission has studied the zoning problem during a period of three years, and has made its public report in the form of the proposed zoning ordinance. Its initial work involved the preparation of maps covering the entire city area which indicate the existing conditions in regard to each of the three major considerations, height of buildings, area of lot covered by buildings, and the uses to which buildings are put. By the use of these maps and from the study of zoning regulations in other cities, the commission has formulated proposed regulations applicable to the different districts into which the city area is divided according to height, area and use of buildings.

Appropriations approximating $13,000 constitute the entire amount made available to the commission during three years. The accomplishment of such a comprehensive study for this meager sum has been due to the fact that it was carried out in conjunction with the bureau of surveys whose chief engineer is a member of the commission. But while the study itself was carefully made despite inadequate funds, there was unfortunately no provision for the publication and wide distribution of the proposed ordinance.

It is also regrettable that numerous public

hearings were not held prior to the introduction of the ordinance into councils, as a result of which apparent defects could have been eliminated, the public could have been educated in the meaning and the importance of such regulations, and a public sentiment would have been created to insure the passage of the ordinance by councils.

Program for the Future

The present zoning commission passes out of existence with the old charter, but there is a provision in the new charter whereby a zoning commission may be appointed by the new mayor. It is advisable that a new commission should be created immediately in order to profit by the public interest in zoning which has just been created. This commission should be provided with funds to publish the proposed zoning regulations and maps, and should institute an educational campaign to inform the public why the regulation of the location, size and use of buildings will promote the public health, safety, order and general welfare. Public hearings should be held to answer questions concerning the proposed regulations. As a result of these hearings apparent discrepancies could be eliminated from the regulations as they now exist so that a new ordinance could be passed without lengthy hearings by the new council.

To all our readers and friends
A Happy New Year

CITIZENS' BUSINESS

BUREAU OF MUNICIPAL RESEARCH

ISSUED WEEKLY AT 805 FRANKLIN BANK BUILDING
PHILADELPHIA. ENTERED AS SECOND CLASS MATTER
JUNE 7, 1913 AT THE POST OFFICE AT PHILADELPHIA,
PA., UNDER THE ACT OF AUGUST 24TH, 1912 —
SUBSCRIPTION FIFTY CENTS THE YEAR.

Here We Stand

No. 398   January 8, 1920

Different conditions may make for different policies governing civic agencies in their respective communities, and changing times will doubtless call for
changing programs. At this "stock taking", we find
certain things on the shelf ticketed FUNDAMENTALS

A New Year and a New Regime

The world stands at the threshold of a new year and Philadelphia is at the beginning of a new municipal administration—the first four-year period under the new charter.

This seems to us an opportune occasion to restate briefly some of the principles and some of the practices of the Bureau of Municipal Research, now in its eleventh year of service to Philadelphia. While the limits of this small folder may not permit an inclusive presentation of the Bureau's position in relation to officials and the public, it is hoped, nevertheless, that some of the more important points may be made clear to new public functionaries, and to citizens unfamiliar with our work, and at the same time that there may be re-emphasis, for our old friends, on certain fundamentals.

Cardinal

In the first place, the Bureau of Municipal Research is non-partisan—*really* non-partisan. That does *not* mean that the contributors, trustees, and staff members may not take sides *as* individuals on local or national issues. They *do,* and their individual opinions vary widely. But the agency, as such, approaches public problems without reference to partisan or factional considerations, with complete open-mindedness, and with but one interest—the public's. No political or religious qualification or disqualification has ever affected the appointment of a member of the staff.

The Bureau is a *fact* agency. It concerns itself with the study of conditions and problems as they are, and it builds its constructive recommendations on conditions as revealed by painstaking study and examination.

The Bureau is a *scientific* agency. In order correctly to interpret facts and to make useful recommendations, it must utilize the technique of the laboratory for accuracy. To do this it must have a trained personnel. Its staff includes representatives of the following professions and fields of training: Law, medicine, engineering, accounting, statistics, pedagogy, business administration, social work, personnel management.

The How

The Bureau is not interested in scandals, exposures, muckraking. Its studies have shown the difficulties—all too frequently underestimated—of the public official, and it co-operates sincerely in the solution of problems whenever co-operative relations are possible. At the same time, it has never promised any officer or board immunity from publicity because pleasant co-operation may have characterized the initial or long-standing relations between such official or body and the Bureau.

The studies in departments have been conducted on the assumption that the responsible official should have the first opportunity to utilize any findings or recommendations that may be of value. This technique has usually been productive of beneficent results.

The Larger Service

Transcending in importance the special study of a given department, bureau or minor community problem, is the work of continuous research in major fields such as the law and structure of our government, and finance. The practical application of this continuous research is illustrated by the form of service the Bureau was able to render during the recent successful charter campaign. Its day-by-day usefulness is illustrated by the Bureau's information service, which is being used by an ever-increasing circle of officials, citizens and students.

Attitude

While the Bureau will strive, for the sake of Philadelphia, for the successful carrying out of the improved charter, its attitude toward the new mayor and council at the start will be precisely as was its initial attitude toward the three preceding administrations under which the Bureau has lived and grown.

The Bureau will not be the apologist for, nor the whitewasher of, any official or any councilman, regardless of his political or factional alignment. Nor will it be hostile to, or captiously critical of, any municipal legislator or administrative officer—be he Guelph or Ghibelline.

The Bureau has exceptional facilities and assembled experience. These it will be glad to have utilized for the purpose of securing more effective and serviceable municipal government. In the future, as in the past, the main concern of the Bureau will be to strive for a city government that shall render to its citizens full value for their taxes and abundant returns for community of effort.

The Bureau asks your co-operation in realizing this goal.

CITIZENS' BUSINESS

BUREAU OF MUNICIPAL RESEARCH

ISSUED WEEKLY AT 805 FRANKLIN BANK BUILDING
PHILADELPHIA. ENTERED AS SECOND CLASS MATTER
JUNE 7, 1913 AT THE POST OFFICE AT PHILADELPHIA,
PA., UNDER THE ACT OF AUGUST 24TH, 1912 —
SUBSCRIPTION FIFTY CENTS THE YEAR—

The Holmesburg Water Purchase

No. 399   January 15, 1920

Arbitrators have placed a lump sum purchase price on the property of the private water companies in Northeast Philadelphia. Are the details of this proposed $850,000 transaction to be explained to the public?

Water Service by Private Companies in Northeast Philadelphia

The Holmesburg, Disston and Philadelphia and Bristol Water Companies supply water to a small portion of the northeastern section of the city, comprising principally about eighty per cent of the forty-first ward. This district lies between the Frankford and Bristol Turnpike and the Delaware River and extends from Tacony to Torresdale. The water companies just named, however, have not extended their mains over the entire territory in which they have been granted permission to operate. At the present time the southern end of the forty-first ward and a certain portion of the thirty-fifth ward, although within the companies' territory, are supplied with water by the city.

Councils Decide to Purchase the Property

Affirming that the growth of the northeast section demands the extension of the municipal water supply, and that it is inexpedient to permit the Holmesburg and Disston Water Companies to continue supplying water in a territory which will ultimately be surrounded by city water mains, councils by ordinance of March 17, 1919 declared the intention of the city to purchase or lease the facilities of these private water companies. By this same ordinance councils also named an arbitrator for the city, who, together with a second arbitrator appointed by the companies, and a third arbitrator to be selected by the two so appointed, should determine the price to be paid by the city for such purchase or lease. These arbitrators, after making an inventory and appraisal of the physical properties and investigating the financial accounts of the companies, have determined upon a purchase price of $850,000. Their report was transmitted to councils on December 3, 1919.

Nature of the Franchises of the Companies

By ordinance approved July 2, 1888, the Holmesburg and Disston Water Companies are permitted to lay water pipe in this northeastern territory with the stipulation that they shall provide hydrants and water for fire protection, and other water for city use except that required by city or county institutions. It is specifically provided that the granting of such permission does not prevent the granting of similar privileges to other companies nor the laying of water pipe in such streets by the city. By ordinance of March 23, 1900, this original franchise was modified to guarantee greater security to investments by the companies. Under the provisions of the Public Service Company Law (Act of July 26, 1913, P. L. 1374) the city may now acquire and operate the water supply facilities belonging to these companies only after approval by the Public Service Commission as evidenced by its certificate of public convenience. This is granted by the commission when it is necessary or proper for the service, accommodation, or safety of the public.

Determination of Fair Compensation

Up to the present date the city and the private water companies have conducted negotiations independently of the Public Service Commission. In order that the proposed transaction may receive public support before being referred to the commission for review the details should be explained to the public.

The arbitrators after an exhaustive investigation of the facts submit only the following report to councils (Appendix to the Journal of Common Council, 1919, vol. 2, Appendix No. 127):

> "We find the price to be paid by the City for the water works, springs, waters, rights to secure water, reservoirs, dams, pumping stations, machinery, lands, buildings, mains, pipes, lines, standpipes, real estate, leaseholds, and all appurtenances and facilities of the Holmesburg, Disston and Philadelphia and Bristol Water Companies, including all pipes, hydrants and water facilities within the grounds of City or County institutions, but not including securities, cash or similar assets held in the treasury of the companies, at eight hundred and fifty thousand ($850,000) dollars."

What sums make up this total price of $850,000? How were they arrived at? What price was initially asked by the companies, and what was the city's proposal? What were the resulting compromises and concessions? What precedents were used in setting property values? These and other questions arise when the proposed purchase is considered, and they are not answered in the arbitrators' report.

It is accordingly urgent that the city council should hold public hearings at which the arbitrators will present the details of their report. It is also essential that the city solicitor should examine the findings in the interest of the public, since certain constituent portions of the recommended purchase price may be based on principles of valuation and compensation concerning which there is a variance of opinion. If these hearings show that the city should not approve the price agreed upon by the arbitrators, then it is suggested that the city and the companies should appeal to the Public Service Commission to investigate the facts and ascertain the fair compensation.

CITIZENS' BUSINESS

BUREAU OF MUNICIPAL RESEARCH

ISSUED WEEKLY AT 805 FRANKLIN BANK BUILDING
PHILADELPHIA. ENTERED AS SECOND CLASS MATTER
JUNE 7, 1913 AT THE POST OFFICE AT PHILADELPHIA,
PA., UNDER THE ACT OF AUGUST 24TH, 1912—
SUBSCRIPTION FIFTY CENTS THE YEAR-

City Hall Courtesy

No. 400   January 22, 1920

> It is the citizen's duty to respect the dignity of the work and the position of the city employe. A corresponding obligation rests upon the city employe to deal courteously with the citizen.

A Change of Heart

An interesting by-product of the recent transition from one administration to another, is the tone of marked courtesy which greets the visitor to City Hall. The official ax is swinging, and official heads are falling into the baskets; suddenly the municipal employes awaken to the fact that the friendship of the public is desirable, and their conduct is molded accordingly. The visitor rubs his eyes and wonders whether these are the same men with whom he dealt only three weeks ago. He recalls particularly the air of supreme indifference which greeted his inquiries. Today, however, a clerk steps briskly up to inquire the visitor's business, and replies are given in a way that seems to show genuine interest on the part of the questionee. The visitor takes his leave, somewhat bewildered by the deference he has encountered; and on his way to the street finds that corridor guards and even elevator men have caught the infection. The change is so startling that he finds it amusing —yet he cannot deny that it is refreshing.

Need There Be a Relapse?

In a few weeks the process of "hiring and firing" will have ceased; our employes at the "Hall" can then be expected gradually to fall back into their old habits. But why need this be so? Is it true that a manly consideration for the rights and sensibilities of others can be brought about only through fear of losing one's job?

Lessons in Politeness

Many private business houses seek to develop habits of courtesy toward customers by definite instruction and training. The result is a distinct gain to all concerned—employer, employes and the public.

Such a course of instruction might be used to good advantage in some parts of City Hall. If anyone doubts this, let him visit the several court rooms while court is in session, and note the manner in which tipstaves and other minor court officials deal with jurors, witnesses and spectators. In some court rooms, decorum and order are maintained without the slightest unnecessary show of authority. In others, the petty authority given these minor employes has so inflated them with a sense of importance that one is outraged by the tone of bureaucratic insolence and by the small acts of tyranny in which they are able to indulge.

A Definite Gain

Courtesy is a distinct asset. Its use inflicts no hardship upon anyone; in the long run it is easier to be courteous than to be overbearing. It is easily within the power of the directors of departments, and of others in authority at City Hall, so to train the habits of their subordinates that the methods of modern business in this respect can be followed. A frank recognition of the undoubted right of the public to considerate treatment in its own offices would go far toward developing that sense of local pride which is at the heart of true civic spirit.

AN INFORMATION DESK

There should be an information desk in City Hall. The building contains 634 rooms, which house more than 100 different offices. A large number and variety of questions are daily put to guards and elevator men which they are unable to answer, and the inquirer is frequently sent from bureau to bureau before he finally secures the information or assistance he set out to find. A single desk, easily accessible on the ground floor, with a well-informed person in charge, would lessen friction, save time and energy, and aid the general efficiency of the municipal force.

CITIZENS' BUSINESS

BUREAU OF MUNICIPAL RESEARCH

ISSUED WEEKLY AT 805 FRANKLIN BANK BUILDING
PHILADELPHIA. ENTERED AS SECOND CLASS MATTER
JUNE 7, 1913 AT THE POST OFFICE AT PHILADELPHIA,
PA., UNDER THE ACT OF AUGUST 24TH, 1912 —
SUBSCRIPTION FIFTY CENTS THE YEAR

A Stitch in Time

No. 401   **January 29, 1920**

Funny, isn't it, to be sounding a Fourth of July warning while blizzards blow and pipes freeze?

Well, when the orgy of noise and slaughter is at hand it is too late!

There is a widespread belief that the casualties from fireworks are everywhere decreasing.   SUCH IS NOT THE CASE.

will be set on fire, and blazing victims will be

sternly that the sale of fireworks is to be prohibited. Then the dealers in fireworks and explosives tearfully exclaim that a terrible injustice is being done. They never expected the heartless officials to forbid them from selling the instruments of destruction. Their stock is all purchased. If they are not permitted to dispose of it, they will lose money. The hard hearts of the city officials are softened by the loss of money of the dealers; and children are sold firecrackers with which to blow off their fingers and set fire to their clothes. And we all have a most miserable Fourth, listening to the incessant boom of the foolish firecracker and wondering whether the next rocket that falls on our roof will necessitate the calling out of the fire engines. As a result of Philadelphia's noisy celebration in 1918, there were 58 persons injured. In 1919 the toll was higher —one death and 144 injuries. What is to be the toll in 1920?

Seize Time by the Forelock

Now is the time to act. In justice to the dealers, action should be taken in *February* rather than in *June*. In former years wild and frantic waving of our arms in June has been of little avail. This year let us consider the matter sanely and sensibly in February.

Council's Responsibility

There is no comprehensive state law on the subject but council should consider its authority under the police power. The matter should be considered thoroughly in every aspect. Council should learn once for all how far its jurisdiction extends in prohibiting the sale of fireworks. Then it should exercise all the authority that it has and pass as drastic an ordinance as possible. In accordance with this ordinance, the orders concerning restrictions should be announced early and strictly enforced by the department of public safety.

An Editorial from the Evening Bulletin of January 24, 1920.

"The Sinking Fund Commission pays 100.054 for two million dollars' worth of the recent issue of municipal bonds which were sold to a syndicate for 100.029, or a gross profit to the latter of about five thousand dollars. But the Commission originally bid 100.076 for the bonds, and therefore may be said to have saved over $5,000 by the transaction. Did the City of Philadelphia lose or gain? Regardless of the answer, it strikes the man on the street that the Sinking Fund Commission, which is the city in one of its forms, ought to be a preferred customer in the sale of municipal bonds."

CITIZENS' BUSINESS

BUREAU OF MUNICIPAL RESEARCH

ISSUED WEEKLY AT 805 FRANKLIN BANK BUILDING
PHILADELPHIA. ENTERED AS SECOND CLASS MATTER
JUNE 7, 1913 AT THE POST OFFICE AT PHILADELPHIA,
PA., UNDER THE ACT OF AUGUST 24TH, 1912 —
SUBSCRIPTION FIFTY CENTS THE YEAR·

Premature Criticism

No. 402   February 5, 1920

It is neither fair nor convincing for a new public official to criticize proposals of the civil service commission before he has had an opportunity of observing their results.

A Word of Caution

To every new public official we would give the counsel "look before you leap." To those new public officials who find some of the restraints of civil service regulations a trifle irksome and who feel impelled to enter at once upon a war of emancipation we would pass on the word of caution "look *twice* before you leap." The merit system is too well established in public sympathy and has too long a record of successful operation to be easily attacked and overthrown.

One of our new city officials has recently come out in opposition to the proposal of the civil service commission that city employes should be promoted in the order of merit as determined by a competitive promotion examination, a limited choice being permitted from among those having the highest rating. His argument was that an employe's fitness for promotion can be determined better by his superior than by a civil service examination.

An Old Story

Strange as it may seem, there is nothing at all novel either in the proposal of the civil service commission or in the argument of the protesting new official. Wherever an effort has been made to insure to the young men and women of the community an opportunity for a career in the public service, a rule similar to the one proposed by the Philadelphia civil service commission has been adopted. In such cities as New York, Chicago, Buffalo, San Francisco and Cleveland; and in such states as Ohio, New Jersey, New York and California, the employes in the service are given a reasonable assurance that promotion will be according to merit by a rule requiring that when an appointing officer wants to make a promotion he must select one of the three persons whose names stand highest on the list of eligibles. As for the objection that an examining board is not as capable of picking out the best qualified men as is the appointing officer himself, we can find it stated and restated in every variety of form in the utterances of spoils politicians in every community where the merit system has ever been considered. Had this objection been permitted to prevail wherever it has been raised, we should still be as completely in the grip of the spoils regime, with all its attendant evils, as we were in the days before the first civil service act was adopted in this country in 1883.

Let's Judge After, Not Before, We Have The Evidence

It would be well, too, for this new official who has made his protest against the new promotion rule to wait until he has an opportunity of observing its results. He may find the promotion examination a much better instrument of selection than he ever dreamed it to be. As a matter of fact the promotion rule in effect in Philadelphia during a considerable period just prior to 1916 was essentially the same as the one now under consideration, and the results during that period appear to have been highly satisfactory. There seems to be no good reason for anticipating less satisfactory results should this rule be reestablished at the present time.

The Civil Service Commission's Opportunity

It is true that the merit system like every other human system may be poorly administered and thus fall short of its highest possibilities. We must look to the civil service commission to make the system produce the best results of which it is capable. At the same time it should not be overlooked that no civil service commission has yet achieved all of the possibilities inherent in the system. In the past there has been a little too much emphasis on the *negative* side of civil service administration and not enough emphasis on the *positive* side. The civil service commission can and should become to the city government what a well organized employment department is to a private business concern. It can and should become much more of a positive aid to administrative officials than it has been in the past. The new civil service law carries out the spirit of this new viewpoint by imposing upon the commission important duties that were not required by the former law. It is now up to the new members of the civil service commission to develop to the full the opportunities for constructive service along employment lines that the new law has opened to them.

The Administrative Official's Duty

The least that the administrative officials of the city can do in making the employment work of the civil service commission a success is to give the commission a chance to work out its own policies in its own way and to withhold criticism until those policies may be judged by their results.

CITIZENS' BUSINESS

BUREAU OF MUNICIPAL RESEARCH

ISSUED WEEKLY AT 805 FRANKLIN BANK BUILDING
PHILADELPHIA, ENTERED AS SECOND CLASS MATTER
JUNE 7, 1913 AT THE POST OFFICE AT PHILADELPHIA,
PA., UNDER THE ACT OF AUGUST 24TH, 1912 —
SUBSCRIPTION FIFTY CENTS THE YEAR-

OF INTEREST

No. 403   February 12, 1920

Laws and ordinances attempt to protect the city's interest in its business relations with contractors, dealers and manufacturers. The latter can and do watch their side of the bargain.

There is no reason why the city's business with banks should not also be conducted with an eye to the city's side of the case.

Cook County's New Deposit Law

An interesting recent bulletin of the Citizens' Association of Chicago discusses the results of their new County Deposits Law, under the operation of which, says the bulletin, $127,000 more interest was paid into the public treasury for the fiscal year ended November 30, 1919, than for the year preceding.

The law requires the county treasurer to account for and pay over all interest on the public funds in his custody. It also requires the selection of depositories by competitive bids. The bulletin goes on to say that this new arrangement is more satisfactory to the banks as well as to the public.

Philadelphia Made One Step Ahead

Six years ago* this Bureau pointed out that the same depositories that were paying the Board of Education 2½% on *active* and *inactive* accounts, were paying the city 2% on inactive and *nothing at all* on active accounts. Later in the year an ordinance changed this situation so that the city now gets the same treatment as the school board on both classes of accounts.

The Bureau buttressed its position on this matter by collating facts from other large cities, and it was found that our city government, even after the increase in the interest rate, fared some-

___
* CITIZENS' BUSINESS No. 97, April 2, 1914.

what worse in this respect than the other leading municipalities.

Interest by Ukase Arbitrary

It strikes us as a little arbitrary for the council to fix a rate of interest on city deposits by ordinance. While we know of no institution that gave up the city's account when the rate went up in 1914, such arbitrary action might have gone to a point beyond which certain of the banks or trust companies (and even perhaps all of them) might have found the city's account unprofitable.

Much fairer, it seems to us, is the system now becoming more and more general, of inviting all eligible banks and trust companies to bid for public deposits. Appropriate regulations governing maximum amounts per class of institution, requirements of notice for withdrawal, etc., have been successfully worked out elsewhere, and would present no difficulties for Philadelphia. Under such a plan one bank might get a small idle deposit at a comparatively high rate, while another would secure an active account, on which it would pay relatively less interest. Moreover, the rates would vary from time to time, with changing-money conditions.

A Square Deal to Both Sides

No one in his senses would want to injure the banks. Yet some of the criticisms directed against those who favored a higher interest rate on city deposits a few years ago, was bitter in tone and assumed both malice and ignorance of the facts.

A fiduciary institution doing business with the city should not be exploited or injured in any way in that relation. On the other hand, it should require no special pleading that the city —a pretty good "account"—should receive as favorable treatment in the matter of interest as any private individual, firm or corporation. Such, in recent years, has not been universally the case.

Not Unimportant!

These little revenues and little expenses are *not* negligible. In these days of rocketing taxes, underpaid teachers, policemen, and firemen, un-mended streets, and other apparently insatiable demands, every hundred thousand—nay, every dollar—must be made to work. Philadelphia had an average daily balance in bank of over $9,000,-000 for 1918. Every quarter-percent per annum on that sum means $22,500—enough to carry the interest and sinking fund charges on about $400,000 of city bonds.

From an editorial, Business Section, Public Ledger, February 5, 1920:

"It is economic illiteracy to make national heroes of prize fighters and pay school teachers such small salaries that in one year 143,000, or 23 per cent of all engaged in the public schools of America have to abandon teaching in order to earn enough to live."

CITIZENS' BUSINESS

BUREAU OF MUNICIPAL RESEARCH

ISSUED WEEKLY AT 805 FRANKLIN BANK BUILDING
PHILADELPHIA. ENTERED AS SECOND CLASS MATTER
JUNE 7, 1913 AT THE POST OFFICE AT PHILADELPHIA,
PA., UNDER THE ACT OF AUGUST 24TH, 1912 —
SUBSCRIPTION FIFTY CENTS THE YEAR

Grandfather's Old Clothes

No. 404   **February 19, 1920**

Who can tell whether "District Peace Judges"
will not be as objectionable a generation hence, if
imbedded in the fundamental law of the commonwealth, as the Philadelphia magistrates are all but
universally admitted to be today?

Good Clothes—Once

In the year 1873 certain eminent citizens decided on a system of courts of justice for the people of Pennsylvania, and wrote their decision into our state Constitution. The system is described in great detail. After providing that—

> The judicial power of this commonwealth shall be vested in a Supreme Court, in courts of common pleas, courts of oyer and terminer and general jail delivery, courts of quarter sessions of the peace, orphans' courts, magistrates' courts, and in such other courts as the General Assembly may from time to time establish—

the Constitution goes into particulars, defines the structure of the court of common pleas for Philadelphia, provides for subordinate officials, such as prothonotaries and court clerks, and generally describes the entire state judicial system. At the time, this system was supposed to have been very well thought out, and to be entirely adequate to the needs of the people.

Outworn and Outgrown

But "the world do move". A half-century has gone by. Problems confront this generation never dreamed of by the men of '73. Yet the system of courts of justice defined by them in the Constitution has not moved—it has remained rigid, fixed, and every effort to do away with any portion of it has met with violent opposition. As a result, the Constitution has "hobbled" our local common pleas courts, so that proper distribution and speedy turnover of work is impossible. The Constitution has fastened on Philadelphia a pernicious system of elected magistrates, who—with certain notable exceptions—have been tools of the political leaders to whom they owed their political existence. The Philadelphia Municipal Court, established in 1913, duplicates much of the work of the magistrates, yet the magistrates cannot be turned out of office, as they are "constitutional officers". Therefore, we have today in our city these two courts side by side with two sets of judges and court employes, and two sets of expense charges helping to make up the tax rate. They are very different in kind, of course, yet the Municipal Court could doubtless arrange to perform the functions of both satisfactorily.

A Few Patches Proposed

The commission on constitutional revision, now sitting at Harrisburg, are considering certain changes in our state judicial system. One proposal is to merge the five courts of common pleas of Philadelphia into one. Another is to abolish the office of magistrate— and create that of "District Peace Judge". The judges of the Superior Court—not mentioned in the present Constitution—are to be given constitutional status, and their term of office lengthened. Other changes in detail have been suggested, but no final recommendations have as yet been made.

New Garments Needed, to Wear for Fifty Years

The provisions that we are placing in the Constitution today, may vitally affect the lives of our children and grandchildren. Who can say what their problems will be? Are we sure that they will require "courts of oyer and terminer and general jail delivery"? Will "District Peace Judges" fully meet the needs of the poor who may crowd their great cities? Who can say that *any* detailed judicial system which we draw up, no matter how conscientiously and carefully, will supply the requirements of this growing commonwealth for the next fifty years?

Let Us Cut the Cloth as We Need It

Human wisdom cannot foresee the grave questions that are bound to arise in our complex civilization in the period during which we may reasonably expect our new Constitution to be in force. When once adopted, experience has proved that amendment is exceedingly difficult. We must have a judicial system capable of growth and adjustment. The problem of seeing that justice is done between man and man is of the most profound nature, requiring constant study, the results of which must be subject to constant revision and improvement. Such a study is not the proper work of a constitutional commission. It is the work of the legislature; the details of our judicial system must be made matter of *law*, not of constitutional provision— and then, if a law is found to be unwise or unworkable, if a court or an official is found to be unnecessary, it is the simplest possible procedure for the legislature to remedy the condition by passing a new law. The Constitution should contain only the broad outline of the judicial plan, stated in most general terms, with full authority given to the legislature to make all details for that plan.

A Pattern

The problem confronting our commission at Harrisburg today is not new. Over a century ago, it faced the men who met in Philadelphia to frame a constitution for the United States. The reports of their debates show that they had the same temptation to fasten a rigid judicial system on a growing America. But the temptation was recognized and resisted; and the result of their labors was one simple sentence. It stands in our national Constitution today, having met the needs and stood the tests of 130 years. It reads as follows:

> The judicial power of the United States shall be vested in one Supreme Court, and in such inferior courts as the congress may from time to time ordain and establish.

We earnestly recommend to the commission that wording similar to this be placed in our State Constitution, that all mention of the details of legal machinery be omitted therefrom, and that broad powers be conferred on our legislature to provide courts of justice for our people as need for the same shall from time to time arise.

CITIZENS' BUSINESS

BUREAU OF MUNICIPAL RESEARCH

ISSUED WEEKLY AT 805 FRANKLIN BANK BUILDING
PHILADELPHIA. ENTERED AS SECOND CLASS MATTER
JUNE 7, 1913 AT THE POST OFFICE AT PHILADELPHIA,
PA., UNDER THE ACT OF AUGUST 24TH, 1912—
SUBSCRIPTION FIFTY CENTS THE YEAR-

The Real Issue in Street Cleaning

No. 405   February 26, 1920

While discussing the percentage of contractors' profits, we should not lose sight of the real issue—municipal operation by 1921—which would abolish these profits.   Isn't it time to begin planning whether we shall institute municipal street cleaning in 1921, and if so, how we shall go about it?

Recently there have been two public controversies in regard to street cleaning. One of these concerned the question of keeping the streets clean in accordance with the terms of the contracts; the other centered upon the percentage of profits being made by the contractors. Both of these subjects are vital issues in the street cleaning situation, but their discussion obscured for the moment the more pressing problem of determining the city's policy with reference to the conduct of street cleaning activities after 1920.

The Real Issue

The new charter provides that after December 31, 1920, the cleaning of our streets and the collection and disposal of city refuse shall be done directly by the city; but that the council, by a vote of a majority of the members elected thereto, with the approval of the mayor, may authorize having this work done by contract, in whole or in part. It is therefore of relatively slight importance what percentage of profits is now being made by the contractors, if the contract method of performing this work is to be discontinued after this year. The important considerations are whether we shall begin municipal work in 1921, and if so, how we shall go about it.

A Matter of Expediency

It is quite true that the question of when we shall have municipal street cleaning is a matter of administrative and financial expediency—

it should not be treated as a matter of political expediency. Most certainly the city should not attempt to "bite off more than it can chew", and should not take over this work any faster than the facilities and organization can be developed. When once the city actually carries on the work, and not simply inspects it, the responsibility will rest directly on municipal officials without other shoulders to shift it to, and there must be an adequate organization to render the service that will be demanded by the public. Having been told in the past that clean streets could be expected only under municipal operation, which was long denied us by the legislature, the citizen will quite naturally expect more effective work when the city assumes charge. The city must therefore plan to conduct this work in a business-like, adequate and effective manner.

Now Is the Time for Planning

In order to give time for study and planning, the date of commencement of municipal operation was set ahead in the new charter to January 1, 1921. However, prior to August 1, bids may be requested for contract work in order to form a basis of comparison with municipal work. Before this step is taken the existing specifications should be closely scrutinized and, if necessary, revised, to provide for the same type of service which it will be planned to render under municipal operation. It will be necessary also to make careful studies of the entire situation to guide the council in making its decision this coming fall.

It is absolutely essential for the city administration to know what plants and equipment will be needed and how they can be acquired; what personnel will be necessary; and what will be the required capital outlay and yearly cost of operation of the municipal organization. **These practical engineering studies should determine the extent to which municipal operation can be applied in 1921 to the street cleaning activities, and to the allied work of ash, refuse and garbage collection and disposal.**

The Next Step

An expenditure of a few thousand dollars to make a complete survey of the street cleaning situation, so that the administration may be wisely guided in making its decisions next fall, is an insignificant amount compared with the enormous sums involved. During the current year the city will spend about $5,000,000 for street cleaning and refuse disposal. If the contract system is dropped, it is apparent that extensive planning will be required to develop the facilities and organization even to spend this amount of money, to say nothing of securing the most economical and effective results.

It is urged therefore that the council provide the means to augment the engineering force of the department of public works for the special purpose of making the necessary studies and plans. This should be done with the least possible delay in order that such work may be completed before the time of decision arrives.

CITIZENS' BUSINESS

BUREAU OF MUNICIPAL RESEARCH

ISSUED WEEKLY AT 805 FRANKLIN BANK BUILDING
PHILADELPHIA. ENTERED AS SECOND CLASS MATTER
JUNE 7, 1913 AT THE POST OFFICE AT PHILADELPHIA,
PA., UNDER THE ACT OF AUGUST 24TH, 1912—
SUBSCRIPTION FIFTY CENTS THE YEAR

In the Spirit

No. 406   March 4, 1920

When the framers of the new charter removed the
correctional functions of the city from the department of public safety, and transferred them to the
welfare department, they were acting in the spirit
of the new attitude towards the punishment of
transgressors.

Time to Think

It is clear to anyone even casually familiar with the city's business that under the old charter—as under the new—the main concern of the director of public safety was the police bureau. Naturally, the bureau of correction occupied a minor place in the attention of any director of the department. Moreover, those who shaped policy for the bureau of correction could not help but regard it largely from the police viewpoint, and it was hardly to be expected that the planning, patience and knowledge could be brought to bear on the city's house of correction that would tend to make it, so far as possible, a *curative* agency, rather than one merely *punitive*.

With the wise provision in the new charter, however, that the welfare department be charged with the correctional activities, there is encouragement for the hope of a new dispensation. There will be the *time* for giving major attention to this activity of our local government, and there should be the *viewpoint* of human service primarily, rather than that of the stern majesty of the law.

Proposed Consolidation of Charities and Corrections

The director of the department of public welfare has had introduced into council an ordinance to consolidate the bureau of charities (in the department of health and charities under the old charter) and the bureau of correction. This, it seems to us, is purely a matter of administrative expediency. In many cities these functions are united. Years ago New York City had charities and corrections in the same department and then separated them. Philadelphia, too, once had them together, but they were divorced in 1903 by an amendment to the Bullitt Act. The general public may also be inclined to regard as details of only administrative interest the titles and salaries proposed for employes and the relatively small financial saving promised.

Enlightened Treatment of First Offenders

But a matter of great social significance, we feel, is the plan of the director of welfare to reorganize the house of correction so as to make it function effectively and humanely as a public agency to save from hopeless ruin those unfortunates who have offended but who have not yet degenerated into hardened criminals.

To carry out this idea of making the house of correction live up to its name, it will be necessary to secure a legislative amendment that would enable judges to commit first offenders to the house of correction instead of to prison. Penologists tell us that commitments to prison tend to turn first offenders into recidivists or chronic criminals. That this is injurious to society as well as to the hapless youths themselves would appear to need no argument.

Other Encouraging Proposals

The director's appealing program has numerous other features which limitations of space prevent our discussing in detail. Foremost in interest among these are proposals for teaching trades to the men and women committed; for wholesome work—much of it out-of-doors in quarry or garden; for entertainments and evening classes; and for concentration on a purpose to salvage so far as it can be done the valuable human material entrusted to the department.

* * * * * *

The department, being new, will doubtless have many interesting plans and programs in recreational and other welfare fields. From time to time, we shall try to summarize these plans and comment on them for the readers of CITIZENS' BUSINESS.

Pol Sci

CITIZENS' BUSINESS

BUREAU OF MUNICIPAL RESEARCH

ISSUED WEEKLY AT 805 FRANKLIN BANK BUILDING
PHILADELPHIA. ENTERED AS SECOND CLASS MATTER
JUNE 7, 1913 AT THE POST OFFICE AT PHILADELPHIA,
PA., UNDER THE ACT OF AUGUST 24TH, 1912 —
SUBSCRIPTION FIFTY CENTS THE YEAR-

How Far Can Civil Service Go?

No. 407   March 11, 1920

A common misunderstanding of the real nature of an
up-to-date civil service examination has been responsible for much of the skepticism as to the suita-
bility of civil service methods for filling high grade
positions.

Wanted: a Substitute

Will some one please suggest a substitute for the term "civil service examination"? Here is an opportunity to serve a good cause in a most effective manner. The term just mentioned is a positive hindrance to the cause of the merit system and ought, if possible, to be abolished. Its connotation is most unfortunate. To the average person it suggests a class-room ordeal in which one's chances of survival vary in inverse ratio to the length of time he has been out of school or college. It is quite natural, therefore, that any proposal to fill high grade positions in the public service by civil service methods should meet at first with a considerable degree of skepticism in many quarters.

New Wine in an Old Bottle

At this moment we ourselves are unable to think of a more suitable term. We may, however, be able to throw a bit of light upon the real nature of an up-to-date civil service examination and thus help to introduce a new meaning into an old term.

As a matter of fact, the more progressive civil service commissions throughout the country have long ceased to rely to any appreciable extent on the somewhat academic test that was used so largely in the early days of the merit system. These commissions now use a series of different tests of a very practical character designed to gauge different qualifications and appropriate for the filling of different types of positions. Carpenters and painters, for example, are no longer asked when Columbus

discovered America, but they are required to demonstrate their skill by doing an actual job of carpen-
tering or painting.

The Un-assembled Examination.

In like manner, applicants for high grade professional, technical or administrative positions are no
longer quizzed in school-room fashion with regard
to this text-book fact or that, but they are invited
to enter a dignified competition in which their past
career and their personality are determining factors
rather than any feat of memory. In examinations
of this character, applicants frequently never meet
together in a single room, but prepare their statements of training and experience in their own private offices or in their homes and send these statements, together with any books or articles they
may have published, to the civil service commission
by mail. In addition they may be asked to discuss
in writing some important technical or administrative problem, and these written discussions, like the
statements of training and experience, may also be
delivered through the mails. All of these evidences
of the qualifications of the various applicants are
then gone over and rated by a board of special
examiners who themselves are professional men or
have had long experience in the kind of work for
which the examination is held. Those applicants
who receive a passing mark in this part of the test
may then be summoned before the special examining board for a personal interview in order that
their personal qualifications may also be taken into

account. Finally, the grades for the various parts of the test are averaged and the successful applicants are placed on the list of eligibles in the order of their rating. This is what is known in civil service parlance as the ''un-assembled examination.''

What It Has Accomplished

Fortunately, it is no longer necessary to argue the efficacy of this kind of test. It sounds like a sensible method and experience has demonstrated over and over again that it produces results. Many important public posts with salaries ranging from $3,000 to $10,000 have been filled not only by the United States Civil Service Commission, but by state and local commissions as well. Men of high standing and national reputation have not hesitated to enter an examination when conducted on such a dignified plane. It has been possible, moreover, for persons who lived in entirely different parts of the country to compete, without being put to the expense of traveling to the place where the examination was held until there appeared a reasonable prospect of appointment.

Making Public Service a Career

In view of the success of this improved type of ''civil service examination'' is there any good reason why we should not proceed with confidence to extend the merit system just as high up in the service as the present law permits us to go? By so doing we shall take a long step toward making public service not merely a blind alley employment but a dignified and honorable career.

BUSINESS

...IPAL RESEARCH

FRANKLIN BANK BUILDING
...AS SECOND CLASS MATTER...
OFFICE AT PHILADELPHIA,
AUGUST 24TH, 1912 —
...CENTS THE YEAR—

in Favor
...ning?

March 25, 1920

...ove question, you might very
... zoning?" Because of the
...o as zoning, it is important
...y what was proposed in the
...ere under discussion several

account. Finally, the grac
of the test are averaged :
cants are placed on the lis
of their rating. This is wha
parlance as the ''un-assen

What It Has Accomplishe(

Fortunately, it is no long
efficacy of this kind. of
sensible method and expe
over and over again that i
important public posts wi
$3,000 to $10,000 have be
United States Civil Service
and local commissions as ˈ
ing and national reputatiˈ
enter an examination wh
dignified plane. It has be
persons who lived in entir
country to compete, withˈ
pense of traveling to the
nation was held until the
prospect of appointment.

Making Public Service a C

In view of the success
''civil service examinatic
reason why we should noⅠ
to extend the merit systeⅠ
service as the present laⅤ
so doing we shall take a
public service not merely
but a dignified and honorˈ

CITIZENS' BUSINESS

BUREAU OF MUNICIPAL RESEARCH

ISSUED WEEKLY AT 805 FRANKLIN BANK BUILDING
PHILADELPHIA. ENTERED AS SECOND CLASS MATTER
JUNE 7, 1913 AT THE POST OFFICE AT PHILADELPHIA,
PA., UNDER THE ACT OF AUGUST 24TH, 1912—
SUBSCRIPTION FIFTY CENTS THE YEAR·

Are You in Favor of Zoning?

No. 409   March 25, 1920

> Before answering the above question, you might very
> reasonably ask, "What is zoning?" Because of the
> many activities referred to as zoning, it is important
> that we understand clearly what was proposed in the
> zoning regulations that were under discussion several
> months ago.

What is Zoning?

The other day we asked a visitor from our neighboring city of Camden whether he was in favor of zoning. Now we didn't intend any offense, and were totally unprepared for his outburst against charging for street car rides according to zones of territory denoted by red ink circles on the city map. That set us thinking. Zoning meant something entirely different to this man from what it meant to us, so we decided to question another person.

The next time we tackled one of our own Philadelphians whom we met in the post office. Yes, he thought zoning was all right, but he'd be hanged if he could remember what zone Kansas City is in, and anyhow the government charges too much for its parcel post service. We replied half-heartedly that maybe that was so, but really we couldn't stop then to discuss it.

A Blessing in Disguise

It will not take a silver-tongued orator to convince the average citizen that he will be benefited by regulations which will improve the tone of the neighborhood in which he lives; which will prevent a public garage from being built across the street from his home; and which will make his work more agreeable on the ground floor of a downtown office building, because the light and air are not cut off by sky-scrapers across the street.

The exercise by the city of control over building operations in the matter of regulating the location, size and use of buildings, is commonly, but unfortunately, spoken of as zoning. Because of the many activities referred to as zoning, it is particularly necessary that the public be fully informed as to its meaning in this instance.

A Few Facts to Remember

A zoning commission was appointed in 1916 and made a report early in November 1919, in the form of a proposed zoning ordinance. This provided for separate regulations of the use to which a building could be put, of the area of lot which could be covered, and of the height to which it could be erected. For the purpose of defining these regulations, there were outlined three groups of districts, *use*, *area* and *height* districts, each group covering the entire city area.

New buildings—for it was not proposed to make the regulations retroactive—would be regulated by these three sets of maps. Under the *use* regulations there are proposed four classes of districts: residential, commercial, industrial and unrestricted districts. Under the *area* regulations there are five classes, in which the area of the lot that may be covered by the building varies progressively from 30 to 95 per cent. The *height* districts are also five in number. In them the permitted building height varies from one to three times the street width, subject to a maximum height limit, and with an additional allowance if the building is set back from the street line.

Education of the Public

Unquestionably all of our citizens are interested in knowing in what classes of use, area and height districts their property will be placed. Hence the proposed ordinance should be given wide publicity, and separate public hearings should be held on the proposed regulations for each section of the city. This important work should be undertaken by the city government. The zoning commission that drafted the proposed zoning ordinance expired with the old charter, but fortunately the new charter authorizes the mayor to appoint a zoning commission. A new commission should be appointed and council should grant the moderate sum needed to carry on a campaign of information.

CORRECTION OF AN ERROR

In CITIZENS' BUSINESS No. 402, devoted to the question of promotion in the city service, we incorrectly listed Ohio among the states and cities which require the appointing officer to choose one of the three persons whose names stand highest on the promotion eligible list. As a matter of fact, under the Ohio civil service law the appointing officer is required to promote the man whose name stands at the head of the list, no choice whatever being permitted. This strengthens the position taken in the number of CITIZENS' BUSINESS in question in which we contended for a promotion rule that would limit the choice of the appointing officer in selecting eligible persons for promotion.

CITIZENS' BUSINESS

BUREAU OF MUNICIPAL RESEARCH

ISSUED WEEKLY AT 805 FRANKLIN BANK BUILDING
PHILADELPHIA. ENTERED AS SECOND CLASS MATTER
JUNE 7, 1913 AT THE POST OFFICE AT PHILADELPHIA,
PA., UNDER THE ACT OF AUGUST 24TH, 1912 —
SUBSCRIPTION FIFTY CENTS THE YEAR—

Our Belated Annual Reports

No. 410   **April 1, 1920**

> The reports of administrative departments could be
> made a vital factor in arousing greater popular interest
> in local public affairs. So long, however, as they con-
> tinue to appear almost a year late and then perhaps in
> uninteresting style they will fail in this important
> mission.

Annual municipal reports of most cities are published long after the year which they record and very frequently they are uninteresting and not really informative. Here and there new standards are being set up but Philadelphia is lagging in the rearguard. Its annual departmental reports are published from six months to a year late and the collected documents are usually published fifteen months after the year which they chronicle.

What the Law Requires

The Bullitt Bill provided that "the several heads of departments shall present to the mayor annually on or before the first Monday of February, a report of their proceedings during the preceding year." The new charter contains practically the same provision. The printing of these reports should be expedited and the citizens informed *promptly* of the activities of the various departments. Here is an opportunity for the new administration to set up new standards both of promptness in publishing reports and of interest of contents.

Why Not Occasional Special Reports?

But why should we wait until the end of the year to know what our city government is accomplishing? Occasional reports on special activities would be of great value and of interest to the citizens. This is a field in which there is plenty of room for improvement. Why should not Philadelphia be in the vanguard of progressive cities in publicity work?

SAUCE FOR THE GOOSE

Several months ago the courts refused to grant an injunction against the Fairmount Park Commission, who had awarded a large contract for some work to a concern which was not the "lowest responsible bidder." The attorney for the commission contended that the laws governing that body—unlike those controlling "city" departments—did not require awarding the work to the lowest bidder, and the court decided accordingly.

To the average citizen who is more interested in good service at minimum cost than in niceties of legal distinction this kind of technicality cannot appeal with much force.

If it is proper to require the school board and the city departments to award contracts to lowest responsible bidders, why should not all boards and departments of local administrative jurisdiction be governed by such a rule?

HOW ABOUT PHILADELPHIA?

Luther Burbank did a great thing for humanity when he "made two blades of grass grow where one grew before." Now if he could only reverse the process and "make one government do where TWO did BEFORE," he would be the benefactor of Los Angeles—both city and county.—*City Club Bulletin of Los Angeles.*

Pol Sci

CITIZENS' BUSINESS

BUREAU OF MUNICIPAL RESEARCH

ISSUED WEEKLY AT 805 FRANKLIN BANK BUILDING
PHILADELPHIA. ENTERED AS SECOND CLASS MATTER
JUNE 7, 1913 AT THE POST OFFICE AT PHILADELPHIA,
PA., UNDER THE ACT OF AUGUST 24TH, 1912 —
SUBSCRIPTION FIFTY CENTS THE YEAR·

A Side Light on Salaries and Wages in the City Service

No. 411   April 8, 1920

In dealing with the problem of salary and wage adjustment in the city service nothing is more important than a clear understanding of all the pertinent facts. Some of these facts are set forth in this number of CITIZENS' BUSINESS.

Meeting an Emergency

The proposed ordinance providing for moderate increases in pay for employes in the Bureau of Water, the Bureau of Highways and the Bureau of Surveys of the Public Works department is to be regarded as distinctly an emergency measure. How great the emergency is may be surmised from the fact that twice within the last six months we have heard of threatened strikes in the Bureau of Water. Happily these strikes have been averted and Philadelphia has been spared the calamity of having its water works shut down. As our Mayor has well put it, however, "we have nothing to crow about." Neither the employes of the Bureau of Water nor the employes in other bureaus and departments of the city government are particularly well provided for on the city payroll. They have, in fact, been compelled to face the ever rising tide of prices with nothing like a corresponding increase in salaries and wages.

The Standardization Program and Emergencies

Since Philadelphia is about to proceed with its program of standardizing salaries it is only natural and proper to defer all questions of payroll adjustment that can be deferred to the time when the whole problem will be dealt with in a comprehensive manner. It should be remembered, however, that as yet the Civil Service Commission has not even secured its appropriation of funds to undertake the work of standardization and that at best it would not be ready to report its plan for councilmanic action much before October. In view of this situation we must not be too inflexible in our determination that all action on salary increases shall wait for the report of the Civil Service Commission. There are bound to be emergencies that cannot be so long deferred.

Present Extraordinary Conditions

The fact is that the employment conditions now confronting the city government are extraordinary in the extreme. It is impossible at existing rates of pay to keep the various bureaus and departments adequately manned and to maintain the morale that is essential to efficiency. Underpayment, moreover, is not confined to one department or to one group of employes; it exists in all departments of the city government and affects practically all groups of employes. Some groups, it is true, have fared better than others, but even the most fortunate ones have fared none too well.

These observations, of course, concern themselves with public services assumed to be essential and with employes assumed to be necessary to those services. This examination of certain

3

pertinent facts must not be susceptible of distortion into a brief for the sinecurist or the chair-warmer.

Facts that Should be Known

Perhaps the most imperative need in the present employment situation is a more general understanding of the facts. If the facts are known beforehand, many a difficulty in wage adjustment that might develop otherwise will never arise. With this thought in mind we have made a comparison of the rates of pay in the various city departments in 1914 with the corresponding rates in 1920 and calculated the increases in salaries and wages during the period between these two dates. In making this comparison we confined ourselves strictly to those positions that were continuous throughout the entire period. It will be noted in the following tables in which the results of this comparison are set forth that the average increase in *salaries* has been only 10.4 per cent without the bonus and 29.2 per cent with the bonus. The cost of living, it must be borne in mind, has gone up more than 85 per cent during the same period. *Wage* scales have advanced 19.4 per cent without the bonus and 41 per cent with the bonus, a somewhat better showing than we have in case of salaries, but still far behind the increase in living costs. These are facts that are of utmost significance in relation to the city's problem of salary and wage adjustment and they ought to be understood not only by our city officials but by all the citizens of Philadelphia.

4

TABLE SHOWING INCREASE IN COMPENSATION FROM 1914 TO 1920 IN SALARIED POSITIONS THAT WERE CONTINUOUS DURING THIS PERIOD. BY SERVICE GROUPS.*

| | PERCENTAGE OF INCREASE | |
SERVICE GROUPS	Without bonus	With bonus
All groups	10.4	29.2
Custodial (caretakers, janitors, storekeepers, watchmen, etc.).	24.4	49.1
Unskilled labor	21.9	46.3
Skilled labor	19.	42.
Protectional (salaried policemen, firemen, and guards)	10.7	31.2
Clerical	8.	27.2
Miscellaneous	6.	25.
Professional and scientific	5.1	21.1
Inspectional	5.	22.7
Executive	2.5	5.1

TABLE SHOWING INCREASE IN COMPENSATION FROM 1914 TO 1920 IN SALARIED POSITIONS THAT WERE CONTINUOUS DURING THIS PERIOD. BY OCCUPATIONAL GROUPS.*

| | PERCENTAGE OF INCREASE | |
OCCUPATIONAL GROUPS	Without bonus	With bonus
All groups	10.4	29.2
Housekeepers	55.2	86.2
Riggers	28.9	54.7
Watchmen	28.9	54.7
Caretakers and janitors	28.9	54.4
Food inspectors	27.7	35.3

* Because of difficulties in making comparisons it has not been possible to include in these tables all of the divisions and bureaus in the departments under city government. The following, however, have been included: Mayor's office; Civil Service Commission; Purchasing Agent; Art Jury; Department of Law; Department of City Transit; Department of Wharves, Docks and Ferries; Department of Public Safety; Department of Public Works (excluding Bureau of Gas); Department of Public Health (excluding Bureau of Hospitals); and Department of Public Welfare (excluding the director's office and Bureau of Constructive Social Service).

5

Occupational Groups (cont'd)	Percentage of Increase Without bonus	With bonus
Enginemen	23.6	48.
Laborers	21.9	46.3
Guards	21.6	45.9
Police matrons	20.9	45.
Hostlers and drivers	20.7	44.5
Drawbridge operators	20.	44.
Miscellaneous skilled workers	18.7	40.7
Woodworkers	18.6	42.4
Statisticians	18.1	32.3
Storekeepers and yardmen	17.1	40.5
Bookkeepers	17.	40.3
Electrical workers	16.1	37.9
Machinists	16.	38.3
Telephone operators	15.3	38.2
Chemists	14.8	28.6
Electrical inspectors	12.8	35.3
Laboratory assistants	12.8	35.3
Inspectors of lighting service	12.7	33.6
Plumbers and steamfitters	12.5	35.
Miscellaneous inspectors	12.5	33.6
Superintendents and foremen	12.2	31.4
Painters	11.7	34.
Motor drivers	11.5	33.7
Blacksmiths	11.1	33.3
Firemen (above rank of firemen, hosemen, and laddermen)	11.	31.9
Recreation instructors	10.5	32.6
Messengers	9.2	31.1
Policemen (above rank of patrolmen)	9.	28.9
Otherwise unclassified	9.	27.1
Disinfectors	8.8	30.5
Inspectors of public works	8.3	25.1
Miscellaneous professional and scientific	8.2	28.
Marine workers	8.1	29.8
Clerks	6.4	24.9
Bacteriologists	6.4	23.2
Stenographers and typists	6.1	27.4
Fire prevention inspectors	6.1	21.8

Occupational Groups (cont'd)	Percentage of Increase Without bonus	With bonus
Detectives	5.6	21.2
Dentists	5.5	24.3
Private secretaries	5.5	13.6
Photographers	5.1	23.5
Institutional attendants	5.	26.
Water service inspectors	5.	23.
Bakers	4.9	25.9
Engineers	4.8	19.5
Civil service examiners	4.8	17.4
Nurses	4.5	24.5
Draftsmen	4.5	24.2
Department officials	4.2	5.5
Inspectors of steam engines and boilers	3.	19.1
Physicians	1.4	12.8
Medical inspectors	.9	19.4
Inspectors of supplies	.0	20.
Inspectors of buildings	.0	13.7
Lawyers	.0	10.4
Executive secretaries	.0	3.3
Bureau chiefs	.8 decrease	4.1

Table Showing Increase in Wage Scales Under the City Government from 1914 to 1920. By Occupational Groups.

Occupational Groups	Percentage of Increase Without bonus	With bonus
All groups	19.4	41.
Metal workers	46.6	75.9
Machinists	36.3	63.7
Boilermakers	35.7	59.
Guards	33.3	60.
Enginemen	28.2	53.8
Hostlers and drivers	26.1	51.3
Electrical workers	25.8	50.9
Blacksmiths	23.4	48.2
Woodworkers	20.1	32.6
Bricklayers	18.3	38.5

OCCUPATIONAL GROUPS (cont'd)	PERCENTAGE OF INCREASE Without bonus	With bonus
Miscellaneous skilled workers....	16.7	38.7
Plumbers and steamfitters	16.6	38.6
Marine workers	14.3	37.1
Elevator operators	14.	34.2
Stonemasons	12.5	35.
Laborers	12.3	34.5
Structural iron workers	11.1	27.8
Painters	9.6	31.5
Riggers	4.7	22.7

STATEMENT OF THE OWNERSHIP, MANAGEMENT, CIR-
CULATION, ETC., REQUIRED BY THE ACT OF
CONGRESS OF AUGUST 24, 1912.

Of *CITIZENS' BUSINESS,* published *weekly at Philadelphia,
Pennsylvania,* for *April 1, 1920.*

State of *Pennsylvania* } *ss.*
County of *Philadelphia*

Before me, a *Notary Public* in and for the State and County
aforesaid, personally appeared *William C. Beyer,* who, having
been duly sworn according to law, deposes and says that he
is the *editor* of *CITIZENS' BUSINESS* and that the following
is, to the best of his knowledge and belief, a true statement
of the ownership, management, etc., of the aforesaid publication for the date shown in the above caption, required by
the Act of August 24, 1912, embodied in section 443, Postal
Laws and Regulations, to wit:

1. That the names and addresses of the publisher, editor,
managing editor, and business managers are:

Publisher, *Bureau of Municipal Research, Philadelphia.*

Editor, *William C. Beyer.*

Managing Editor, *None.*

Business Managers, *None.*

2. That the owners are:

Bureau of Municipal Research. No capital stock.

3. That the known bondholders, mortgagees, and other security holders owning or holding 1 per cent or more of total
amount of bonds, mortgages, or other securities are:

None.

(Signed) *William C. Beyer*

Sworn to and subscribed before me this 26*th* day of *March,*
1920.

(Signed) *Martha H. Quinn.*

[SEAL] (My commission expires *January 16, 1923.*)

CITIZENS' BUSINESS

BUREAU OF MUNICIPAL RESEARCH

ISSUED WEEKLY AT 805 FRANKLIN BANK BUILDING
PHILADELPHIA. ENTERED AS SECOND CLASS MATTER
JUNE 7, 1913 AT THE POST OFFICE AT PHILADELPHIA,
PA., UNDER THE ACT OF AUGUST 24TH, 1912 —
SUBSCRIPTION FIFTY CENTS THE YEAR

Conciliation and Small Claims Courts

No. 412	April 15, 1920

"To the poor the Courts are a maze,
If he plead there all his life,
Law is so lordly;
And loath to end his case;
Without money paid in presents
Law listeneth to few."

Vision of Piers Plowman

The Situation in Philadelphia

Smith walked into the office of his Attorney. The following conversation took place:

Smith: I have a small bill against Brown which he refuses to pay. He says the work I did for him was of poor quality, and I know there was nothing wrong with it. There is no use arguing with him any longer, so I shall have to sue.

Attorney: How much is the bill?

Smith: Seven dollars.

Attorney: I am afraid it won't pay you to sue. It will cost you more than Brown owes you. If you go before a magistrate you must pay out $3.50 for costs; in addition it will cost you at least $10.00 for my own fee. If you get judgment before the magistrate, Brown can appeal to the Municipal Court. You would then have to go through the whole thing again. There would be another fee to pay me, of course. In the end, if you won, all you would get back would be $7.00 and your costs —plus $3.00 towards my fee. So the suit would cost you at least $7.00, and you have to consider the value of your own time.

Smith: How about bringing suit at once in the Municipal Court?

Attorney: There the costs would be at least $6.00; $10.00 if either of you want a jury trial. You take a chance on losing whatever you pay for costs; and of course the question of my fee would come in. It wouldn't pay you.

Smith: I might handle the case without a lawyer.

Attorney: You can do that if you wish. Have you ever tried it?

Smith: No.

Attorney: I thought not. If you can afford the time, go to it. Only don't blame me if Brown's lawyer puts it all over you.

Smith: Do you mean to say that here in Philadelphia there is no way to enforce the collection of an honest claim for $7.00?

Attorney: Theoretically there is. As a practical matter there is not. You had better cross the amount off your books and forget it.

So Smith proceeds to "forget it." Or, he proceeds to do the direct opposite—to burn with a sense of indignation at the law which refuses to grant him justice, and to add this incident to his score of general resentment against courts and lawyers.

The Danger

Here we have tried to epitomize a serious condition which exists in Philadelphia, a condition far more serious than most people think possible. Each year there occur in our city thousands of cases similar to the one described above, where the outcome is a flat denial of justice. Theodore Roosevelt, in speaking on this subject, once said:

> "People of means and leisure have no conception of the amount of misery due to the causes which lie behind these small suits. They represent in the aggregate an extraordinary amount of bitterness, and they ferment into economic unrest, violent social revolt, and much individual crime and failure."

The bitterness and unrest, we submit, are caused not by the suits themselves, but arise when men of small means are unable, as they are in Philadelphia, to get a fair hearing for their just complaints.

The Situation in Other Cities

In 1912 there was established in the city of Cleveland a Small Claims Court, with jurisdiction over suits involving not more than $35.00. Every effort was made to reduce technicalities, costs and delays to a minimum. A trial in this court is simply a meeting before the judge, who endeavors to get at the facts in the quickest and most practical way, disregarding if advisable technical rules of evidence. Lawyers are unnecessary, as the judge cares for the interest of all parties. The total expense of a trial is in the neighborhood of 75 cents. The judgment rendered is a common sense judgment, dealing directly with the facts. In one case, where a claim was made for the conversion of a pair of shoes, the judge instead of giving a judgment for money damages simply ordered the shoes returned. The report of another case is as follows:

> Defendant admitted he owed plaintiff four dollars, but refused to pay it because plaintiff had insulted his wife. Plaintiff denied that he had personally insulted her, but admitted that one of his employes

might have done so. The court ordered plaintiff to
telephone the wife apologizing for anything that had
been said. Plaintiff did so, using the telephone in
the judge's room. Plaintiff was then given judgment
for four dollars.

The success of the Cleveland court in dealing with
this class of cases has led to the establishment of
similar tribunals in New York, Chicago, Baltimore,
Minneapolis, and a number of other cities. These
courts differ in many ways but their guiding principle
is the same—speedy and inexpensive justice for the
poor.

Conciliation

Many of these small claims courts apply the principle
of conciliation. The procedure is most simple. Before a case comes to trial the judge brings both parties
together, either with or without attorneys and witnesses,
and tries to induce them to settle their differences. He
hears both sides briefly, explains the law bearing on
the case, points out the chances of victory on each
side, if necessary refers to the expense of lawyers and
witnesses, and by every legitimate means strives to
bring about a settlement. If he succeeds, he issues a
certificate to that effect which has the force of a
judgment. If he does not succeed, the case goes to
trial, and no reference whatever is made to the attempt
at conciliation. There are no costs whatever. This
form of procedure has been adopted in a number of our
larger cities, and wherever tried it has met with marked
success.

A Step Forward

It is gratifying to note that a number of public-minded
and influential citizens of Philadelphia are today considering the establishment of Conciliation and Small
Claims Courts under the jurisdiction of our Municipal
Court. It is proposed that a bill providing for these
tribunals shall be presented to the Legislature of 1921.
In the meantime the subject should be given exhaustive
study, so that the most successful method in operation
in other communities may be adopted in the courts of
Philadelphia.

CITIZENS' BUSINESS

BUREAU OF MUNICIPAL RESEARCH

ISSUED WEEKLY AT 805 FRANKLIN BANK BUILDING
PHILADELPHIA, ENTERED AS SECOND-CLASS MATTER
JUNE 7, 1913 AT THE POST OFFICE AT PHILADELPHIA,
PA., UNDER THE ACT OF AUGUST 24TH, 1912 —
SUBSCRIPTION FIFTY CENTS THE YEAR

Common Sense, as Well as History

Constitutional Comments, No. 1

No. 413 April 22, 1920

Thirty-one states amend their constitutions by
action of ONE legislature, ratified by popular vote.

The Demand for General Revision

The conclusion of the hearings at Harrisburg makes it evident that it is time for us to sit up and realize the real need for constitutional revision.

That conclusion was foreshadowed a month ago by the number of changes recommended in the Revision Commission's own preliminary draft. It was buttressed by the arguments presented before the Commission in hearings which have extended over the past three weeks. Several facts are evident from the hearings: First, that the Commission's wise changes are in the main approved. Second, that where difference of opinion was evident it was not because less revision was needed, but revision of a different kind. Third, that there is demand for still more changes than were first suggested by the Commission.

A Flexible Constitution Needed

To whatever action this may lead on the part of the Commission and of the next legislature, it is an indication too plain to remain unheeded that we are in a period when constitutions must be flexible. For thirty years following the adoption of the Constitution of 1873 there was a period of stability in public affairs. Practically no changes were made in our state constitution. Practically none were needed. No one, however, would be rash enough to contend that we are still in that period. Beginning with the very opening year of the twentieth century, effort after effort has been made to amend the constitution and keep the state balanced amid the shifting economic and political issues of the time. The present constitution is *not* the Constitution of 1873, for since its adoption it has been amended *twenty-one* times, *eighteen of them since 1901.*

The Present Amending Process is Inadequate

In addition to the eighteen amendments thus adopted, seventeen amendments proposed by the legislature failed.

If the ordinary amending process of our constitution is adequate, is it not a strange contradiction that the constitution should now be so badly in need of *general* revision?

The fact is that only five of the seventeen amendments which failed were rejected by the people. Twelve of them never got to the people. One of the twelve was counted out by the attorney general on a technicality arising from inexcusably bad bill-drafting. The remaining eleven were *killed in a second legislature*, because the amending article of the present constitution requires that before an amendment can be voted on by the people it must be passed by *two successive* legislatures.

The Fruits of This Process in the Past

By reason of this cumbersome requirement, the consolidation of common pleas courts in Philadelphia and Allegheny counties approved by the legislature of 1907 was delayed until 1911 for Allegheny county, and has not even yet been permitted in Philadelphia. By virtue of the same requirement, the legislature of 1911 blocked the abolition of magistrates' courts in Philadelphia. Again in 1911 and 1917 by reason of this requirement the legislature defeated amendments designed to abolish the tax paying qualification for voters, and to provide for excess condemnation. By virtue of the same requirement the governor was able during the session of 1915 to prevent the abolition of the office of Secretary of Internal Affairs. The incumbent for whom the office was preserved has died, and the last legislature had to transfer several bureaus to that department in order to give it an excuse for existence.

The Part of Wisdom

It is perfectly evident that no one would write into a constitution a clause stipulating that the constitution *could not* be amended. To do so would be in effect to invite revolution. The effect of making it *difficult* to amend a constitution is to invite discontent. No wise man plugs up the spout of a steaming tea kettle. No wise state in a period of change makes or leaves its constitution difficult to amend.

The Modern Tendency Toward an Easier Amending Process

The tendency among American states has been steadily toward an easier amending process—the unrestricted proposal of amendments by the action of one legislature, and adoption by a majority of the persons voting thereon at the next election.

Of the nineteen constitutions adopted since 1885, all but three have provided for action by one legislature only, and two other states, by amendment, have made similar provision; and of the thirteen states that still require action by two legislatures, two—Massachusetts and Nevada—provide also that amendments may be proposed by popular initiative.

Keeping the Ship Afloat

Those of us who believe in democracy—who believe in its inherent ability to adapt itself to changing needs and conditions—realize that the main effort in a storm must be to keep the ship afloat. When one of the prerequisities is sensible shifting of the ballast, it is folly to nail the ballast down.

With this number of CITIZENS' BUSINESS we begin a series of comments on matters arising from the Constitution of Pennsylvania, especially as they affect Philadelphia's municipal interests.

CITIZENS' BUSINESS

BUREAU OF MUNICIPAL RESEARCH

ISSUED WEEKLY AT 805 FRANKLIN BANK BUILDING
PHILADELPHIA. ENTERED AS SECOND CLASS MATTER
JUNE 7, 1913 AT THE POST OFFICE AT PHILADELPHIA,
PA., UNDER THE ACT OF AUGUST 24TH, 1912 —
SUBSCRIPTION FIFTY CENTS THE YEAR

Incorporated Districts?

Constitutional Comments, No. 2

No. 414   **April 29, 1920**

Section 5 of the proposed new article on Municipalities would permit the legislature to create "incorporated districts" and confer upon them "one or more of the powers vested by law in the municipalities within their respective boundaries and additional powers. . ."

Our Spreading Cities

Arbitrary political boundaries are not the lines that determine natural communities, and with the steady improvement of means of communication and travel, the frontiers of our local jurisdictions have tended to become less and less significant socially and economically. With the growth of our cities we have found suburban areas developing which in some cases have even exceeded the populations of the mother-cities. Those living in the suburbs are citizens of the metropolitan center in every respect except the political. One would expect to see a rapid absorption of the surrounding suburban area by most of our cities.

Political Barriers Still Up

In point of fact, whether because of inertia, village pride, or political obstruction, we find that most of our large cities have not absorbed the belt of contiguous communities that would naturally be a part of their bodies politic. In Pennsylvania, our two large cities, Philadelphia and Pittsburgh, are excellent illustrations of metropolitan areas in all but political unity.

It is inevitable that certain governmental activities would extend normally over all or part of the area embraced in the natural district, and that this normal functioning is often hampered by artificial restrictions. This is conspicuously true of a number of activities in the field of public works.

The Commission's Proposed Relief

The constitutional revision commission realized this situation, as has every citizen or group in touch with municipal affairs. To permit the legislature to relieve this unnatural restraint, the commission included in its tentative draft the section referred to on the front of this leaflet.

The intent is commendable. There must be some means of carrying on the business of local government without arbitrary and purely legalistic restrictions, but there are dangers in the commission's suggestion, and we think there is a better way.

Expand the City

In the first place, we believe in the natural expansion of cities. Most of the movements in suburban towns against annexation appear to us as pure reaction against the march of progress— pure provincialism, tinctured at times with sordid considerations.

Whenever possible, growing cities should plan ahead with a view to adding to their political jurisdictions such contiguous areas as are reasonably and appropriately to be considered as belonging to the same communities. With this thought in mind we should begin to disregard mere imaginary boundary lines and also such natural boundary lines as are not economically or socially significant. It must be admitted, of course, that state lines are more serious barriers than county or city boundaries, and there is no immediate proposal for ignoring them in schemes for municipal development. But the minor political sub-division will have to face consolidation, absorption, elimination even, to conform to the need of the city whose economic "parasite" the residential suburb usually is.

But When You Can't Expand

There are cases, however, where expansion is impossible or undesirable. Moreover, there are public works enterprises in which two or more urban communities may find it advantageous to pool their activities but their community of interest does not extend to *all* municipal functions and a merger would not be justified.

In such cases, it would be simpler to have the municipalities *contract* to engage in the joint undertaking, turning the management over to a commission or individual, and bearing the initial outlay and operating costs in proportions agreed upon.

Danger in Incorporated Districts

The danger in the proposal tentatively set up by the commission is twofold. The first danger is the one found by experience to be the result in other states—that constitutional or statutory debt limits and taxing limits have been exceeded by this tempting device of creating new forms of municipal corporations. This is important to the taxpayer who foots the bills, but is not so important, we think, as the injury to the morale of democratic institutions by the complications that must result from the lengthening of the ballot and the multiplying of territorial jurisdictions, both of which are inherent in this scheme.

Look at the structure of Chicago's local government and be warned in time!

In a subsequent number of this series of Constitutional Comments we hope to analyze briefly another proposal affecting cities, which is somewhat akin to the plan discussed above.

BUSINESS

TIAL RESEARCH

FRANKLIN BANK BUILDING
AS SECOND CLASS MATTER
OFFICE AT PHILADELPHIA,
AUGUST 14TH, 1912 —
CENTS THE YEAR—

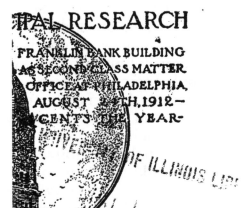

tan Areas

'omments, No. 4

May 13, 1920

mocracy is its ability to fix
nment upon the individual
ructure of government and
ty, the more directly is the
he exercise of this authority
dual citizen.

But When You Can'

There are cases, how
impossible or undesirab
public works enterprise:
urban communities may
pool their activities b
interest does not exten
tions and a merger wou

In such cases, it woul
municipalities *contract*
undertaking, turning th
commission or individua
outlay and operating co
upon.

Danger in Incorpora

The danger in the pr
by the commission is tv
is the one found by ex
in other states—that cc
debt limits and taxing li
by this tempting device
municipal corporations.
taxpayer who foots the
portant, we think, as th
democratic institutions 1
must result from the l
and the multiplying of
both of which are inhere

*Look at the structure
ernment and be warned*

In a subsequent number
·tional Comments we hope
proposal affecting cities, wl
plan discussed above.

CITIZENS' BUSINESS

BUREAU OF MUNICIPAL RESEARCH

ISSUED WEEKLY AT 805 FRANKLIN BANK BUILDING
PHILADELPHIA. ENTERED AS SECOND CLASS MATTER
JUNE 7, 1913 AT THE POST OFFICE AT PHILADELPHIA,
PA., UNDER THE ACT OF AUGUST 24TH, 1912—
SUBSCRIPTION FIFTY CENTS THE YEAR—

Metropolitan Areas

Constitutional Comments, No. 4

No. 416   May 13, 1920

> The test of successful democracy is its ability to fix the responsibility for government upon the individual citizen. The simpler the structure of government and the less diffused its authority, the more directly is the ultimate responsibility for the exercise of this authority brought home to the individual citizen.

In a recent issue of CITIZENS' BUSINESS we discussed the problem of suburban areas and touched upon the dangers of creating incorporated districts for the joint handling of problems common to two or more communities within such areas, suggesting as a better plan the handling of such problems by joint contract.

The Contractual Method of Carrying Out Joint Undertakings

In order to bring this suggestion concretely before the Commission on Constitutional Revision and Amendment we have submitted to the Commission a draft of a substitute for its proposed section on incorporated districts. This substitute section provides that municipalities may contract with each other for the acquisition and maintenance of public works, utilities and improvements in which they may have a joint interest. It goes on to state also that such contracts may provide for the creation of boards of commissions to effect the purposes of such contracts, *but that no such board shall have the power to levy taxes or to borrow money.*

Such a section in the Constitution would, we believe, enable the various communities in a metropolitan. area to solve their joint problems by the making of contracts or agreements among themselves much as individuals contract to carry out plans in which they 'are jointly interested. This solution would be more satisfactory and would be accomplished with much less demoralization to the citizenship concerned than if the same ends were reached by setting up one 'or more incorporated districts and delegating to them some of the powers properly belonging to the cities, boroughs or townships comprising them.

Neither New nor Novel

That such a scheme involves no new concept of the functions of municipalities, is attested by the numerous inter-city and inter-county bridges. We further find that the Pennsylvania School Code of 1911 provides that two or more adjoining school districts may, by written agreement between their several boards, establish and maintain joint high schools, or other schools, pro-rating the costs among the districts that are parties to the agreement. Similarly, by an act of the legislature in 1917, we find that two or more municipalities may by written agreement establish and maintain libraries. This concept, we believe, could well be extended to contracts involving more elaborate public works of common benefit to several municipalities.

Brings Home Responsibility

Furthermore, the plan of accomplishing purposes common to several municipalities by means of joint contracts does not violate the principle we have set forth on the first page of this leaflet. Under its operation, the citizen will feel his responsibility for his own local government. True, this government may be a party to a number of independent contracts covering various phases of public works or improvements, but the same officials are responsible for all these contracts insofar as they affect the particular community in question. The citizen will be called on for taxes to meet the cost of the various improvements for which his community contracts, but *all* his taxes will be levied by the same taxing body and will be accounted for by the same auditor or controller. If the taxes are out of proportion to the benefits received, or if the auditor's report does not show a proper expenditure of the money received from his taxes, our citizen will know that the responsibility is his for the selection of the *single* local government chargeable with this state of affairs.

Incorporated Districts Diffuse Responsibility

By way of contrast let us consider briefly the situation we would have if the same community secured these improvements by becoming a part of, let us say, a half dozen incorporated districts. These districts would probably not have the same boundaries, each being created for a certain specific purpose. Our citizen of "Borough A" would enjoy the same advantages of water works, sewage disposal, fire protection, and other community services and would be taxed quite as much as under the other plan to pay for them. In this case, however, he would pay some of his tax to "Borough A", some to "Water District B", and some to "Sewer District C"; and in order to know how his taxes have been expended he would have to read the reports of *all* these various districts. When he goes to the polls, his sense of personal responsibility must necessarily be weakened by the extent to which he is called on to exercise his franchise for the officials of so many independent municipalities.

Is it not wiser to strengthen our citizen's feeling of responsibility for the right conduct of his local government by keeping to the absolute minimum the number of such local governments for which he is to be held responsible? Does it not make for simplicity to accomplish public improvement in metropolitan areas by contractual association of the municipalities concerned rather than by the creation of additional overlying municipalities with independent powers and separate officials? Let us hold to our fundamental principle of responsibility and simplicity and not diffuse authority and complicate the structure of local government by the creation of endless incorporated districts.

CITIZENS' BUSINESS

BUREAU OF MUNICIPAL RESEARCH

ISSUED WEEKLY AT 805 FRANKLIN BANK BUILDING
PHILADELPHIA. ENTERED AS SECOND CLASS MATTER
JUNE 7, 1913 AT THE POST OFFICE AT PHILADELPHIA,
PA., UNDER THE ACT OF AUGUST 24TH, 1912 —
SUBSCRIPTION FIFTY CENTS THE YEAR—

State Aid

Constitutional Comments, No. 5

No. 417   May 20, 1920

We feel that the Commission's proposals for meeting Pennsylvania's state aid problem are a step forward. The problem is a knotty one, and its solution presents plenty of room for honest difference of opinion.

The Commission's plan prohibiting grants to specific institutions ought to discourage log-rolling, at least, and it ought to encourage a state-wide social outlook instead of the prevalent local vanity.

In Other Jurisdictions

The constitution of Massachusetts is one of a dozen or more state constitutions that are very positive and very clear in their prohibition against granting public moneys to charitable or educational institutions not wholly under state control. In Massachusetts, however, an appropriation in payment for specific services is permitted, and is granted to a few institutions. Other states are less rigid in this matter, and we find a considerable variety in the practices of the different legislatures in this regard—a few giving considerable amounts in lump-sum grants; some giving relatively small amounts on a service per capita basis. Some states allow subventions only to certain types of institutions or agencies, while five or six states cover practically the whole field of human altruistic effort. Space does not permit more than this general reference, as citations of illustrations would fill more lines than are contained in this leaflet.

In Pennsylvania

In this commonwealth we have a policy that may be regarded as the antithesis of that of New Jersey, Illinois, Ohio, and a number of other important states that grant no subsidies whatever. Not only do we give grants of state money each biennium to a widely diverse and lengthy list of private agencies and institutions, but each legislature appropriates sums for this purpose far greater than is appropriated in any other state, and these appropriations represent a far larger percentage of the entire expenditures of the state than do analogous grants in any other state.

Hence we see that in addition to the natural query as to the wisdom of our method as a social policy, its economic and financial significance is very great.

Many of those who have followed this subject in

recent years have been impressed with the fact that
state grants have frequently been made on a basis
seemingly arbitrary, for we find institutions of kindred
functions and similar size receiving very different allot-
ments. We find some agencies neither asking nor receiving state aid, while others secure their major revenue from that source.

Above all, we find certain phases of necessary public
charity (e. g., the care of the feebleminded) not adequately developed, in the judgment of those competent
to appraise these activities.

It was but to be expected, therefore, that proposals
would be offered to amend our constitution so as to
change this situation.

The More Advanced Proposal

Boiled down, the more drastic proposal sought to
prohibit legislative appropriations *after 1935*, to agencies not exclusively under state control. It also sought
to prohibit such grants at once in any amount over
60 per cent of the cost of free service rendered by any
agency, and it provided for the gradual reduction of
state aid to 10 per cent of the cost of such free service,
in the period intervening until after 1935. Provision for
exacting conformity to standards of excellence was
also included in this proposal.

What the Commission Recommends

The foregoing proposal was again debated at last
week's sessions of the revision commission, but a majority of the members, sincerely convinced of the benefit
and propriety of the present subsidy system, voted
down this amendment. Thus the commission's tentative draft is likely to be recommended to the people
in the new constitution. This tentative draft reads:

Appropriations for charitable or benevolent purposes
may be made to a class or classes of institutions not

under the absolute control of the commonwealth, but engaged in work or service deemed by the general assembly to be for the public good, provided such work or service conforms to such standards of excellence as may be prescribed by law, or by an executive agency created by law. Every such appropriation shall be made by a vote of two-thirds of the members elected to each house. Institutions receiving such appropriations shall be subject to inspection by the commonwealth, according to law, and shall make report to the general assembly, or to such person or persons as it may designate, of the precise use made of such appropriation.

Under this plan, an appropriation to *a particular institution* would be unconstitutional. The emphasis on standards is very definite, and even though grants are to be by *classes* of agencies, a two-thirds vote is required for each item of appropriation, as at present.

In the section of Article III that establishes a budget system for Pennsylvania, the commission has set up additional protection in the paragraph:

. In submitting proposals for appropriations to charitable, educational or benevolent institutions not under the absolute control of the commonwealth, the governor shall at the same time submit a plan of distribution among the classes of institutions to be benefited. No bill shall ever appropriate any definite sum of money to any such institutions or designate any one or more of such institutions as beneficiaries; but all bills containing such appropriations shall appropriate a gross sum to be distributed among a class or classes of such institutions (as such class or classes may be defined by law) only in accordance with a plan uniform in its application to all the institutions, corporations or associations in any class, said plan to be prescribed by general law or by an executive agency created by law.

* * * * * *

We are not attempting to go into a number of the important sociological and administrative details of the problem in this bulletin. We are attempting in this series of Constitutional Comments merely to touch the high spots of such of the topics as we shall be able to treat.

By permission, we are glad to be able to refer any reader of CITIZENS' BUSINESS to the Public Charities Association of Pennsylvania, 403 Empire Building, Philadelphia. The staff of that association has collated a great deal of information on this subject and will furnish printed matter or will reply to specific inquiries.

CITIZENS' BUSINESS

BUREAU OF MUNICIPAL RESEARCH

ISSUED WEEKLY AT 805 FRANKLIN BANK BUILDING
PHILADELPHIA. ENTERED AS SECOND CLASS MATTER
JUNE 7, 1913 AT THE POST OFFICE AT PHILADELPHIA,
PA., UNDER THE ACT OF AUGUST 24TH, 1912—
SUBSCRIPTION FIFTY CENTS THE YEAR-

On Its Way

No. 418   May 27, 1920

One of the most important matters that will confront the city government this coming Fall will be the recommendations of the Civil Service Commission in regard to the standardization of salaries and conditions of employment in the city service.

Philadelphia Falls in Line

It is indeed cause for gratification that the work of employment standardization in the city service is at last under way. We say "at last" because it has taken about six years of persistent effort to secure an earnest beginning on this important work. During these six years over a dozen other cities, counties and states throughout the country have followed the pioneer example of Chicago and standardized their services or begun to standardize them. Among them are the cities of Oakland, Pittsburgh, New York, Seattle, Milwaukee, Cleveland, Akron, St. Louis, and Baltimore; the counties of Los Angeles and Milwaukee; and the states of New York, Ohio, New Jersey, and Massachusetts. To this list should be added also the government of the Dominion of Canada and our own federal government. And now Philadelphia, too, is falling into line.

The Mandate to Proceed

The Civil Service Commission, in proceeding with this work, is carrying out the mandate of the new city charter which requires the Commission to standardize the service. There is, however, also the mandate of actual conditions in the city service which call loudly for some constructive measure of correction. The inequalities of pay for similar work, the lack of definite lines of promotion, and the gross underpayment in practically all departments of the city government cannot be permitted to continue much longer without inviting disaster. How fully this situation is appreciated by those in closest touch with conditions is evidenced by the fact that not only the Civil Service Commission, but also the entire City Council, the departmental officials, and the employes appear to be heartily in favor of the standardization program.

The Commission's Task Not Easy

The task undertaken by the Civil Service Commission is not an easy one. It involves devising standards of work, of qualifications for appointment, and of compensation affecting more than twelve thousand municipal employes. The Commission will be required to pass upon many knotty questions of employment policy which cannot be side-stepped in any honest effort to devise employment standards. Among other things, it will be necessary to decide whether the bonus system is to be continued or not; to what extent the current market value of services rendered by city employes is to be taken as a guide in fixing salaries and wages; to what extent the cost of maintaining a given standard of living is to be taken as a guide; whether a distinction in pay is to be made between lines of work usually performed by single persons and lines of work usually performed by persons with families to support; whether men and women are to receive equal pay for similar services; whether promotions are to be confined within departments or permitted across departmental lines; what groups of employes should be paid for over-time work; and many other questions of equal importance.

The Need of Much Pertinent Information

To pass intelligently and fairly upon these questions will require not only a broad-minded approach to the whole problem, but also a mass of pertinent information. Without this information the Commission cannot be sure of the correctness of its decisions, the City Council will not be able intelligently to appraise the Commission's recommendations, and the taxpayer will have no evidence before him to justify his approval of the manner in which his councilman votes on these recommendations.

Some Specific Lines of Inquiry

It will be necessary, therefore, to ascertain the employment practices in other jurisdictions, to find out what rates of compensation private employers are paying, to compute the cost of different standards of living at current prices, and to know definitely all the significant facts relating to existing conditions in the city service. Most of the last mentioned information will be supplied to the Commission in the questionnaires which the employes in the various departments have been asked to fill out. This information, however, will be of little value unless the returned questionnaires are carefully edited and much of it even then will be of no value unless the data in the questionnaires are tabulated. All of this involves a great deal of work, but if the final report of the Civil Service Commission is to be of merit, this work must be performed.

The Best Is None Too Good for Philadelphia

Once more let us express gratification at Philadelphia's start on a program of employment standardization. But let us not forget that merely to start is not the whole performance. Philadelphia should not be content with anything short of the best piece of work of its kind that has yet been done in this country.

CITIZENS' BUSINESS

BUREAU OF MUNICIPAL RESEARCH

ISSUED WEEKLY AT 805 FRANKLIN BANK BUILDING
PHILADELPHIA. ENTERED AS SECOND CLASS MATTER
JUNE 7, 1913 AT THE POST OFFICE AT PHILADELPHIA,
PA., UNDER THE ACT OF AUGUST 24TH, 1912—
SUBSCRIPTION FIFTY CENTS THE YEAR

STREET CLEANING UNDER THE NEW CHARTER

No. 419   **June 3, 1920**

After years of agitation for municipal street cleaning, the new charter actually requires its initiation in 1921, subject to the power of a majority of the 21 councilmen and the mayor to authorize contract performance in any or all of the street cleaning and refuse disposal activities. The legislature has decided the issue as to the means of performance, but the loophole provided will be useful if any of these activities are impracticable of municipal operation in 1921.

It is gratifying to note that studies are in progress for providing a fact basis upon which to determine the policy of the city administration relative to municipal street cleaning in the year 1921. Before discussing the scope of such an investigation, it may be of advantage briefly to review the events of the recent past relating to this proposition.

The New Charter Reverses the Old Procedure

It was not until the new city charter went into effect that Philadelphia was given a free hand to decide its own policy in performing street cleaning and the allied activities of ash, rubbish and garbage collection and disposal. Not only had previous legislative provisions compelled us to perform these functions by contract, but we were restrained from contracting for a longer period than one year. It is unnecessary now to discuss the disadvantages relating to the former means of performing this work because the new charter practically reverses this old procedure. Article XX, Section 5, provides that after December 31 of this year these activities shall be performed by municipal forces, unless a majority of all the members elected to the council, with the approval of the mayor, shall authorize the performance by contract of any or all of the functions enumerated above. It is important to note that the council and the mayor must concur in any decision to reverse the mandatory provision for municipal work. The council, it would appear from the law, cannot override the mayor's veto in this case.

In direct contradiction to the former legislative provisions, therefore, the new charter specifies municipal street cleaning, but in order to permit a certain measure of home rule, provides that the council and the mayor may jointly authorize the performance of any such work by contract when it is to the best interest of the city to do so. The burden of proof, however, falls squarely upon those who would seek to continue contract street cleaning, because if they do not succeed in marshalling a majority vote of the 21 councilmen and in obtaining the approval of the mayor for contract work, municipal operation will automatically be the legal requirement in the year 1921.

A Street Cleaning Investigation Authorized

The whole proposition can be boiled down to the question of the practicability of performing the street cleaning and refuse disposal activities by municipal forces in 1921. This is an engineering question pure and simple, and the council and the mayor displayed excellent judgment in approving unanimously an ordinance authorizing the director of public works to prepare plans and cost estimates of the cleaning of the streets and the collection and disposal of refuse, including the cost of the purchase, construction or lease of such plants as may be necessary. An appropriation of $25,000 was authorized for the employment and pay of the necessary experts, engineers and other assistants required to carry on this investigation.

What the Investigation Should Disclose

Definite studies are now under way by the department of public works which will indicate the practicability of performing the street cleaning and refuse disposal activities by municipal forces in 1921. If municipal operation is impracticable in 1921, or if it is to the best interests of the city to authorize contract performance in any or all of these activities, the department will recommend under what form of contract and specifications this work should be advertised.

The report from this investigation will be received with much interest by all citizens who desire better street cleaning service. It is not municipal work, but contract work, that is on the carpet, because municipal work is given the preference by the new charter and it will automatically go into effect if contract work is not specifically provided. It is quite necessary, however, that the city should definitely determine that it can conduct each one of these activities by municipal forces in 1921 before it decides to follow out the charter provisions for municipal work in that particular activity.

If it is necessary to contract for the performance of any or all of the four activities—street cleaning, ash, rubbish and garbage collection and disposal—in 1921, such a decision should be made while there is adequate time remaining to insure real competitive bidding for the work. These conditions call for a quick survey of conditions and immediate consultation with practical specialists in street cleaning activities. To be of any real use, the results of the study should be available well before August first.

Pol. Sci.

CITIZENS' BUSINESS

BUREAU OF MUNICIPAL RESEARCH

ISSUED WEEKLY AT 805 FRANKLIN BANK BUILDING
PHILADELPHIA ENTERED AS SECOND CLASS MATTER
JUNE 7, 1913 AT THE POST OFFICE AT PHILADELPHIA,
PA., UNDER THE ACT OF AUGUST 24TH, 1912 —
SUBSCRIPTION FIFTY CENTS THE YEAR·

Gathering Momentum

Constitutional Comments, No. 6

No. 420   June 10, 1920

The movement for a new constitution for Pennsylvania is well under way. The preliminary or winnowing out process is over and the second step is beginning.

Ending the First Phase

When the Commission on Constitutional Amendment and Revision adjourned for the summer on May 13, it had just finished three strenuous days of deliberation, during which the debates and discussion were of a much higher order than is usually found in public legislative bodies. While of necessity those proposals that found no supporters were automatically dropped, such suggestions as were sponsored by a mover and a seconder received careful attention, and a number of decided improvements were written into the tentative new constitution. In fact, practically every article appears to have been made clearer, stronger, and better by the commission's latest efforts; though Article V, on the judiciary, while improved in certain minor respects, seems to be in as discouraging a condition now as before, especially in those aspects in which Philadelphia is most concerned.

The "Committee on Style"

There is hope, however, even for Article V. Before adjournment the commission authorized the chairman to appoint a "Committee on Style", and the resolution authorizing this appointment gave important duties and powers to this committee, including the right not only to make improvements in the style of the second draft, but also to recommend "any changes in substance" approved by the committee. To the style committee was entrusted also the power to recommend the manner in which the commission's final proposals should be laid before the people.

On this body were appointed seven of the most active and interested members of the commission, with the chairman and secretary, *ex officiis*, and there is every reason to hope that during the summer they will work out verbal and substantive improvements of great value. The smaller body will be able to do better and more rapidly the detail work, and most of their recommendations will probably be ratified by the commission, though the latter's right to review is in no way abridged.

The appointment of this style committee was a great step forward. Experience has often shown the advantage of this procedure. A recent local example was furnished by the citizens' committee which drafted the new city charter. That body turned the detail drafting over to a committee of fifteen, which in turn assigned parts of the work to smaller subcommittees. Thus rapid progress was assured, but the scrutiny of the larger body remained as a check on the work of the subordinate groups.

This style committee should be able to wrestle with such unfinished and peculiarly difficult jobs as the judiciary article. They should produce a draft, or perhaps alternative drafts, that will commend themselves to the revision commission and eventually to the people of Pennsylvania.

A FEW NUGGETS

Some of the constructive forward steps taken by the commission at its last session are listed below. If opportunity offers, we hope to be able to treat of some of them at greater length in this series of Constitutional Comments.

1. The merit principle is established in the civil service of the state and of its subdivisions.
2. Optional home rule charters for cities are made possible. Proportional representation in municipalities is made optional.
3. The rule-making power of the supreme court is expanded. The non-judicial functions of judges are reduced. The subject of ''justice to the poor'' is given recognition.
4. The way is open for shortening the county ballot.
5. A state-wide agency for supervising finances of local governments is not only permitted but is virtually required.
6. The state sinking fund provisions are strengthened.
7. The constitutional provisions determining debt limits of municipalities are made much simpler and clearer.
8. The way is opened for the assessment of benefits against all properties whose value is enhanced by any kind of public improvement.
9. The effective consolidation of Philadelphia city and county is made possible, and unified financial control is made mandatory.
10. The article on education is bettered in several respects.
11. The direct invitation to the legislature, in the preliminary draft, to create overlapping municipalities is eliminated, and a safe workable provision for necessary joint public works and kindred undertakings between municipalities is set up.

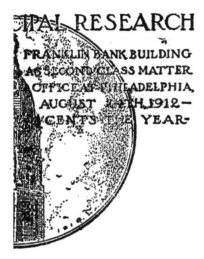

BUSINESS

:IPAL RESEARCH

FRANKLIN BANK BUILDING
AS SECOND CLASS MATTER
OFFICE AT PHILADELPHIA,
AUGUST 14TH, 1912 —
CENTS THE YEAR-

:achers'
Increased?

June 24, 1920

> hastening ills a prey,
> lates, and men decay:"
>   *—The Deserted Village*

treat of some of them a
series of Constitutional Cc

1. The merit principle i
service of the state :

2. Optional home rule cl
possible. Proportion
nicipalities is made o

3. The rule-making pow
is expanded. The 1
judges are reduced.
to the poor" is given

4. The way is open fc
ballot.

5. A state-wide agency
of local governments
is virtually required.

6. The state sinking
strengthened.

7. The constitutional pr
limits of municipalitì
and clearer.

8. The way is opened fo
fits against all prope
hanced by any kind c

9. The effective consolid:
and county is mad
financial control is m

10. The article on educat
respects.

11. The direct invitation
preliminary draft, to
nicipalities is elimina
provision for necessaì
kindred undertakings
set up.

of Sci

CITIZENS' BUSINESS

BUREAU OF MUNICIPAL RESEARCH

ISSUED WEEKLY AT 805 FRANKLIN BANK BUILDING
PHILADELPHIA, ENTERED AS SECOND CLASS MATTER
JUNE 7, 1913 AT THE POST OFFICE AT PHILADELPHIA,
PA., UNDER THE ACT OF AUGUST 24TH, 1912 —
SUBSCRIPTION FIFTY CENTS THE YEAR

Can Teachers'
Salaries be Increased?

No. 422   June 24, 1920

"Ill fares the land, to hastening ills a prey,
Where wealth accumulates, and men decay:"
—*The Deserted Village*

An Open Memorandum on the School Salary Situation

SUBMITTED BY THE BUREAU OF MUNICIPAL RESEARCH OF PHILADELPHIA

to

THE BOARD OF PUBLIC EDUCATION , THE CITIZENS' COMMITTEE ON TEACHERS' SALARIES, THE TEACHERS,

and

THE PUBLIC

For some weeks this Bureau has been urged to go into the question of teachers' salaries. This memorandum was released on June 10 to the members of the Board of Public Education, the members of the citizens' committee on teachers' salaries, and the newspapers. It seems to us that it contains matter of interest to the readers of CITIZENS' BUSINESS.

What the Teachers Demand

Briefly stated the demands of the teachers are as follows:

Each teacher is to receive for 1920 a bonus of $400, being $40 a month for the ten school months of the calendar year and of this the bonus for the first six months, or $240, is to be paid to the teachers before the end of June.

As there are approximately 6,500 employes affected, it will be seen that the amount required for the year approximates $2,600,000 and that of this sum $1,560,000 would have to be paid in cash this month.

The Problem

Assuming that the school board recognizes the justice of the teachers' demand and that it is willing to accede thereto if it can find a way to do so, the problem is (1) how to find a means of

2

increasing the board's *appropriating power* for 1920 by the sum of $2,600,000, and (2) how to finance the immediate *cash requirement* of $1,560,000.

It is submitted that under the law, under the present financial situation of the school board, under its existing commitments and the immediate demands on it, and in accord with the principles of safe financing, both of these essential requirements can be met.

An Important Differentiation

Before proceeding to a more detailed elaboration of the suggestions hereinafter outlined, it is essential to draw a distinction between the two great purposes that are served by what are known as temporary loans.

One purpose served by temporary loans is the one used very skillfully and effectively by the board ever since the separation of the schools from the city government. It is the use of temporary loans merely as a means of *cash financing*. In other words, the temporary loan is floated to bring money into the treasury in *anticipation* of the collection of taxes; i. e., merely to provide the cash necessary to meet, now, cash demands which otherwise would only have to be postponed until other cash came in.

As distinguished from borrowing merely to secure cash, is the employment of temporary loans as a basis for increased *appropriating power*. For this end they have not usually been availed of by the Board of Education, although the language of the school code very properly does not prohibit their use for this purpose.

To illustrate by analogy—the City of Philadelphia formerly had only one form of temporary loan, and it used the one form for both purposes. Under the new city charter, however, there are *two* forms of loan permitted—*temporary loans* for the purpose of securing cash to meet requirements, and *emergency loans* which enable the city to secure additional appropriating power.

If used for this latter purpose, the proceeds of such a loan are equivalent for appropriating purposes of additional tax money, and are not a charge against the revenue from taxation until the year in which such temporary loans fall due.

This is the kind of use of temporary borrowing power to which any governmental body would undoubtedly resort in case of great catastrophe. It is, of course, a basic assumption that both the Board of Education and the Citizens' Committee recognize just as acute a crisis in the situation caused by the inadequacy of teachers' salaries, and that they are both striving for the best interests of the schools and of the children.

It is absolutely essential for clear thinking on the problem before us that we keep separate and distinct in our minds these two uses for which it is possible for the Board of Education to employ temporary loans.

An Important Legal Power

Another matter which should be taken into consideration as an essential factor in working out this problem is the fact that under section 508 of the school code the board has the power to issue temporary loans to mature any time within two years. This point has apparently not been brought out in this discussion up to this time, and it is very important for the reason that it makes it possible to plan ahead in financing beyond the next legislative session and if necessary over into 1922, and the possible usefulness of this power in the present emergency will be alluded to hereafter.

The Problem Analyzed

In a paragraph above it was pointed out that it is necessary to do two things: (1) to provide additional appropriating power of $2,600,000, and (2) to provide cash immediately to the amount of $1,560,000.

The logical manner in which to approach this two-fold problem is to recognize at once that the major problem is the provision for the entire year 1920 of such additional appropriating power as is required; and after the necessary legal and financial details are worked out for settling that part of the problem, turn to the lesser problem, the solution of which is in a measure contingent upon the solution of the first and which will be found to be simple after the first is disposed of.

Additional Appropriating Power

An examination of the "balance sheet" of the Secretary of the Board of Education as of the close of May 31, 1920, and an examination of the books of the Board of Education prove conclusively that all appropriations thus far made by the Board of Education for the year 1920, other than appropriations based upon permanent loans already issued, are supported by conservative estimates of the revenue receipts (taxes, state school appropriations, etc.) of 1920 and that not one cent of these appropriations is based upon temporary loans or any of the possible temporary borrowing capacity of the school district.

This is conclusive evidence of the fact that the temporary loans already issued or authorized are for the purpose merely of providing cash enough to meet obligations as they fall due and that such loans have not been used for additional appropriating power. This simplifies the problem considerably.

It is understood that the board's secretary told the Citizens' Committee that virtually the entire temporary borrowing capacity of the board had been "appropriated" and that there would be no additional appropriating power from this source.

An examination of the books of the Board of Education shows that the Secretary meant either that the cash derived from these temporary loans was needed to meet its immediate disbursement requirements or that as soon as the cash was borrowed an equivalent amount was appropriated for the repayment of that borrowing under "Item 9. Debt Service." It is clear that from an accounting and financial viewpoint this type of "appropriation" is wholly different from the regular form of "appropriation," which is an authorization to make an expenditure or to incur a liability.

All the temporary borrowing can be paid off not later than August 31, 1920, when the bulk of the tax money will have been paid into the school treasury, which being done the board will have at its disposal once more its entire 2/10% temporary borrowing capacity, which amounts to approximately $3,850,000.

From a recent statement it appears that there is now available for further appropriation for any purpose $590,862. It may be, and in fact has been claimed, that this amount will be needed before the end of the year for purposes to which the school board is already committed. At all events, any such commitment was apparently not so binding as to cause the board to appropriate the sum; and the sum has remained legally available for appropriation for *any* purpose.

To secure additional appropriating power for 1920 the board can avail itself of the following possibilities:

(a) Sale of unused real estate, not less
than $600,000

(b) Transfer from item 6a of the
budget, for land and buildings, the
unexpended balance as of June 9,
at least 90,000

(c) Transfer from item 5 of the budget, for repairs, the unexpended
balance as of June 9, at least 500,000

(d) Maximum temporary loan available after August 31, because tax
money coming in will enable the
board to cancel previous tempor-
ary loans 3,850,000

$5,040,000

There is, therefore, apparently, a grand total
of $5,630,862 available.

These items are justified by the following:

(a) The sale of unused real estate is already
approved by the finance committee and it is probably, therefore, unnecessary to submit any
further arguments on this point, but in general it
should be said that since the Board of Education has in the past practiced the wise policy of
providing for a portion of its capital outlays out
of revenue each year, the sale of this relatively
small amount of permanent property for expense
purposes in the emergency should not be open to
criticism, especially as the amount is small enough
to make up easily in the near future if the board
is able to resume its policy of providing for some
of its permanent acquisitions out of current revenue.

It is important to point out that the amount
estimated as realizable on this real estate will fur-

nish additional appropriating power *even before the cash is received.* Under the law an estimated receipt furnishes a basis on which an appropriation can be made, and it is not necessary to have the cash in hand before it is appropriated any more than the taxes must be collected before they are appropriated.

(b) The budget item for land and buildings being for the acquisition of permanent property, it is justifiable to transfer these items from the general account (tax budget) to the loan account and to provide for them out of a permanent loan to be presently issued.

(c) Items for repairs, of course, ordinarily should be met out of revenue, "maintenance" being usually and properly interpreted as expense. It is not recommended that the money necessary to take care of maintenance items be provided from long term loans, but in this emergency it would be perfectly proper to finance this item out of a short term "permanent" loan, thus recognizing the principle that long term financing for such items is not to be indulged in, and at the same time easing the present pressure on the available appropriating power of the board.

(d) When the bulk of the tax money will have been paid into the treasury any outstanding temporary loan of the board can be repaid and then the board can avail itself of an additional appropriating power to the extent of two-tenths of 1 per cent of the property subject to taxation for school purposes in the school district.

This is Conservative

From the foregoing it will be seen that on a very conservative basis the board could commit itself for 1920 to *over twice as large an amount*

8

as is required to meet the teachers' request for a $40 per month bonus. It should be pointed out as an example of the conservatism of this calculation, that there are additional items that might be brought in to increase this figure, e. g., the 6% reserve for uncollectible taxes appears to be too large under present real estate conditions, as it is reported that taxes are being collected very much more effectively than has been the experience in most recent years. It might also be pointed out that some other receipts probably will be greater than the estimates and that these, together with unused and merging balances of appropriations at the close of the year, will provide a "surplus" at the beginning of 1921. At the beginning of this year, for instance, this surplus totaled $202,000. However, in order to be extra conservative, it is not advocated that reserves be reduced or that surpluses be counted upon.

The Question of Cash

The remaining problem, then, is to secure cash sufficient to pay all or a considerable part of the $1,560,000 necessary to give each teacher $240 before the end of June as a bonus of $40 per month for the first six months in the year. As a part of this program it will be necessary to issue a permanent loan or loans sufficient to put cash in the school treasury to meet immediate needs. It should be pointed out most emphatically in this connection that it is *not* advocated to use long term loans to pay expenses. These long term loans are for the acquisition of land, buildings, etc., but their proceeds may be available temporarily to meet immediate cash requirements as has been done very properly by the board on innumerable occasions in the past. The loan for permanent improvements might run for 20

9

or 30 years and might be authorized for $2,000,-
000, the entire amount to be floated, or such
amounts from time to time as are required. In
addition it might be feasible to authorize a loan
of $500,000 to run for 3 to 5 years to offset
the repair items already referred to.

The item (a), sale of unused real estate, referred to in the preceding section, should also
be realized in cash as soon as possible and the
Board of Education can doubtless either negotiate a sale or make some financial arrangement
whereby this cash can be received in the very
near future. For immediate purposes, estimat-
ing the receipts from real estate $600,000, less
than $1,000,000 temporary advance from loan
funds is needed to meet the needs of the teachers for the bonus before vacation time.

Anticipating Appropriating Power

Having pointed out that the appropriating
power for the balance of the year, after taking
into account the revival of the temporary borrowing capacity after August 31, will be more
than twice as large as will be necessary to take
care of the entire $2,600,000 yearly bonus, and
having shown just above how the school board
can arrange to get cash for the payment this
month of the first six months' bonus to the teachers, it is perhaps in order to point to the fact
that the school board can immediately anticipate
as much of this additional appropriating power
as it will need to take care of the $1,560,000
bonus to be paid this month.

The board could authorize payment out of
item 1 of the budget, for teachers' salaries,
(which on June 4 had an unexpended balance of
more than $4,000,000), the present salaries plus
the $40 per month bonus for the first six months.
In other words, the board might authorize pay-

ment out of that item at once of the $1,560,000 bonus for the first six months, which, including salaries, would use up of that item by June 30 approximately $6,960,000. For the last four months of the school year, there would be required on the existing salary basis plus the proposed bonus about $4,640,000, but there would be left in the item a balance of only $2,040,000 ($9,000,000 minus the above withdrawals to June 30 of $6,960,000). At the very worst, therefore, there would remain to be made up $2,600,000, which could be financed at the first meeting in September by the use of that amount of temporary loan, out of the board's temporary borrowing power of $3,850,000. In view of the proceeds of the sale of real estate, the transfer of items, and the appropriating power already available (to all of which we have previously referred), much less than $2,600,000 will actually have to be borrowed. It will be noted that the entire temporary borrowing power of two-tenths of 1 per cent can be available by the first meeting in September, because of the fact that the bulk of the taxes will have been received by August 31.

Taking Care of 1921

It will now be seen that the power of the school board to borrow on temporary loans up to two years is very important. Committing itself to increased salaries for teachers this year means that it will have the problem of increased needs for its 1921 budget. We, therefore, propose that the temporary loans issued this fall for affording increased appropriating power be made to mature during 1922, so that the amount of such loans will not be a charge against the board's revenue for 1921.

In the meantime, the board has power to increase the school tax rate for 1921 to 8 mills, which, even if the assessments are not increased a single dollar, should bring in approximately $2,000,000 additional revenue for 1921. All but about $600,000 of the increased salaries that will have to be met again in 1921 as the result of granting the teachers' present demands, will thus be taken care of with this increased tax revenue. Probably the remaining $600,000 could be taken care of by arranging that all capital outlays in 1921 be provided for by loan funds instead of out of tax moneys. It is, therefore, apparent that 1921 need not be burdened with any difficult problems as a result of acceding to the teachers' present demands for the $40 per month bonus. As for succeeding years, the legislature which meets in January 1921, only seven months hence, can be successfully appealed to by the Board of Education to afford any relief that may then be necessary. The legislature will be ever so much more likely to afford such relief if the school board has acted in the emergency and has thus demonstrated without the slightest question that such relief is necessary, than if the school board were to depend on the legislature without first making use of every resource at its command to meet emergencies as they arise.

Conclusion

All of the plans outlined above are legal, workable and susceptible of immediate and satisfactory application.

It is clear, therefore, from these facts, and from the further fact that the entire net debt of the school district is less than one-half of its allowable borrowing capacity, that the board's finances are in excellent shape, and that the present critical situation in the matter of teachers' salaries can be met on a safe, conservative basis.

CITIZENS' BUSINESS

BUREAU OF MUNICIPAL RESEARCH
OF PHILADELPHIA

**AN AGENCY OF 2000 CITIZENS
COOPERATING IN THE EFFECTIVE
DISCHARGE OF CIVIC DUTIES,
EQUIPPED TO INTERPRET AND SOLVE
TECHNICAL PROBLEMS OF GOVERNMENT**

Who Spends Your Money?

No. 423   **July 1, 1920**

> The Philadelphia taxpayer is in the unfortunate
> plight of having a large part of his contribution spent
> in ways over which he and his councilmen have no
> direct control.
>
> "And how his audit stands who knows, save
> Heaven?"—Hamlet, Act III.

THE DAY IS COMING SOON, we hope, when Pennsylvanians who do not live in Philadelphia will stop telling Philadelphia how it must spend the money which its citizens pay into the city treasury.

Representation Without Taxation

It has long been the practice to establish by legislative enactment or constitutional provision various kinds of governmental agencies in Philadelphia, and to compel the city to pay for them. The practice of spending other people's money cannot be expected to produce economy any more in government than in private life. No one but a Philadelphian will be annoyed by a high tax rate in Philadelphia. Is it fair to allow people who are not affected by the tax rate to have anything to do with creating it?

If the existence of a governmental agency in Philadelphia is of such state-wide importance that the legislature is moved to establish it, why shouldn't the cost be met out of the state's revenues? If this were done, perhaps the state would temper the liberality with which it bestows courts, commissions, boards, etc., upon the city, and provides for their maintenance out of city funds.

Slight Consolation

In many cases the legislature tells the city just what the bill will be. This method has one merit at any rate: by appropriating the specified amount council can forestall the collection of it, or any part of it, by mandamus.

Even this crumb of comfort is denied, however, in a multitude of cases in which officers and agencies other than the council are authorized by the legislature and constitution to use their own discretion in determining what the city must contribute to their support. Probation officers, stenographers, clerks, tipstaves, criers and others—too numerous to mention in this bulletin—are appointed in numbers and at salaries over which the council has no control. Their salaries are by law a charge on the treasury, and, if not appropriated by council, are sued for and ordered by mandamus to be paid.

Diffused Authority spells Irresponsibility

This is part of what the city calls its "Mandamus Evil." We intimated in a recent issue of CITIZENS' BUSINESS that perhaps it is not aptly so termed. The evil lies in the fact that the power to spend the city's money is so widely distributed that the citizen's efforts to fix the responsibility for wasteful government are almost certain to result in confusion, discouragement and indifference. Courts, commissions, boards, officers, and the legislature itself, share with council the responsibility for the disposition of the city's funds. All but council are saved the embarrassment of levying taxes to meet the obligations they incur or create; and council, which has the burden of levying all the taxes, can justly disclaim responsibility for a large, but indefinite part, of the levy.

Only by a miracle can efficient and economic administration of the city's affairs result from such a system. We feel, however, that miracles of this sort do not occur with sufficient frequency in Philadelphia to justify making them our sole reliance. We, therefore, advocate a change of system: that all power and discretion in spending the city's money be vested in the tax levying body—the council. If inefficiency should then exist, it would not be attributable to difficulty in placing the responsibility where it belongs.

Prospects of Relief

Unfortunately there is no prospect that the state will cease saddling charges on the city treasury; or that all discretion to determine the amount of such charges will be delegated to the city council. There is a prospect, however, that an increased control of the city's financial affairs will be vested in the council. This we hope to see accomplished by the incorporation in the constitution of two recommendations tentatively adopted by the Commission on Constitutional Amendment and Revision. These provisions will not solve the problem completely; they will not vest in council complete control over the "Mandamus Evil"; but they are steps in the right direction.

The more far-reaching of these two recommendations is tentatively numbered as section 14-B of article XVIII-A and reads as follows:

> In any county whose boundaries coincide with or lie wholly within the boundaries of any city, all county officers, and judges, other than the judges of common pleas and orphans' courts, and all state or county officers whose salaries or expenses are payable, in whole or in part, out of funds receivable by any city or county officer shall submit to the chief executive of the city, in the manner and the time required of city officers, estimates of the needs of their respective offices and courts. The city council or other body vested by law with the power of appropriation shall have the same control over appropriations for the support of such offices and courts as it has over appropriations for the support of city offices, except that the general assembly may fix the salaries of such officers and judges.
>
> In any such county any or all county offices may be abolished by law and the functions and powers pertaining to any such office may be transferred to any officer or officers of such city.

The other recommendation is tentatively numbered as section 20 of article XVIII-A and reads as follows:

> No debt shall be contracted or liability incurred by any municipal commission, board, officer, employe or other agency, except in pursuance of an appropriation previously made therefor by the municipal government.

In order to conserve the resources of the Bureau for its constantly increasing activities, the Board of Trustees wish to see CITIZENS' BUSINESS made self-supporting, and have, therefore, fixed the subscription price at $1 per year, effective July 1.

CITIZENS' BUSINESS is issued weekly at 805 Franklin Bank Building, Philadelphia. Entered as second class matter June 7, 1913, at the Post Office at Philadelphia, Pa., under the Act of August 24, 1912.

CITIZENS' BUSINESS
BUREAU OF MUNICIPAL RESEARCH
OF PHILADELPHIA

**AN AGENCY OF 2000 CITIZENS
COOPERATING IN THE EFFECTIVE
DISCHARGE OF CIVIC DUTIES,
EQUIPPED TO INTERPRET AND SOLVE
TECHNICAL PROBLEMS OF GOVERNMENT**

A Many-Sided Question

University of Illinois Library,

Urbana,

Ill.

No. 424   **July 8, 1920**

While we have consistently taken the stand that we
do not favor any action by the city that will injure
the banks or be unfair to them, we insist, as a citizens'
agency, that the city is entitled to as favorable arrangements as is any private depositor.

The Two Proposals

On June 21 there was a hearing before the Finance Committee of Council on a proposed ordinance to increase the rate of interest on city deposits from 2½ to 3 per cent and to provide insurance or collateral to protect the city against loss from failure of a bank, as is now provided for school district deposits, but not for city deposits.

The Lesser Problem

In our judgment, the question of requiring the banks to protect the city against loss in case of bank failure, whether such protection be through insurance or through deposit of approved investment securities, is less important than the matter of interest on the city's balances. While the future may show greater losses to the city than has the experience of recent years, we are inclined to the opinion that a judicious placing of deposits could reduce this risk to proportions that would not be serious. This would be the case even more certainly if the economical policy of smaller cash balances was carried out.

The bankers, naturally enough, oppose insuring the city's deposits. They base this on the cost, and also on principle, as they declare it to be bad banking practice to insure depositors. They also object to furnishing collateral, although this would probably prove more acceptable to the banks than furnishing a surety company's bond.

The deposits of the commonwealth and of every school district in the state are required by law to be protected. The proponents of the measure argue by analogy that the city's deposits —being the public's property—are equally entitled to protection.

Pittsburgh's Choice and the Result

We have obtained some interesting information from Pittsburgh officials. Formerly that city had its deposits secured, but found that it could get more interest from the banks on unsecured deposits. Accordingly, the proper authorities decided to discontinue the security provision.

Pittsburgh invites annual bids on city deposits and for the current year it receives 3¾ per cent on its most active account and 3.57½ per cent to 3.83 per cent on its other active accounts. Deposits are also distributed in smaller amounts to other banks and trust companies, but none at less than 3 per cent. The School District of Pittsburgh receives 3 to 4 per cent interest on its deposits and, in addition, has them secured.

State and Nation—Other Cities

Other large cities—New York, Chicago, Boston—report higher interest on their deposits than Philadelphia gets. On the other hand, the last published sworn statement of the auditor general and state treasurer showed that Pennsylvania had about $18,000,000 in banks at 2 per cent. The state's deposits are all secured.

We are informed that the Federal government receives only 2 per cent on its deposits—unsecured—whereas the government's deposits of postal savings moneys earn 2½ per cent and are secured.

Points to Consider

So many elements enter into this problem that we favor postponing final action for a little while, to enable councilmen, the banks, and citizens to throw more light on certain phases of the question.

For instance, the proposed ordinance provides for a maximum of $8,000,000 in the active depositories, and fails to stipulate that any of the deposits should be distributed to the banks on a basis proportionate to their combined paid in capital and surplus. This, it is pointed out, might invite favoritism. The ordinance has been criticized, too, on the ground that it is too rigid— that adjustments in the interest rates should be provided for at frequent stipulated intervals.

These, and a number of associated points will be discussed, if conditions permit, in later bulletins. In the meantime we urge the fullest publicity and the most candid discussion. As there is no occasion for haste, the issue should be settled, so far as these are ascertainable, on its merits.

CITIZENS' BUSINESS is issued weekly at 805 Franklin Bank Building, Philadelphia. Entered as second class matter June 7, 1913, at the Post Office at Philadelphia, Pa., under the Act of August 24, 1912.

CITIZENS' BUSINESS
BUREAU OF MUNICIPAL RESEARCH
OF PHILADELPHIA

**AN AGENCY OF 2000 CITIZENS
COOPERATING IN THE EFFECTIVE
DISCHARGE OF CIVIC DUTIES,
EQUIPPED TO INTERPRET AND SOLVE
TECHNICAL PROBLEMS OF GOVERNMENT**

The City's Wage Policy

No. 425   **July 15, 1920**

> By what standards of adequacy is the city to be
> guided in determining its salary and wage schedule
> this coming fall? The answer to this question will
> be of vital importance to the efficiency of Philadel-
> phia's government.

THE work of employment standardization carried on under the supervision of the Civil Service Commission has reached the stage where information is being collected as to proper rates of pay for the various classes of employment in the city service. This information will consist partly of comparative salaries and wages paid in private establishments in Philadelphia, partly of comparative rates paid in other governmental services, and partly of facts concerning the cost of living.

Questions That Facts Alone Won't Settle

It is hardly possible to over-emphasize the importance of all of this information in arriving at a fair salary and wage schedule for city employes, but it would be delusion to assume that the mere collection of information of this character will settle automatically all questions of wage policy that will confront the city government. For example, after it is known what private establishments are paying for a particular class of work, there still remains the question whether the city ought to conform exactly to that rate or whether there are considerations that would warrant the payment of a lower or a higher rate. Again, the story told by cost of living data may not harmonize at all with the standards of compensation found to exist in private employment. Should this prove to be the case it will be necessary to decide upon a definite policy as to the relative weight to be given to these two factors in wage determination.

The Outstanding Question

The question of outstanding importance, however, will be whether the city government is to be looked upon as an unimportant overhead organization, the functioning of which is a matter of indifference to most of the citizens of Philadelphia; or whether it is to be regarded as an essential enterprise, the efficiency of which must be maintained at all hazards. If the former is to be our attitude, there is little point in adjusting salaries and wages with any thought of adequacy; in fact, it would be more consistent to discontinue the city government entirely. If, however, we take the attitude that our city government is an essential enterprise, then it follows as the night the day that all the factors that make for its efficiency must be taken into account, including adequate compensation of the men and women who do the city's work.

Our City Government an Essential Enterprise

Now, we believe that our city government *is* an essential enterprise. We believe its efficiency ought not only to be maintained but improved. And we are convinced that the efficiency of our city government cannot be improved or even maintained for any length of time at its present level with a working force that is underpaid. *Hence we believe in adequate compensation of all essential city employes.* We believe that the city government should adopt standards of compensation which, with other conditions of employment, will enable the city to compete successfully with other employers in getting the best talent available within and without its boundaries. And this, we believe, *in the long run will make for economy in public expenditures instead of extravagance.*

But Drones Are Not Essential

As for those employes who are superfluous, whose presence serves only to pad the payroll, we have not a dram of sympathy to waste in their behalf. The only proper solution of this problem is their speedy elimination from the service, and this solution we urge with all our might. The city hall drone, whether he is on the city payroll or the county payroll, is a positive obstacle to fair treatment of other municipal employes, and *he ought to be tolerated as little by his fellow workmen as by the tax-paying public.*

OUR LAST NUMBER went to press on Thursday, July 1, and on Tuesday, July 6, council's finance committee met and approved an ordinance on city deposits that incorporates a number of suggestions contained therein. This ordinance was reported favorably to Council on July 7.

While we are at it we wish to record a slight error in that issue—CITIZENS' BUSINESS No. 424. The hearing alluded to in the opening sentence was on June 28, not June 21. It was impossible to correct all of the edition in time for mailing.

CITIZENS' BUSINESS is issued weekly at 805 Franklin Bank Building, Philadelphia. Entered as second class matter June 7, 1913, at the Post Office at Philadelphia, Pa., under the Act of August 24, 1912. Subscription, One Dollar a year.

P Sci

CITIZENS' BUSINESS
BUREAU OF MUNICIPAL RESEARCH
OF PHILADELPHIA

AN AGENCY OF 2000 CITIZENS COOPERATING IN THE EFFECTIVE DISCHARGE OF CIVIC DUTIES, EQUIPPED TO INTERPRET AND SOLVE TECHNICAL PROBLEMS OF GOVERNMENT

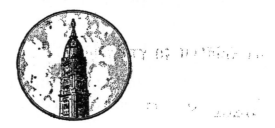

What is a Bureau Member?

No. 426   July 22, 1920

> If any be a hearer of the word, and not a doer, he is like unto a man beholding his natural face in a glass; for he beholdeth himself, and goeth his way, and straightway forgetteth what manner of man he was.　　　　　*—The Epistle of James.*

IT is important that each member of the Bureau of Municipal Research take account in his own heart and remember what manner of member he is. Effective membership extends beyond financial support.

A Definition

Membership in the Bureau exists by virtue of one's financial support of the organization, coupled with a desire to be a part of this citizens' agency. It consists in thus grouping oneself with some 2,000 like-minded citizens for the performance of certain civic duties that can better be performed collectively than individually.

These duties relate to scrutiny, criticism and advice in matters of public affairs requiring time and knowledge for their understanding. Lacking the time and knowledge, citizens generally ignore these highly important civic duties, or perform them only indifferently.

Others—meaning members of the Bureau of Municipal Research—by group action maintain a paid staff of specialists (1) equipped to analyze technical problems of government, (2) responsible to citizen control, *and to no other influence whatsoever,* (3) for reinforcing citizen cooperation with public officials in technical matters, and (4) to report facts on which intelligent public opinion and action may be based.

From Genesis to Revelation

This is the beginning of Bureau membership. But the business of a Bureau member is continuous—and ought to be arduous whenever the times have a tendency to become disjointed. Beyond the financial obligations of membership* there are three prime obligations that Bureau members should regard as resting on them.

Dynamic Support

Every member should make it his duty as a citizen to give the weight of his influence to the principles and policies of good government which *his* Bureau advocates, (1) by his share of the public opinion, (2) by propaganda among his friends and neighbors, (3) by making his attitude and desires regarding public matters known to his legislative representatives and other public servants.

Intellectual Support

Every member should make it his duty as a citizen to know how the Bureau is performing its work, in order that his dynamic support may be intelligent and conscientious. This can be done (1) by reading Citizens' Business, (2) by following newspaper references to Bureau

---

*Contributing members pay $100 or more per year
Sustaining " " 50 per year
Cooperating " " 25 " "
Annual " . " 10 " "
Associate " " 5 " "

activities, (3) by correspondence and personal inquiries, suggestions, and conferences with the Bureau staff on civic matters.

Promotional Support

Every member should make it his duty as a citizen, and as a member of the Bureau, to increase the resources of the Bureau to the highest possible power (1) by his own financial contribution, (2) by making the nature and activities of the Bureau known to others, (3) by obtaining new members from among his circle of associates.*

Continuity of Organization Needed

Assumption of Bureau membership implies no obligation to continue from year to year; but continuity of organization is essential. Obviously, so long as democratic government exists, the responsibility of citizen supervision continues; and so long as citizen supervision is a duty, the necessity for independent and competent inquiry into facts is paramount. This is the motive spirit of the Bureau, and the reason why only citizen cooperation can give trustee supervision and technical staff activities their maximum force.

---

*The Secretary of the Bureau will be glad to suggest to any member interested in such an effort a simple plan based on successful experience.

CITIZENS' BUSINESS is issued weekly at 805 Franklin Bank Building, Philadelphia. Entered as second class matter June 7, 1913, at the Post Office at Philadelphia, Pa., under the Act of August 24, 1912. Subscription, One Dollar a year.

CITIZENS' BUSINESS

BUREAU OF MUNICIPAL RESEARCH
OF PHILADELPHIA

AN AGENCY OF 2000 CITIZENS
COOPERATING IN THE EFFECTIVE
DISCHARGE OF CIVIC DUTIES,
EQUIPPED TO INTERPRET AND SOLVE
TECHNICAL PROBLEMS OF GOVERNMENT

Where There's a Will
There's a Way!

No. 427   July 29, 1920

The administration is faced with the necessity either
of speedily preparing for municipal street cleaning in
1921 in accordance with the mandatory provisions of
the charter, or of justifying the continuance of contract work to the people.

The street cleaning problem once more holds the center of the stage. After the struggle over this subject in the charter revision work had resulted in the winning of the fight for municipal street cleaning, the public considered the question settled and simply waited for the new administration to put the new method into effect.

The Charter Requirements

Today the administration is faced with the necessity either of speedily preparing to carry out the mandatory provisions of the charter requiring municipal operation in 1921, or of justifying the continuance of contract work. Article XX, Section 5 of the charter provides that after December 31 of this year street cleaning and the collection and disposal of city wastes shall be performed directly by the city, unless contract operation of any such work shall be authorized by a vote of eleven councilmen with the approval of the mayor. If council and the mayor do not expressly authorize contract work, municipal operation will automatically become the legal requirement for 1921. Either the council or the mayor, in standing out for strict compliance with the charter, can insure municipal street cleaning in 1921, for the decision for contract work must be made concurrently, and it does not appear from the law that the council can override the mayor's veto.

Recommendations of the Commission of Engineers

To furnish information for use in determining the course to be adopted for 1921, a commission of engineers was recently sent to fifteen of the larger

American cities to observe street cleaning conditions. This tour was *not* taken in order to compare contract and municipal street cleaning, for it was already known that no large city except Philadelphia employed contract forces to clean the streets, and therefore only municipal work could be observed. But it was deemed advisable to find out what difficulties are being encountered in municipal work, and whether these conditions would justify Philadelphia in postponing the initiation of municipal street cleaning.

In their report which has already been made public, all three of the engineers recommend that street cleaning and garbage collection be performed by municipal forces in 1921; two of them recommend that ash and rubbish collection be done directly by the city in 1921, while the third, in order to reduce the work necessary to take all of these functions over at one time, recommends that contract ash and rubbish collection be continued for one year longer. The divergence in these recommendations is slight and relatively unimportant, since street cleaning is the matter of major consideration.

Is Municipal Work Practicable for 1921?

The engineers' report sets forth in no uncertain terms the disadvantages of contracting for street cleaning on the present basis, although after the charter revision work any further demonstration of this fact seems to be as unnecessary as the piling up of arguments that the world is round. In fact, the decision for municipal street cleaning was virtually made when the charter was adopted, and now the problem has been resolved into a determination of whether it is practicable to initiate municipal work in 1921 as is set forth in the charter.

The Essentials of Municipal Operation

Certain definite things are essential to starting municipal street cleaning in 1921: Plant and equipment, a labor organization, an administrative or directing bureau staff and adequate operating funds. Plant and equipment involve a capital outlay which cannot be made available from a popular loan at the November election in time to be of use, but the amount necessary however lies within the remaining borrowing capacity of council.

The development of a labor organization will present many difficulties, it is true, and while future conditions may be uncertain, the city can much better afford to take a chance on adverse labor conditions than can the individual contractors who will charge the city for the chance which they must take.

Reorganization of the street cleaning bureau is necessary to provide engineering personnel, supervisors and foremen to handle the labor force, but this change will not increase the office payroll because the present inspectors will be no longer needed.

Operating funds in the 1921 budget probably will not exceed the 1920 appropriations unless labor and material prices increase, but in this event contract prices would also be higher for 1921. After all, the citizens are ready to go the limit of expense if clean streets can be obtained by municipal work.

CITIZENS' BUSINESS is issued weekly at 805 Franklin Bank Building, Philadelphia. Entered as second class matter June 7, 1913, at the Post Office at Philadelphia, Pa., under the Act of August 24, 1912. Subscription, One Dollar a year.

CITIZENS' BUSINESS
BUREAU OF MUNICIPAL RESEARCH
OF PHILADELPHIA

AN AGENCY OF 2000 CITIZENS
COOPERATING IN THE EFFECTIVE
DISCHARGE OF CIVIC DUTIES,
EQUIPPED TO INTERPRET AND SOLVE
TECHNICAL PROBLEMS OF GOVERNMENT

The Sinking Fund Once Again

No. 428   August 5, 1920

Quite apart from the question of the public morals
involved in secrecy in the financial affairs of a
democracy is the very practical question of whether
the sinking fund is wasteful or not.

SO much discussion has been centered about the city's sinking fund that it will doubtless be of interest to readers of CITIZENS' BUSINESS to have set forth concisely a few of the more important legal and administrative facts affecting the ·fund and the commission that administers it.

Legal Status

The sinking fund as at present constituted owes its existence to an ordinance of Councils approved January 29, 1855, and the commission to an ordinance approved May 9, 1857, as amended on June 19 of the same year.

The commission consists of the Mayor, the City Controller and one citizen to be elected annually by the City Council in July. As the ordinance provides that the elected commissioner is to hold office until his successor is chosen, unless sooner removed by resolution of Council, the practise for many years has been to omit the annual elections and to continue the incumbent indefinitely.

The structure and essential functioning of the commission as set up in these ordinances have never been modified by conflicting provisions in statutes or in the constitution. The Bullitt Act of June 1, 1885, contained an article reading "The sinking fund commission shall continue as now established by law," which was repeated in the new city charter of June 25, 1919.

Answerability

In the ordinance of May 9, 1857, the duties of the commissioners are enumerated and they are, among other things,

> "To report their proceedings and the state of the fund in their charge to the Councils, quarterly, and whenever required to do so by the said Councils."

In conformity with this legal duty, the commissioners

make quarterly reports, albeit not very informative ones, to the Council. Recognition of this duty is contained in the reports; for instance, the last one began with the words: "In compliance with the provisions of the Ordinance of Councils Approved May 7,* 1857, the Commissioners of the Sinking Fund of the City of Philadelphia respectfully present their report for the quarter ending . . . ."

Recent History

A considerable amount of significant information about the sinking fund was published for several years in the City Controller's annual reports and budget statements up to and including the budget statement of October 1916. The required reserves were set forth, and much satisfaction was expressed with the fact that there was a surplus over and above the requirements.

This situation might have gone along without raising any questions for a still longer period were it not for the fact that the autumn of 1916 marked an important epoch in Philadelphia's municipal finances. It will be recalled that it was then that the traditional fixed tax rate of $1.00 was abandoned for a rate fixed after councilmanic decision on the budget. As a natural result, the inadequate dollar tax had to give way to a higher figure and as rising taxes are never popular there followed a keener scrutiny of requests for appropriations.

The practise for many years had been for Councils to vote the budget requests for the sinking fund without so much as a single question as to their adequacy, inadequacy, or excessiveness. This scrutiny and ques-

*This has been cited by the Sinking Fund Commission for a number of years as the ordinance "Approved May 7" but in the printed ordinances of 1857 (p. 189) the Mayor's approval is dated May 9.

tioning resulted in a surrender by the sinking fund commissioners of over a million dollars which did not belong to any sinking fund. This move lessened the 1917 tax burden to that extent—about seven cents in the tax rate.

By the budget season of 1917 it appeared that the 25 cent tax increase of the previous year would have to be followed by a further and a larger raise, so that those responsible for fiscal policy found it necessary to examine more exhaustively into every request. Coupled with this increasing difficulty of making both ends meet, it was observed that all information concerning the much-vaunted sinking fund surpluses had been completely suppressed since the million-dollar surrender of the previous year.

Accordingly, Councils asked for certain light on the condition and the operations of the sinking fund in a resolution passed unanimously in November 1917.

Curiosity Revived

So much in the management of sinking funds of the type of Philadelphia's is technical in character that it is easy to confuse the lay citizen and difficult to make clear the vital issues that are involved.

Costs of government are continuing to rise, and he is rash indeed who predicts lower taxes in Philadelphia in the near future.

Hence councilmen, officials and citizens wonder why there is a veil of secrecy about the city's $40,000,000 financial pocket, and newspaper stories hinting at possible irregularities or improprieties recall the fact that Councils' "14 points" of 1917 remain unanswered to this day.

At its last session before the summer recess the new small City Council passed unanimous resolutions again asking for light on the sinking fund. No doubt some helpful and illuminating figures will be available for budget-time.

CITIZENS' BUSINESS is issued weekly at 805 Franklin Bank Building, Philadelphia. Entered as second class matter June 7, 1913, at the Post Office at Philadelphia, Pa., under the Act of August 24, 1912. Subscription, One Dollar a year.

CITIZENS' BUSINESS
BUREAU OF MUNICIPAL RESEARCH
OF PHILADELPHIA

AN AGENCY OF 2000 CITIZENS
COOPERATING IN THE EFFECTIVE
DISCHARGE OF CIVIC DUTIES,
EQUIPPED TO INTERPRET AND SOLVE
TECHNICAL PROBLEMS OF GOVERNMENT

Contract Bids and Equipment Prices

No. 429   **August 12, 1920**

Because no decision could be made prior to August 1
on a street cleaning program for 1921, the mayor has
invited a full set of bids to protect the city. He has
also asked for prices on new and used equipment.

The Mayor Asks for Bids

On July 30 the mayor advertised for contract bids on street cleaning and the collection and disposal of city wastes and for the furnishing of new and used equipment for municipal operation. Printed specifications for contract work have since been made public and specifications for equipment will shortly be available.

Why Bids were Invited

The mayor was advised by legal counsel that under the provisions of the new charter, unless bids were invited prior to August first, that contract work in none of the above functions could be undertaken in 1921. According to this interpretation of the law, if bids had not been invited before the above date, municipal operation would have been the only course open for 1921.

The mayor has stated that such advertisement is not a commitment to contract street cleaning, but was undertaken to protect the city's interest in the event that it is impracticable to initiate the full program of municipal work required by the charter. Contract performance of all or part of these functions can be substituted for the mandate of the law only by the concurrence of council with the mayor and not by the mayor alone, although the mayor holds the strategic position in this decision.

Since the charter provides that "the mayor or

the council *may* . . . invite bids for such work," such advertisement is *optional* and *not obligatory*. It was superfluous, therefore, to have invited bids for any part of the work which could have been definitely put on the slate for municipal operation prior to August 1. Evidently it was not possible for the mayor to decide by that date to what extent municipal operation could be inaugurated for 1921 and a full set of bids was invited as a safeguard.

Possible Complications from Contract Bids

While it is true that the asking of bids for street cleaning does not actually commit the city to contract work, yet it obscures the main issue. Of greater importance than the delay involved in the actual solution of the problem, is the fact that irrelevant questions will creep into the discussion which may confuse the public.

The claim may be advanced that the new specifications, together with a firmer determination on the part of the administration to produce results, will improve conditions. Such an argument, however, should not mislead us for we know from past experiences that it is next to impossible to produce any set of specifications which will protect the city's interest so long as the work cannot be measured.

Again it may be claimed that new contractors will give the city a better deal. In the first place it is doubtful whether much new competition will appear under existing conditions. In the second place even if new competitors should enter the field, nothing will be gained by "swapping horses," when what we need is a boat which we can operate easily to the shore.

These and other stock arguments will bob up now that bids have been asked and will stay with us until the administration takes a firm stand for municipal street cleaning, which as yet it has not done. Fundamentally, contract street cleaning is the wrong remedy for the disease of dirty streets for which *municipal operation* has been prescribed.

Bids which are to the Point

The real issue in the street cleaning problem is the determination of the practicability of municipal operation for 1921. The mayor's action in asking bids for the furnishing of new and old equipment is a big step in this direction. When the proposals are received on September 15 definite information will be at hand as to the availability and cost of such equipment. In order to conserve time after September 15 when even a few days' delay may be disastrous, appraisals of used equipment should be made prior to that date by the citizens' appraisal commission advocated by the mayor in a communication to council. While a special appropriation for such work has been requested, but has not yet been granted, there are other funds already available to start this work, and it should be undertaken at once.

CITIZENS' BUSINESS is issued weekly at 805 Franklin Bank Building, Philadelphia. Entered as second class matter June 7, 1913, at the Post Office at Philadelphia, Pa., under the Act of August 24, 1912. Subscription, One Dollar a year.

CITIZENS' BUSINESS

BUREAU OF MUNICIPAL RESEARCH
OF PHILADELPHIA

**AN AGENCY OF 2000 CITIZENS
COOPERATING IN THE EFFECTIVE
DISCHARGE OF CIVIC DUTIES,
EQUIPPED TO INTERPRET AND SOLVE
TECHNICAL PROBLEMS OF GOVERNMENT**

The City Impotent

No. 430   **August 19, 1920**

Having given the city the right to pass ordinances, the legislature should complete the job by giving also the power necessary to compel obedience to them.

Toothless Ordinances

Unless expressly authorized by the legislature, a municipality, while it can impose a fine for violation of an ordinance, cannot imprison the culprit upon his failure to pay the fine. Such is the rule of the common law, and it has never been changed by our state legislature. In consequence, the city's police ordinances are, for the most part, ineffective, antiquated, unused, and in large measure unknown.

They cannot carry heavier penalties than fines. They might even then be respected, if there were a sure way to collect the fines, but a fine imposed for violation of an ordinance is nothing more than a debt due the city, and can be collected only in the manner in which other debts are collectible. Enforcement of ordinances under these conditions is a process that is slow, cumbersome, and expensive, and what is worse, in many cases futile, since the type of citizen who offends most flagrantly is usually execution-proof.

A Little Salutary Discomfiture for Offenders

If a police officer sees a violation of an ordinance and is willing to arrest the offender, a certain degree of salutary discomfiture can be inflicted. A magistrate can then compel the offender to give bail to insure his appearance at the hearing of the case, and if bail is not entered, can order imprisonment until the hearing.

One who is placed in this dilemma will no doubt hesitate before attempting another violation—at least in the presence of an unfriendly policeman. Comparatively few violations, however, are seen by officers, and of those that are seen, some are not followed by arrests. The power to arrest, therefore, does not materially increase the effectiveness of the ordinances.

Statutes are Clumsy Substitutes for Ordinances

Lacking the power to keep its own house in order, the city finds itself under the necessity of appealing to the legislature for statutes to meet conditions which are essentially local and which could be met much more intelligently and expeditiously by its council. Thus appealed to, the legislature may enact the desired law, and it may not. If it does, and the law proves unsatisfactory in any particular, the city waits two years more—not for a change in the law—but for an opportunity to ask the legislature for a change.

Municipal Street Cleaning Will Accentuate the Problem

The city's helplessness in enforcing its ordinances is a matter of especially grave concern in these days when municipal street cleaning and collection and disposal of refuse are being planned. The assumption of this work by the city will inevitably accentuate existing problems and bring to the fore new problems, the solution of which will require new regulations. As the city's experience ripens, these regulations will no doubt need frequent revision. The statutes bearing on street cleaning and the prevention of street littering are even now unsatisfactory. Are we to be left under the changed conditions to the mercies of a legislature which convenes once in two years? Is it not more to be desired, in fact will it not be imperative, that the situation be controlled by the council—which is constantly on the scene, and which meets weekly? But the situation cannot be controlled by council unless the legislature accords greater dignity to council's ordinances.

The Legislature's Little Joke

Back in 1901 the legislature apparently entertained some notion of giving cities the right to put teeth in their ordinances, but its good intentions too quickly evaporated. With the approval of the governor, given May 11, 1901, the legislature placed the following gem on the statute books—we hesitate to call it an act or a law:

> The several cities of this Commonwealth shall have power to regulate the police thereof, and to impose fines, forfeitures and penalties for the violation of any ordinance, and provide for the recovery and collection of the same, and in default of payment to provide for confinement in the city or county prison, or to hard labor upon the streets or elsewhere for the benefit of the city: *Provided, That this act shall not apply to cities of the first, second and third class.*

It will be remembered that as early as 1888 the Supreme Court had decided that under the present constitution more than three classes of cities could not exist. No doubt the other cities of the commonwealth join Philadelphia in the thought that it is high time the inane proviso to the act of 1901 be repealed.

How do you like our new dress?

The last eight issues of CITIZENS' BUSINESS have appeared under a new cover design. The new design is a temporary measure, advanced by a friend of the Bureau as an improvement over our previous cover. What do you think of it? Is it an improvement, or do you prefer the old one? Or have you a third suggestion, that will better them both? Write the Bureau of Municipal Research your comments; because we all want CITIZENS' BUSINESS to hold constantly the top notch of attractiveness. That is one way it makes friends for better government.

CITIZENS' BUSINESS is issued weekly at 805 Franklin Bank Building, Philadelphia. Entered as second class matter June 7, 1913, at the Post Office at Philadelphia, Pa., under the Act of August 24, 1912. Subscription, One Dollar a year.

f. Sci

CITIZENS' BUSINESS
BUREAU OF MUNICIPAL RESEARCH
OF PHILADELPHIA

**AN AGENCY OF 2000 CITIZENS
COOPERATING IN THE EFFECTIVE
DISCHARGE OF CIVIC DUTIES,
EQUIPPED TO INTERPRET AND SOLVE
TECHNICAL PROBLEMS OF GOVERNMENT**

Progress in Sinking Fund Affairs

o. 431   August 26, 1920

Herein are set forth two recent sinking fund developments of considerable importance; and two future steps of great significance are indicated.

Noteworthy Development No. 1

The last two weeks have produced two noteworthy developments. Under date of August 12 the commissioners of the sinking fund replied to a resolution, unanimously adopted by council on July 27, requesting the commissioners to furnish certain information regarding their failure to bid for bonds awarded July 19 to the Drexel and Company syndicate, and regarding their purchase almost immediately thereafter of $3,000,000 of those bonds at a profit to the syndicate of $7,500. By replying as they did, the sinking fund commission reversed a policy which they had maintained for several years, and once more recognized the authority of council over the sinking fund. Those who have been following the sinking fund controversies of the last few years will appreciate the significance of this reversal of policy.

Noteworthy Development No. 2

Closely upon the heels of this response to the request of the local legislative body came the award of a new issue of city bonds on August 18. That the bond awarding committee was influenced by the criticism that followed the transactions which the sinking fund commission was asked by council to explain, is more than apparent. Contrary to the two immediately preceding bond awards, the "all or none" bid was rejected; only bids above par were accepted; and the sinking fund was awarded the full amount of bonds it wanted ($1,000,000 worth), thus saving the city from a loss such as those which it sustained inexcusably on several former occasions. Incidentally, an incentive was created for independent banking houses and investors to bid directly for future issues of city bonds; notice was served upon all to offer premiums if they wish to be reasonably certain of not having their bids passed by; and, last but not least, the commissioners of the sinking fund were given a practical demonstration in sinking fund and city finance.

Future Step No. 1

Having re-established their recognition of the authority of council over the sinking fund, it is next in order for the sinking fund commission to furnish council with that wealth of information asked for in another unanimous resolution of July 27. This information is due on or before September 7. In view of certain assertions made by the commission in the not distant past, and especially in view of the fact that some of the most important features of this information have been deliberately suppressed ever since 1916, when the former councils made use of similar facts that until then were freely and even boastfully published in the annual reports and budget statements of the city controller, this information will prove extremely interesting.

Future Step No. 2

Another of several steps which the commissioners of the sinking fund should take promptly is that of complying with the provision of section 8 of article 18 of the new city charter which requires cancellation of city bonds in the sinking fund up to the amount of money set aside for the payment of the particular issue of bonds.

Whatever may be said against complying with

this requirement insofar as bonds issued prior to the date of the approval of the new city charter are concerned, there is absolutely no justification, legal or otherwise, for failure to carry out both the spirit and the letter of the requirement in question as regards bonds issued since that date.

Full and immediate compliance will harm no one; will greatly simplify sinking fund administration and borrowing capacity calculations; will make the sinking fund actually "sink" debt as promptly as possible; will point to the wisdom of issuing serial bonds and having them mature in such manner as to "eat up" whatever sums are required to be set aside for their payment as soon as that money is required to be set aside; and will produce still other desirable results which space does not permit us to elaborate at this time.

Difficult as the Philadelphia city cleansing problem is, both physical and administrative, it can doubtless be solved in a satisfactory manner—due allowances being made for the inheritance of past evils and for dilatoriness—if it is handled in a business-like engineering way. There are plenty of engineers connected with the city administration of Philadelphia who could bring order and efficient service into municipal cleansing in Philadelphia if they were given free hands and wholehearted backing. We do not mean to say that this is not the intent of the administration, nor that the bids now being asked may not be used as a step to that end, but in this respect the administration is on trial not only before Philadelphians but the rest of the country as well.

Editorial—*Engineering News-Record,*
August 12, 1920.

CITIZENS' BUSINESS is issued weekly at 805 Franklin Bank Building, Philadelphia. Entered as second class matter June 7, 1913, at the Post Office at Philadelphia, Pa., under the Act of August 24, 1912. Subscription, One Dollar a year.

CITIZENS' BUSINESS
BUREAU OF MUNICIPAL RESEARCH
OF PHILADELPHIA

AN AGENCY OF 2000 CITIZENS
COOPERATING IN THE EFFECTIVE
DISCHARGE OF CIVIC DUTIES,
EQUIPPED TO INTERPRET AND SOLVE
TECHNICAL PROBLEMS OF GOVERNMENT

Let's Not be Penny Wise!

No. 432   **September 2, 1920**

After having worked out a plan for the classification
of positions and the standardization of salaries in the
city service, we must not fail to take all measures
necessary to make this plan permanently effective.

It would be most unfortunate if the work of employment standardization now in progress under the supervision of the civil service commission should be hampered by short-sighted economy. There is real danger, however, that this may prove to be the case. The nature of this danger will appear from the following statement of facts:

The Contract

By an ordinance of council approved on April 16, 1920, the civil service commission was granted an appropriation of $30,000 to proceed with the classification of positions and the standardization of salaries in the city service, as provided in the new charter. At the time when this ordinance was under consideration it was the plan of the commission to have the work of classification and standardization done under contract by an outside consulting firm rather than by a special staff of its own. The ordinance, therefore, was framed so as to permit, if not indeed to compel, the performance of this work by contract. Immediately upon approval of the ordinance, the commission proceeded with its plan and awarded the contract for the work to a consulting firm at a price of $19,250. Under the terms of this contract the final report of the consulting firm must be furnished to the commission not later than September 15 of this year.

The Continuous Task

It is obvious, however, that the rendering of a report does not constitute the completion of the task which is required of the commission by the new charter. As a matter of fact there are certain features of this task that never can be completed but will call for continuous attention. Even after the new classification has been put into effect and the standard rates of compensation have been applied to all positions in the city service, new positions that may be created from time to time will have to be classified, and adjustments will have to be made in the classification of old positions. Whenever a department wishes to reorganize some of its activities, the commission will be confronted with a problem of classification. Neither can we assume that the standard rates of pay that now are considered fair will not be in need of frequent revision to conform with changes in the market value of personal service and in living costs. In short, after the outside consultants have folded up their tents and departed, there will still remain the important task of putting the new plan into effect and of keeping it in operation. This will require the continuous services of at least one person who has a thorough understanding of all the problems involved.

Training a Man for the Task

When the contract with the consulting firm was drawn up, this situation was fully appreciated. In fact it was stipulated in the contract itself that the consulting firm "will render such instructions and information as may be desired in reference to the work covered by the contract to the members of the civil service commission, and to such employes and examiners of the commission as may be detailed by the commission for such instruction."

The Commission's Request for a Larger Staff

At the same time the commission found its examining staff inadequate to perform even the current work of conducting examinations, to say nothing of keeping in close touch with the work of classification and standardization. Accordingly, about the same time when council was requested to provide funds for classification purposes, the commission asked for a larger appropriation for its other activities, including two additional examiners and a classification staff. In requesting a classification staff, the commission hoped to obtain authority for the employment of persons who could be detailed to the consulting firm for instruction and to whom could be entrusted the important work of maintaining and perfecting the classification after the departure of the consultants.

An Unfortunate Veto

Misfortune, however, befell the ordinance embodying the request of the commission. Council saw fit to pare down the salaries asked for, to eliminate one of the two additional examiners, and to reduce the size of the classification staff to one classifier. With this modification, the measure was passed on to the Mayor. He made a further reduction in the salaries and also vetoed the other additional examiner and the one remaining classifier. As a result of this action, the commission has been greatly handicapped in its work of examining applicants, and has had no one whom it could detail to the outside consultants for instruction. Up to the present time no employe of the commission has been so detailed, and September 15, the date when the consulting firm will probably leave the city, is almost upon us!

The Real Object of the Recent Protest

In this connection it should be mentioned that the public protest of two weeks ago was not against the appointment of a classifier, but rather against what appeared an attempt to set aside an eligible list of classifiers and to employ by round-about methods a person who had not even taken the examination for the position of classifier. That nearly all of the newspapers in the city rallied to the support of proper governmental methods when this situation came to light is most gratifying.

The Need of the Hour

For the present, this protest appears to have been sufficient to prevent the carrying out of an apparently questionable procedure. The consideration of greatest urgency at this moment is the appointment of a classifier. An eligible list is ready, but the authority to employ a classifier without further action by council is doubtful. If the city solicitor, who has been asked for an opinion, should rule that no part of the $30,000 appropriated for classification purposes can be used for the employment of a classifier, then council should take immediate action granting specific authority to employ such a person. The funds are there—it would be simply a matter of amending the ordinance of April 16.

CITIZENS' BUSINESS is issued weekly at 805 Franklin Bank Building, Philadelphia. Entered as second class matter June 7, 1913, at the Post Office at Philadelphia, Pa., under the Act of August 24, 1912. Subscription, One Dollar a year.

CITIZENS' BUSINESS

BUREAU OF MUNICIPAL RESEARCH
OF PHILADELPHIA

AN AGENCY OF 2000 CITIZENS
COOPERATING IN THE EFFECTIVE
DISCHARGE OF CIVIC DUTIES,
EQUIPPED TO INTERPRET AND SOLVE
TECHNICAL PROBLEMS OF GOVERNMENT

The Cost of a Workingmen's Standard of Living in Philadelphia at August 1920 Prices

No. 433   September 9, 1920

In this issue the living cost figures contained in
the Bureau's report published in October 1919 by
the Macmillan Company under the title "Workingmen's Standard of Living in Philadelphia" are

The Initial Investigation

It will be recalled that during the period from August 15, 1917 to May 15, 1918 the Bureau of Municipal Research of Philadelphia made a field investigation of living standards and living costs of workingmen's families in all the more important industrial sections of this city. In the course of our investigation, schedules of income and expenditures were obtained from 395 families. Of these, 260 schedules proved acceptable for tabulation and analysis. With this information as a basis, we proceeded to devise a standard of living that would be expressed in terms of actual goods and services instead of merely in terms of dollars and cents which so quickly lose their meaning in these days of fast changing price levels. By expressing the standard of living in this manner we can readily ascertain its current cost at any time by simply revising the price figures appearing opposite the various commodity and service items listed in the standard. The results of our effort together with a detailed statement of our findings were published in book form in October 1919 by the Macmillan Company under the title "Workingmen's Standard of Living in Philadelphia".

The Cost of Living in 1918 and in 1919

In this publication it was shown that at autumn 1918 prices the annual income necessary to enable a workingman's family of five persons to maintain a fair standard of living was $1,636.79. The following year this figure was revised to conform with prices as they obtained in November, 1919, and the new annual cost was found to be $1,803.14 which represented an increase of slightly more than 10 per cent over the cost at autumn 1918 prices. A detailed statement supporting this new figure was published on December 4,

Our Findings in August 1920

On account of the pronounced interest that has been shown in this information not only locally but in all parts of the country, and especially on account of the immediate usefulness of information of this character in connection with the classification of positions and standardization of salaries which the city government of Philadelphia is now pushing to completion, it has been deemed wise to publish another revised statement showing the cost of maintaining our suggested standard of living at the present time. We therefore ascertained this cost at August 1920 prices and found it to be $1,988.32 or a little over 10 per cent higher than it was at November 1919 prices. In the following pages our latest findings are set forth in detail. A brief summary of these findings together with a comparison of this year's figures with those of previous years is shown in the table below:

CHANGES IN COST OF LIVING IN PHILADELPHIA

Classes of expenditure	Autumn 1918	Nov. 1919	Aug. 1920	From autumn 1918 to Aug. 1920	From autumn 1918 to Nov. 1919	Fro Nov. 1 to Aug. 1
All classes	$1,636.79	$1,803.14	$1,988.32	21.5	10.2	10.3
Specified standard	1,352.72	1,490.20	1,643.24	21.5	10.2	10.3
Housing	240.00	300.00	336.00	40.0	25.0	12.0
Fuel and light..	75.00	84.23	98.10	30.8	12.3	16.5
Food	660.09	674.30	681.82	3.3	2.2	1.1
Clothing	299.43	346.63	439.37	46.7	15.8	26.8
Carfare	35.40	35.40	35.40	.0	.0	.0
Cleaning supplies and services	42.80	49.64	52.55	22.8	16.0	5.9
Unspecified standard*—21% of cost of specified standard.	284.07	312.94	345.08	21.5	10.2	10.3

*For a list of the classes included in the unspecified standard see page 11.

It will be noted that the standard is divided into two parts, the *specified* standard and the *unspecified* standard. In the *specified* standard are included those items or classes of the household budget for which the requirements could be set forth in terms of actual goods and services, and in the *unspecified* standard are included those classes that could not readily be set forth in this manner. It has been shown by investigation, however, that the classes comprising the *unspecified* standard normally constitute about 18 per cent of the total household expenditures of workingmen's families or equal about 21 per cent of the expenditures included under the *specified* standard. Hence the use of the method employed above in determining the amount for the *unspecified* standard.

The Original Standard Left Substantially Intact

Except for a few minor changes made for the sake of greater exactness, the items and quantities listed in the standard herein described are substantially the same as those appearing in CITIZENS' BUSINESS No. 393 and in "Workingmen's Standard of Living in Philadelphia." The only changes in quantities will be found under the heading of "cleaning supplies and services" where the allowances of shoe polish, starch, and stove polish have been reduced and the allowances of shaves, haircuts, and clothespins have been increased. These reductions and increases, however, so nearly offset each other that the changes in the total cost figures from year to year may confidently be taken to represent only changes in retail price levels and in no sense alterations in the standard itself.

The Bureau wishes to acknowledge at this time its appreciation of the generous and courteous co-operation of those who furnished the necessary information for this inquiry.

REQUIREMENTS AND COST, AT AUGUST 1920 PRICES, OF A FAIR STANDARD OF LIVING FOR A FAMILY OF FIVE, CONSISTING OF PARENTS, BOY OF 13, GIRL OF 10, AND BOY OF 6

TOTAL.. $1,988.32

SPECIFIED STANDARD............................ $1,643.24

Housing—annual rent............................. $ 336.00
    Two-story house, with six rooms, facing street; bathroom including toilet, washstand, and tub; laundry tubs; furnace; and facilities for cooking and lighting with gas.

Fuel and Light

	Unit	Price per unit	Annual quantity	Annual cost
Total.......	...	...	...	$98.10
Coal, pea.....	ton	$12.50	2½	31.25
Coal, stove....	ton	15.30	2½	38.25
Gas.........	1000 cu. ft.	1.00	26	26.00
Matches......	box of 500	.05	52	2.60

Food

	Unit	Price per unit	Annual quantity	Annual cost
Total.......	...	...	...	$681.82
Bread and cereals	...	...	......	*135.46*
Bread.......	16 oz. loaf	$ .09	988	88.92
Buns........	15 oz. doz.	.20	41.6	8.32
Rolls........	24 oz. doz.	.22	26	5.72
Cakes, misc....	lb.	.35	13	4.55
Cornmeal.....	lb.	.06	26	1.56
Cornstarch....	16 oz. pkg.	.11	13	1.43
Flour, wheat..	12 lb. bag	.98	13	12.74
Macaroni.....	12 oz. pkg.	.12	13	1.56
Oatmeal......	lb.	.07	52	3.64
Rice.........	lb.	.18	39	7.02
Meats and fish...	...		...	*121.94*
Beef, equal parts of brisket, chuck, and round........	lb.	.25	286	71.50
Chicken.......	lb.	.45	26	11.70
Fish, fresh....	lb.	.18	78	14.04

Unit	Price per unit	Annual quantity	Annual cost
. . .	. . .	. . .	*$169.65*
lb.	$ .09	13	1.17
lb.	.34	26	8.84
doz.	.63	78	49.14
qt.	.15	728	109.20
lb.	.10	13	1.30
. . .	. . .	. . .	*47.45*
lb.	.65	26	16.90
lb.	.24	32.5	7.80
lb.	.35	65	22.75
. . .	. . .	. . .	*65.09*
2 lb. head	.06	39	2.34
2 lb. bunch	.10	39	3.90
doz. ears	.30	13	3.90
4 oz. head	.06	13	.78
lb.	.03	91	2.73
pk.	.48	78	37.44
pk.	1.00	1	1.00
pk.	.70	4	2.80
pk.	.60	4	2.40
pk.	.60	13	7.80
. . .	. . .	. . .	*11.83*
19 oz. can	.16	13	2.08
19 oz. can	.15	13	1.95
19 oz. can	.15	52	7.80
. . .	. . .	. . .	*22.75*
pk.	.60	13	7.80
doz.	.50	19.5	9.75
pk.	.80	6.5	5.20
. . .	. . .	. . .	*4.81*
lb.	.22	13	2.86
15 oz. pkg.	.30	6.5	1.95
. . .	. . .	. . .	*47.19*
24 oz. can	.14	19.5	2.73
lb.	.19	234	44.46
. . .	. . .	. . .	*28.08*
8 oz. can	.22	13	2.86
lb.	.36	52	18.72
lb.	.50	13	6.50

Food—*Continued*

	Unit	Price per unit	Annual quantity	Annual cost
Miscellaneous....	...	...	...	$27.57
Baking powder	3 oz. can	$ .07	11	.77
Ice...........	25 lb. piece	.18	120	21.60
Pickles.......	8 oz. bottle	.15	26	3.90
Salt..........	4 lb. bag	.10	13	1.30

Clothing

	Price per article	Annual quantity	Annual cost
Total................................	...	...	$439.37
Husband..............................	...	...	*102.80*
Caps, wool and cotton mixture, 30% wool, lined or unlined......................	$ 1.50	1	1.50
Hats, soft or stiff felt, medium grade.....	4.00	½	2.00
Hats, cheapest straw, stiff brimmed......	2.00	½	1.00
Sweaters, 60% wool....................	6.50	½	3.25
Overcoats, overcoating, 40% wool........	25.00	⅓	8.33
Suits, cheviot or cassimere, 50% wool....	25.00	1	25.00
Extra trousers, worsted face, cotton back.	5.00	1	5.00
Overalls, denim.......................	2.50	2	5.00
Working shirts, cotton flannel or flannelette...............................	2.00	2	4.00
Working shirts, cotton shirting..........	1.75	2	3.50
Dress shirts, printed madras............	2.50	2	5.00
Collars, stiff or soft washable...........	.27	6	1.62
Ties, silk and cotton, four-in-hand.......	.75	3	2.25
Suspenders, cotton or lisle elastic web....	.75	1	.75
Belts, cheap leather...................	.70	½	.35
Handkerchiefs, cotton.................	.15	6	.90
Nightshirts (homemade), 5 yds. 36 inch muslin, thread, and buttons...........	2.00	1	2.00
Nightshirts (homemade), 5 yds. 27 inch outing flannel, thread, and buttons.....	2.00	1	2.00
Summer underwear, sets, Balbriggan.....	1.25	3	3.75
Winter underwear, sets, 25% wool.......	2.50	1	2.50
Socks, common cotton.................	.25	12	3.00
Shoes, gun-metal welt.................	6.50	2	13.00
Shoe repairs, half-soled and heeled.......	2.25	2	4.50
Rubbers, storm......................	1.25	1	1.25
Gloves, knitted yarn, 75% wool.........	1.00	1	1.00
Garters, cotton elastic web.............	.35	1	.35

Wife			$100.7
Hats, plain velvet, little trimming			2.00
Hats, plain straw, little trimming			4.00
Coats, Kersey cloth, pile fabric, cheviot, or mixtures			12.50
Wash dresses (homemade), 6 yds. 36 inch percale or 32 inch gingham, thread, and buttons			7.13
Suits, wool poplin or other material, 50% wool			12.50
Skirts, serge, panama cloth, or plaid mixtures			7.50
Shirtwaists (homemade), 2½ yds. 40 inch cotton voile or 36 inch lawn, thread, and buttons		3	4.44
Shirtwaists, washable silk		½	2.50
Petticoats (homemade), 3¾ yds. 36 inch muslin, cambric, or sateen, thread, and buttons	2.11	2	4.22
Corsets, standard make	2.50	1	2.50
Corset covers, cambric with narrow embroidered or lace edging	75	2	1.50
Summer underwear, cotton ribbed union suits	1.00	3	3.00
Winter underwear, winter weight cotton union suits	2.00	2	4.00
Nightgowns (homemade), 4 yds. 36 inch muslin, or 27 inch outing flannel, thread, and buttons	1.63	2	3.26
Handkerchiefs, cotton	.15	6	.90
Gloves, cotton or chamoisette	1.00	1	1.00
Aprons (homemade, bungalow), 5 yds. 36 inch figured percale or 32 inch gingham, thread, and buttons	2.48	3	7.44
Stockings, plain cotton	.33	9	2.97
Shoes, gun-metal welt	7.00	2	14.00
Shoe repairs, half-soled and heeled	2.25	1	2.25
Rubbers, storm	1.10	1	1.10
Boy, age 13		...	*94.61*
Caps, wool and cotton mixture, 30% wool, lined or unlined	1.50	1½	2.25
Hats, wool and cotton mixture	1.75	½	.88
Sweaters, 60% wool	5.00	½	2.50
Overcoats, overcoating, 30% wool	15.00	½	7.50
Suits, 60% wool, cassimere, union cheviot, or suiting	13.00	1½	19.50
Extra trousers, 35% wool, union cheviot ..	2.50	1	2.50

Boy, age 13—Continued

Extra trousers, cotton khaki...........		
Blouses (homemade), 2½ yds. 36 inch percale or 32 inch gingham, thread, and buttons.............................		
Collars, stiff or soft washable...........	27	
Ties, silk Windsor...................	50	
Belts, cheap leather.................	50	
Handkerchiefs, cotton................		
Nightshirts (homemade), 3½ yds. 36 inch muslin, thread, and buttons..........		
Nightshirts (homemade), 3½ yds. 27 inch outing flannel, thread, and buttons.....		
Summer underwear, sets, Balbriggan.....	75	
Winter underwear, sets, winter weight cotton, fleece-lined.......................		
Stockings, cotton ribbed...............	30	
Shoes, gun-metal welt.................		
Shoe repairs, half-soled and heeled.......	2.00	
Rubbers, storm......................	1.00	
Gloves, fleece-lined, cotton back........		
Garters (homemade), 1 yd. cotton elastic web..............................		

Girl, age 10...............................

Hats, tailored straw....................	3.00	
Hats, velveteen or corduroy.............	3.00	
Sweaters, worsted face, cotton back......		
Coats, cheviot, 50% wool...............		
Wash dresses (homemade), 4½ yds. 32 inch gingham or chambray, thread, and buttons...............................		
Petticoats (homemade), 2 yds. 36 inch muslin and 2½ yds. lace or edging, thread, and buttons..................	2½	2.7
Petticoats (homemade), 2 yds. 27 inch outing flannel and thread.............	2	1.6
Drawer waists, muslin..................	3	1.9
Drawers (homemade), 2 yds. 36 inch muslin and thread......................	6	4.9
Union suits, cotton, fleece-lined..........	2	2.5
Nightgowns (homemade), 3 yds. 36 inch muslin, 1½ yds. lace or edging, and thread............................	1	1.3
Nightgowns (homemade), 3 yds. 27 inch outing flannel and thread.............	1	1.2
Handkerchiefs, cotton..................	6	.7

Girl, age 10—Continued

Article	Price per unit	Annual quantity	Annual cost
Gloves, fleece-lined, cotton back..........	$ .75	1	
Stockings, cotton ribbed................	5.0	12	
Shoes, gun-metal welt..................	4.50	4	
Shoe repairs, half-soled and heeled.......	1.75	2	
Rubbers, storm.....................	1.00	1	
Garters (homemade), 1 yd. cotton elastic web...........................	.25	2	
Ribbons, 1 yd. 3 inch silk face..........	.50	8	
Boy, age 6.....................	...	...	
Caps, wool and cotton mixture, 30% wool.	1.25	1½	
Sweaters, worsted face, cotton back......	4.50	1	
Overcoats, overcoating or union cheviot, 30% wool.......................	10.00	½	
Wash suits (homemade), 2½ yds. 36 inch percale or 32 inch gingham, thread, and buttons.........................	1.34	6	8.0
Ties, silk Windsor....................	.50	1	.5
Handkerchiefs, cotton.................	.10	6	.6
Nightgowns (homemade), 3 yds. 36 inch muslin, thread, and buttons..........	1.27	1	1.2
Nightgowns (homemade), 3 yds. 27 inch outing flannel, thread, and buttons.....	1.27	1	1.2
Drawer waists, muslin.................	.65	3	1.9
Drawers (homemade), 1½ yds. 36 inch muslin and thread...................	.63	4	2.5
Union suits, cotton, fleece-lined.........	1.25	2	2.5
Stockings, cotton ribbed..............	.50	18	9.0
Shoes, satin calf, machine sewed or nailed	3.00	3	9.0
Shoe repairs, half-soled...............	1.75	2	3.5
Rubbers, storm.....................	1.00	1	1.0
Gloves, fleece-lined, cotton back........	.75	1	.7
Garters (homemade), 1 yd. cotton elastic web...........................	.25	2	.5

Carfare

	Unit	Price per unit	Annual quantity	Annual cost
Total....................	...	...	...	$35.4
Carfare of husband...........	ride	$.05	604	30.2
Carfare of family............	ride	.05	104	5.2

Total......................	...			**$52.55**
Personal......................	...			*23.98*
Toilet soap.................	small bar			7.00
Toothbrush.................	brush			1.25
Toothpaste or toothpowder....	3 oz. tube or 4 oz. box	24	12	2.88
Combs, hard rubber..........	comb	25	1	.25
Hairbrushes, wooden back.....	brush	75	½	.38
Shoe polish.................	2¼ oz. box	12	6	.72
Barber's services:				
Husband.................	shave and haircut	55	12	6.60
Children.................	haircut	35	14	4.90
Household......................	...			*17.73*
Laundry soap................	½ lb. bar	.08	120	9.60
Starch.....................	lb.	09	6	.54
Bluing.....................	½ pt.	05	24	1.20
Clothesline.................	yd.	02	5	.10
Clothespins.................	doz.	03	2	.06
Stove polish................	3¼ oz. box	07	13	.91
Furniture polish............	½ pt.	14	4	.56
Cleanser...................	14 oz. box	06	36	2.16
Collars sent to laundry.......	collar	05	52	2.60
Unspecified cleaning supplies and services—26% of cost of specified requirements.................	...			*10.84*

UNSPECIFIED STANDARD—21% of specified standard...... **$345.08**
Including the following classes: health; furniture and
furnishings; taxes, dues and contributions; recreation
and amusements; education and reading; insurance;
and miscellaneous expenditures.

CITIZENS' BUSINESS is issued weekly at 805 Franklin Bank
Building, Philadelphia. Entered as second class matter June 7, 1913,
at the Post Office at Philadelphia, Pa., under the Act of August 24, 1912.
Subscription, One Dollar a year.

THIS issue of CITIZENS' BUSINESS is especially designed in size and style for insertion in "*Workingmen's Standard of Living in Philadelphia*" as a supplement to the latter.

CITIZENS' BUSINESS

BUREAU OF MUNICIPAL RESEARCH
OF PHILADELPHIA

AN AGENCY OF 2000 CITIZENS
COOPERATING IN THE EFFECTIVE
DISCHARGE OF CIVIC DUTIES,
EQUIPPED TO INTERPRET AND SOLVE
TECHNICAL PROBLEMS OF GOVERNMENT

A Phase of the Mandamus
Question

No. 434   September 16, 1920

The power of our courts to finance themselves without responsibility to those who pay the bills, violates
the fundamentals of democracy and tends inevitably
to reduce the courts in the public esteem.

THE things that have been said in recent months about municipal court mandamuses make it necessary at the outset to emphasize the point of this bulletin. Let it be understood that we are not criticising the municipal court's use of its mandamus power, or intimating an abuse of it. Our attack is upon the existence of such power in the municipal court—or in fact, in any court. On this count, needless to say, the legislature and not the municipal court is the true defendant.

Just for Instance

Solely, therefore, for purposes of illustrating a principle, let us consider a specific case—the payroll for municipal court probation officers.

For 1919 council appropriated $363,350 to pay salaries of probation officers of the municipal court. According to the city controller's report $70,050.45 more was paid to satisfy mandamuses. This year the appropriation is $410,850.

Is too much being spent for probation officers? We do not say so. Our point is, rather, that no one knows whether too much is being spent. The only proper measure of what should be spent is the desire of those who "put up" the cash—the taxpayers. Perhaps they would choose to spend as much or more if theirs were the choice. Unfortunately the choice is not theirs, so that there is no way to compare what is spent with what they desire to spend.

Autocracy Not Yet Extinct

A statute gives the president judge of the municipal

court authority to appoint a chief probation officer at a salary not to exceed $5000, "and such additional probation officers and employes as he may determine at salaries not to exceed $2500 a year."

If the taxpayers think their bill for probation officers is excessive what recourse have they? Their council cannot be held responsible. What it does not appropriate may be mandamused. It appropriated $410,850 this year, not in the belief that that amount was what ought to be spent, but with the knowledge that it would be spent whether appropriated or not.

Municipal court judges, it is true, are elected by Philadelphians, but this does not give the taxpayers command of the situation. The presidency of the court, in which the power in question is vested, comes by appointment of the governor from judges already elected. A displeased and patient electorate could refuse to return a president judge at the end of his ten year term of office, but the governor and not the voters will pick the next president judge.

Apparently the fight against autocracy is not yet won.

Concerning Anomalies

The unlimited power of the municipal court to spend money for probation officers is not unique in this state. The municipal court has other powers fully as broad, and the powers of the municipal court are matched in other courts.

Outside of Pennsylvania, however, courts are seldom free from the necessity of living within appropriations made by the legislative branch of either the state or municipal government. Where such freedom does exist in other states it is not usually found in lower courts. The federal judiciary spends what congress allows it, and no more. *Such power to finance itself as our municipal court has is not entrusted even to the United States supreme court.*

The reason is clear. Judges usually are given long and secure terms of office in order that the influence of personal exigencies may be reflected as little as possible in their decisions. For obvious reasons legislative bodies, whose proper functions include the levying of taxes and the spending of the proceeds, are elected at much shorter intervals. Long terms of office and money-spending powers are utterly incompatible. A judge with power to spend public moneys is an anomaly; as much of an anomaly as would be a legislature with members elected for life terms, or a supreme court elected every year.

The Prestige of the Bench Suffers

Apart from the impossibility of effectual ballot control over expenditures made by judges, but equally worthy of serious consideration, is the fact that the bench is likely to lose dignity and prestige by performing non-judicial functions. The fitness of judges to hold their offices should depend solely upon their ability and fairness in administering the law. Are elections to the bench some day to hinge upon promises of the candidates to economize in their use of public funds?

That this would be a calamity probably the judges themselves would be the first to agree. Yet it is well within the range of possibility if the money-spending powers of our courts are not revoked.

"Government is a contrivance of human wisdom to provide for human wants."—Burke.

CITIZENS' BUSINESS is issued weekly at 805 Franklin Bank Building, Philadelphia. Entered as second class matter June 7, 1913, at the Post Office at Philadelphia, Pa., under the Act of August 24, 1912. Subscription, One Dollar a year.

CITIZENS' BUSINESS
BUREAU OF MUNICIPAL RESEARCH
OF PHILADELPHIA

AN AGENCY OF 2000 CITIZENS
COOPERATING IN THE EFFECTIVE
DISCHARGE OF CIVIC DUTIES,
EQUIPPED TO INTERPRET AND SOLVE
TECHNICAL PROBLEMS OF GOVERNMENT

The Mayor Announces His Policy on Street Cleaning

University of Illinois Library,

Urbana,

Ill.

No. 435   September 23, 1920

The announcement by the mayor that the city will do its own street cleaning is his first definitive statement of policy on this subject since his inauguration. It is to be hoped that this important victory will not be negatived by subsequent announcement that only a portion of the city will participate in this benefit.

T HE mayor is reported as having announced that the city will do its own street cleaning in 1921. Details as to how this plan will be carried out or whether it will include all districts of the city have not been made public, at the time of our going to press. An item of $1,000,000 for the purchase of plant and equipment has been added to the popular loan bill by the finance committee.

Review of Past Events

Although we have discussed the several phases of the street cleaning problem in former numbers of CITIZENS' BUSINESS, it may not be amiss to review the more important steps in the settlement of this issue. The new charter removes previous restrictions against municipal work and requires that the city shall clean the streets and collect and dispose of refuse by municipal forces beginning January 1, 1921, unless a majority of all members elected to council, with the approval of the mayor, shall decide to continue contract work in whole or in part. Municipal work, therefore, is the legal requirement for the year 1921, unless expressly set aside by a vote of eleven councilmen with the approval of the mayor.

On the request of the mayor, council early in May appropriated $25,000 to the department of public works for a complete investigation of the street cleaning and refuse collection problems. As a part of this investigation a commission of three engineers was sent to fifteen of the larger American cities to observe street cleaning conditions and to report their findings to the city government. The engineers' report has been made public. It disclosed the fact that Philadelphia alone of all large American cities still contracts for street cleaning and that our city has very little company among other cities in contracting for the collection of refuse. The report serves as a fitting sequel to the work of the charter revision committee and clinches the fact that municipal work is the only proper method of performing street cleaning services.

Contract Bids Were Asked

The engineers' report was submitted to the mayor on July 12, only a short time before council took its summer recess. Just prior to August 1, the mayor exercised the optional authority given to either the mayor or the council by the charter and advertised for bids for the cleaning of the streets and the collection and disposal of refuse by contract in 1921. While the charter states that such advertisement *may* be undertaken to determine whether it is to the best interests of the city to contract for work of this character, such a step was not necessary if municipal operation had been definitely decided upon. It was apparently impossible, however, to formulate the 1921 program before August 1, and, to protect the city, a complete set of bids was invited for contract performance. Proposals were also asked for the furnishing of new or used equipment with which the city could perform these services by municipal forces. Thus full provision was made for two alternative courses of action and the administration declined to indicate what program would be recommended for 1921 until the bids had been opened. Such postponing of the announcement of administrative policy led to a feeling of uneasiness and uncertainty in many quarters as to whether the administration would support the charter provision for municipal street cleaning. This condition was largely due to the fact that the mayor since his inauguration had not taken a stand for municipal street cleaning on principle, regardless of whether it was expedient to initiate it in 1921 as provided in the charter.

Cost as Well as Service Favors Municipal Work

The bids opened on September 15 showed that contractors are still anxious to perform work of the indefinite and uncontrollable nature of street cleaning. That fact could have been easily foreseen without the asking of bids. Some new competition appeared, and while this resulted in reducing the contract prices in two districts, the combined bids for the entire city are nearly 25 per cent above the current year's costs. This fact still further strengthens the argument in favor of municipal street cleaning, and makes it just so much more important to obey the mandate of the charter, for it is evident that by so doing the profit of the contractors can be saved to the taxpayers and used for repairing streets and for other beneficial work.

We have consistently contended that *service* is the fundamental consideration in the street cleaning issue. This is our contention still. When, however, the factors of *cost as well as service* unite in favor of municipal work, the argument is irrefutable.

Other Steps Still Necessary

Any fears that contractors would not sell their present equipment or that manufacturers could not furnish the necessary articles in time to be of use in 1921, were completely dispelled by the offers of used and new equipment opened on September 15. Initial steps to secure a million dollars from the popular loan for the purchase of plant and equipment have been taken, as noted above. It is important that this item should be so worded as to preclude the possibility of an interpretation that such a sum must cover the full needs of the administration. Larger funds for the purchase of plant and equipment must be obtained if a full program of municipal work is to be initiated. But other sources of money are available and the sum to be included in the popular loan bill should not become the main consideration in determining the extent to which municipal street cleaning is to be inaugurated in 1921.

CITIZENS' BUSINESS is issued weekly at 805 Franklin Bank Building, Philadelphia. Entered as second class matter June 7, 1913, at the Post Office at Philadelphia, Pa., under the Act of August 24, 1912. Subscription, One Dollar a year

CITIZENS' BUSINESS
BUREAU OF MUNICIPAL RESEARCH
OF PHILADELPHIA

AN AGENCY OF 2000 CITIZENS
COOPERATING IN THE EFFECTIVE
DISCHARGE OF CIVIC DUTIES,
EQUIPPED TO INTERPRET AND SOLVE
TECHNICAL PROBLEMS OF GOVERNMENT

The Water Report

No. 436   September 30, 1920

The engineers' report presents estimates of expenditure for the development of water supply facilities sufficient for an indefinite period. These estimates may seem staggering, but it must be borne in mind that the investment will be spread over a number of years and will provide a dependable, adequate and wholesome water supply.

O N September 15 the board of consulting engineers appointed two months previously to investigate needed betterments and extensions of the Philadelphia water works, made its report to the mayor, and on September 21 this report was transmitted to council. It is, therefore, timely to point out the significance of the appointment of this board and to indicate briefly the substance of its principal recommendations.

A Problem That Will Not Down

After years of discussion and procrastination with a problem that progressively became more acute, a commission on the extension and improvement of the water supply was appointed in 1899 to make recommendations for its solution. This commission reported to the then mayor of the city on September 15, 1899. The commission's report discusses thoroughly the abandonment of local sources of water in the two rivers and the securing of supplies farther afield. With the adoption of the recommendations of the commission to install sand filters and to develop and extend the facilities for pumping locally from both the Delaware and Schuylkill rivers, it was generally felt that with the completion of this program an ample and thoroughly satisfactory supply of water was assured for an indefinite time, and that the consideration of distant sources of supply was dismissed for at least a generation or two.

Within two decades, however, Philadelphia's water problem has again become so acute that it has resulted in the appointment of a board of consulting engineers. The commission of 1899 looked into the future with all the technical knowledge then available and concluded that slow sand filtration applied to the waters of the Delaware and the Schuylkill rivers would render these supplies suitable for the city's need for many years to come. Unforeseen developments, however, have arisen, such as extensive industrial pollution of the rivers, particularly in the matter of coal tar wastes, which at times impart to the water a highly objectionable odor and taste, and which cannot be completely removed by existing means of purification; and the increased draft on the Schuylkill which is likely soon to exhaust the flow of the river during the dry season.

A New Program

To meet these new developments the report now before council recommends the immediate construction of a storage reservoir on the Perkiomen, initially to increase the dry season flow of the Schuylkill, but later to fit into a plan for the complete abandonment of the Schuylkill. The program further contemplates the ultimate abandonment of the Delaware supply at Torresdale, a corresponding development of the Neshaminy and possibly of the Tohickon watersheds and an additional supply available by pumping from the Delaware above Trenton. Execution of this program will render available a supply estimated at 700,000,000 gallons daily—sufficient to provide for the city's needs for an indefinite period.

The report emphasizes the continued necessity for filtration even after these new sources of supply have been developed, but recommends in the extension of the filtration system the use of rapid sand filters rather than the slow sand type originally installed.

It is gratifying to note that the engineers are not proposing a huge plan of construction that must be completed as one unit in order to become available, but rather a comprehensive program extending over a number of years designed to keep the city's water supply system well in advance of actual needs, utilizing to the fullest extent the present equipment in filtration plants and pumping stations, and possessing sufficient flexibility to be capable of modification in engineering details as may seem advisable from time to time.

Financial Aspects

In setting forth their plans for a progressive development of the water supply system, the consulting engineers have had constantly in mind the financial limitations of the city and have suggested a construction program involving an outlay of about $35,000,000 during the next six years. This they consider to be well within the resources of the city and will be sufficient not only to inaugurate work on the major portions of the project recommended, but also to permit vitally necessary improvements and extensions to the existing works. Completion of the entire project is estimated to cost, at present prices, $135,000,000. So flexible are the proposed plans and so well linked up to the existing works that their execution can be accomplished little by little, and the cost distributed over a considerable period.

A Stitch in Time

In addition to their recommendations for a future supply, the engineers have examined carefully the existing system and have pointed out wherein it is defective and needs immediate improvement. Their conclusions relative to the arrangement of distribution mains, pumping machinery and other details are largely technical in nature and need not be commented on here, but we would call especial attention to their observations on the deferred maintenance of the plant of the water bureau. They point out that during the war period the water system suffered greatly from lack of adequate funds to keep up normal maintenance, and that every-day operation cannot be made dependable even after the recommended extensions and betterments have been secured unless ample yearly appropriations are made for upkeep. To quote from the report, "Abnormally deferred maintenance develops an extravagant situation which costs more to correct with the lapse of each month of deferment. More than that, existing conditions threaten to shorten needlessly the life of some of the structures and equipment, with the consequently increasing liability of serious interruptions in water supply. *If uncorrected, it will mean a water famine before long."*

Lack of adequate appropriations is an old story in the history of the water bureau. It is sincerely to be hoped that with this report before them, whatever their decision may be as to the program of future development, the present council will not fail to provide adequate funds for maintenance of the existing water works.

CITIZENS' BUSINESS is issued weekly at 805 Franklin Bank Building, Philadelphia. Entered as second class matter June 7, 1913, at the Post Office at Philadelphia, Pa., under the Act of August 24, 1912. Subscription, One Dollar a year.

CITIZENS' BUSINESS
BUREAU OF MUNICIPAL RESEARCH
OF PHILADELPHIA

AN AGENCY OF 2000 CITIZENS COOPERATING IN THE EFFECTIVE DISCHARGE OF CIVIC DUTIES, EQUIPPED TO INTERPRET AND SOLVE TECHNICAL PROBLEMS OF GOVERNMENT

November First

No. 437   October 7, 1920

Is there any public office in Philadelphia that is more vitally related to our welfare than that of superintendent of schools?

The Quest for a New Superintendent of Schools

An important date for Philadelphians to bear in mind at present is November 1. When we remember that on that day the position of superintendent of schools in Philadelphia will become vacant through resignation of the present incumbent and that no decision has been made as to his successor, we feel that it is uncomfortably near.

The quest for a new superintendent is of the utmost gravity and should be conducted with thoroughness, broadness of vision, and a determination to be satisfied with nothing but the best. We undoubtedly need a person of courage and initiative, capable of originating and directing school policies, and at the same time possessing a personality that will inspire the confidence both of the board of education and of the teachers in our schools. We need a superintendent who will be able to bring together all those interested in education and yet one who has the courage of his convictions and who will not brook interference in his professional duties.

Paving the Way for the Right Man

To secure such a person it will be necessary, of course, to increase the salary that the position pays. It is out of the question to hope that a satisfactory candidate will present himself for a salary of $9,000, which is the amount that the position now pays. Contrast this salary with those paid elsewhere:

Chicago	$12,000
New York	$12,000
Pittsburgh	$12,000
Jersey City	$10,500

Moreover, the practice of electing the superintendent for only one year, in accordance with the present custom, is unfair. No sooner does he have his work well under way, than the prospect of standing for reelection looms up before him, a prospect that is likely to affect his initiative and the conduct of his work. He needs the confidence and assurance that a more permanent tenure of office would give him, in order that he may plan his work more extensively and carry out his duties more efficiently. With this end in view he should be appointed for an indefinite term, and the school code should be amended, if necessary, to make this possible.

The Best Available

Thus far report has it that no applications have been received from prospective superintendents. However, the names of a number of prominent educators are before the committee that is to make the decision. The ultimate choice must be a careful one for much is at stake. Among a certain group, there seems to be considerable sentiment in favor of a Philadelphian for the position. In our local enthusiasm, let us not lose sight of the entire field at our command. Let us not discriminate against a suitable person because he happens to be or not to be a Philadelphian. Whether we obtain a man or a woman, whether the new superintendent be a local product or one secured from elsewhere, let us be perfectly sure that he is big enough to fill our needs, that he is the best person available for the position.

STATEMENT OF THE OWNERSHIP, MANAGEMENT, CIRCULATION, ETC., REQUIRED BY THE ACT OF CONGRESS OF AUGUST 24, 1912.

Of *CITIZENS' BUSINESS*, published *weekly at Philadelphia, Pennsylvania,* for *October 1, 1920.*

State of *Pennsylvania* } *ss.*
County of *Philadelphia* }

Before me, a *Notary Public* in and for the State and County aforesaid, personally appeared *William C. Beyer,* who, having been duly sworn according to law, deposes and says that he is the *editor* of *CITIZENS' BUSINESS* and that the following is, to the best of his knowledge and belief, a true statement of the ownership, management, etc., of the aforesaid publication for the date shown in the above caption, required by the Act of August 24, 1912, embodied in section 443, Postal Laws and Regulations, to wit:

1. That the names and addresses of the publisher, editor, managing editor, and business managers are:
Publisher, *Bureau of Municipal Research, Philadelphia.*
Editor, *William C. Beyer.*
Managing Editor, *None.*
Business Managers, *None.*

2. That the owners are:
Bureau of Municipal Research. No capital stock.

3. That the known bondholders, mortgagees, and other security holders owning or holding 1 per cent or more of total amount of bonds, mortgages, or other securities are:
None.

(Signed) *William C. Beyer*

Sworn to and subscribed before me this *22d* day of *September, 1920.*

(Signed) *Martha H. Quinn.*

[SEAL]   (My commission expires *January 16, 1923.*)

CITIZENS' BUSINESS is issued weekly at 805 Franklin Bank Building, Philadelphia. Entered as second class matter June 7, 1913, at the Post Office at Philadelphia, Pa., under the Act of August 24, 1912. Subscription, One Dollar a year.

CITIZENS' BUSINESS

BUREAU OF MUNICIPAL RESEARCH

ISSUED WEEKLY AT 805 FRANKLIN BANK BUILDING
PHILADELPHIA ENTERED AS SECOND CLASS MATTER
JUNE 7,1913 AT THE POST OFFICE AT PHILADELPHIA,
PA., UNDER THE ACT OF AUGUST 24TH, 1912 —
SUBSCRIPTION ONE DOLLAR THE YEAR

Free Justice

No. 438   October 14, 1920

> By establishing a small claims court and a municipal bureau of legal aid Philadelphia has taken steps of far reaching importance.

IT seems quite probable that years to come will appraise the recent organization in Philadelphia of a municipal bureau of legal aid and a small claims court as events of the deepest significance.

The Bureau of Legal Aid

The bureau of legal aid was established by council in the city's newly created department of public welfare "for the purpose of providing legal aid and assistance for those who are in need thereof and who for financial reasons are unable to retain private counsel." Philadelphia can now boast of being the largest city in the United States with a municipally supported legal aid agency.

The bureau began work August 1. That the institution has already won the confidence of those it was designed to benefit is attested by the fact that about 250 applications for assistance are now being received each week—a rate of more than 12,500 a year.

The present policy of the bureau is to decline to give aid in negligence and divorce cases: divorce cases, for ethical reasons, and negligence cases, because attorneys can readily be found who will handle them on a contingent fee basis. In criminal cases the bureau has offered to act as "public defender."

Conciliation First

An attempt at conciliation is the first approach of the bureau to the problems of its clients. If this were its only function its existence would be justified. Most disputes can be amicably adjusted if a disinterested third party will go to the trouble of bringing the dis-

legal situation which confronts them. The bureau of
legal aid is just such a third party. The results of its

aid will undoubtedly give relief where relief is sorely needed. Yet their real importance probably lies not so much in what they are today as in what they may become in the future. It has been the tendency of institutions which have their origins in the needs of less fortunate members of society to expand into agencies which serve all of us. Consider, for example, our public school system.

The constitution of 1838 directed the legislature to establish schools "in such manner that the poor may be taught gratis." Within a third of a century the conception of public schools had undergone a remarkable change. The constitution of 1873 directed the legislature to provide for a system of schools "wherein *all* the children of this commonwealth above the age of six years may be educated."

Are "poor men's courts" to run the same course? Certainly it is difficult to justify making any man, rich or poor, pay for what the state defines as his right, and now that the tendency is to give "free justice" to the poor it will be more difficult than ever to find reasons for denying it to those who are not so poor. We need not be surprised, therefore, if, as the years roll on, we see a gradual extension, both in the kinds of cases handled by the small claims court and the bureau of legal aid, and in the classes of people who may take advantage of their services.

A Teacher's Reward

We have just learned of a teacher who started poor twenty years ago and has retired with the comfortable fortune of fifty thousand dollars. This was acquired through industry, economy, conscientious effort, indomitable perseverance, and the death of an uncle who left her an estate valued at $49,999.50.—Seneca Vocational School.

CITIZENS' BUSINESS

BUREAU OF MUNICIPAL RESEARCH

ISSUED WEEKLY AT 805 FRANKLIN BANK BUILDING
PHILADELPHIA. ENTERED AS SECOND CLASS MATTER
JUNE 7, 1913 AT THE POST OFFICE AT PHILADELPHIA,
PA., UNDER THE ACT OF AUGUST 24TH, 1912 —
SUBSCRIPTION ONE DOLLAR THE YEAR·

That $33,000,000 Loan

No. 439   October 21, 1920

Herein are a few pertinent comments on a matter of immense importance to all Philadelphians.

The People's Veto Power

On October 1 the council passed, and the mayor approved, an ordinance authorizing the creation of a loan up to a total of $33,000,000 for certain specified purposes, for each of which a definite portion of the total is allotted. Ordinarily, the approval of an ordinance by the mayor makes that ordinance effective. But in this particular case, the ordinance must be referred to the people for their approval or rejection, in much the same manner as *all* ordinances must be referred to the mayor for his approval or rejection.

The Nature of this Power

Except in the case of ordinances for the payment of what have come to be known as "moral claims", the rejection or veto of an ordinance by the mayor does not of itself kill or render the ordinance ineffective, for the council may pass it over the mayor's veto by a three-fifths vote of all the members elected to that body. But just as the mayor has an absolute veto in the case of ordinances for the payment of moral claims, so have the people an absolute veto over this $33,-000,000 loan ordinance. If on November 2 next more people vote against this ordinance than vote in its favor, the ordinance is killed and made as ineffective as though council had never passed it.

"All or None"

In the case of ordinances making appropriations the mayor has, in addition to the right to veto an ordinance as a whole, the very valuable right to disapprove or reduce any appropriation item. But in the case of all other ordinances the mayor must approve or reject each ordinance as a whole. Similarly, the people must approve or reject this $33,000,000 loan ordinance as a whole. They cannot, by their votes at least, approve certain items in the loan ordinance and reject others. All the items are bound together—united they must stand, or united they must fall.

Hamstringing the People

The effect of forcing the people to vote upon the $33,000,000 loan as *one* proposition, instead of making it possible for them to pass upon the individual items on their respective merits, is distinctly bad.

If, as many assert, there are items in this loan ordinance that should not be approved, because they are inherently bad, or untimely, or extravagant, or because of other reasons, such items should be made ineffective, without in any way endangering or delaying the others. And the items that really merit approval should be made effective, without carrying along any of those that deserve to be rejected. Each item should be viewed and rated on its own merits. The bad should not pull down the good, nor should the good carry along the bad.

To force the people to approve or reject the $33,000,000 loan as an undivided proposition is to prohibit them from exercising their right of franchise in an intelligent and discriminating manner. Largely because of the mistaken idea that the rejection of this loan by the people on November 2 would result in a year's postponement of certain necessary public improvements, or because of the feeling that the cost of a special loan election would be too great for the advantages to be obtained from a rejection of the loan in its present form, the people are encouraged in their readiness to assume that the loan ordinance is worthy of their approval, and are discouraged from considering and evaluating the individual items.

The Law

The law does not require each item comprised in a proposed loan to be submitted separately to the people, nor does it prohibit the submission to the people of each distinct proposition for which money is proposed to be borrowed. The council had it within its power to submit separately each item now comprised in the $33,000,000 loan, but perhaps because of precedent, or because of a feeling that all the items would meet with the approval of the people even were they voted on separately, or possibly for other reasons, the council combined all the items into a single proposition.

4

What a Rejection Cannot Do

But suppose it were possible for the people to vote on the individual items, would council be prohibited from borrowing a million dollars for a given purpose, if the people were to vote down an identical item? The answer is, no!

As the state constitution and the statutes are now worded, the rejection by the people of a loan item does not operate as a prohibition against council. It merely operates to keep that proposed loan from being charged up against the people as an "electoral loan." If the council has sufficient "councilmanic borrowing capacity" it can pass another ordinance and create the rejected loan without assent of the people. It is clear, therefore, that the rejection by the people of items that fall within the amount of the councilmanic borrowing capacity is, at the most, merely an expression of opinion, which the council may lawfully disregard if it so desires. It is neither dictation nor a mandate—it is merely advisory in character.

Surely, there is need for a more effective referendum. At present it partakes of much of the nature of a farce.

What Those Loan Items Are

Below is given a complete list of the items comprised in the proposed $33,000,000 loan, together with the amount allotted to each. The wording is identical with that of the loan ordinance.

It will be noticed that a number of these items begin with the word "toward." This word has much legal significance. In most cases it has been inserted in these items so as to make it possible to *spend* larger sums of money for the purposes specified than the ordinance provides, or so as to make it possible to *begin* a given project on a scale that will cost more money than the ordinance provides. A typical example of this is the item of $1,000,000 "toward the construction of building or buildings for the Juvenile, Domestic Relations and other branches of the Municipal Court". It is freely admitted that this $1,000,000 represents less than one-fifth of the probable cost of the proposed improvement and that other millions will have to be provided later to complete the building that is to be begun after this loan ordinance is approved by the people.

There are many cases where the use of the word "toward" is highly desirable. For instance, in the case of a large program the ultimate cost of which cannot be predicted years in advance of its completion, the use of this language enables the financing to be elastic instead of rigid. On the other hand, its use in the case of items that are comparatively small and the execution of which spreads over but a short period of time, invites extravagances, loose planning, and similar evils.

Items and amounts in the loan ordinance

Grading streets ....$	750,000
Paving streets	500,000
Improvement of country roads	250,000
Toward the extension of Bensalem avenue and Holme avenue branches of the Roosevelt Boulevard, and acquisition of property	800,000
Construction of bathing beaches and appurtenant work	500,000
Toward the extension and paving of Delaware avenue, from Laurel to Dyott street, including acquisition of property	750,000
Improvement of Delaware avenue, from Snyder avenue southward	800,000
Construction of main sewers; *Provided,* Four Hundred Thousand (400,000) dollars of this amount shall be expended toward the extension and construction of the Rock	

6

Run Main Sewer in the Forty-second ward 1,500,000

Toward the construction and extension of main sewers in Bigler and Packer streets 500,000

Construction of branch sewers 1,000,000

Construction of bridges 400,000

Toward acquisition of property, erection and construction of sewage treatment plants and intercepting sewers 1,500,000

Extension and improvement of water supply. 3,105,000

Improvement of Independence Hall group of buildings 200,000

Improvement of parks and squares 100,000

Construction of comfort stations 100,000

Improvement of South Second Street Market 40,000

Toward erection of building for municipal purposes on site owned by the City of Philadelphia in Germantown 450,000

Toward the purchase and erection of plant, buildings, ground and equipment for the cleaning of streets, the collection of ashes and rubbish and the collection and disposal of garbage 1,000,000

Construction of new police and fire stations 500,000

Toward the construction of new elevators in City Hall 500,000

Purchasing new fire apparatus 550,000

Toward completion and equipment of the Frankford Elevated Railway, from Front and Arch streets to Rhawn street 3,500,000

Toward the construction of connection of Market Street Subway and Frankford Elevated Railway 100,000

Erection and improvement of swimming pools and bath houses 300,000

Construction of buildings and improvements at House of Correction 50,000

Acquiring property for and completion and equipment of playgrounds 650,000

Toward the acquisition of land and the improvement, development and equipment of playgrounds, parks and recreation centres in the congested and thickly populated parts of the City in the area bounded by Susquehanna avenue, Washington avenue, Broad street and the Delaware River 500,000

Construction of and improvement to buildings at Brown's Farm 50,000

Purchase and equipment of receiving shelter for children 25,000

Toward the construction and improvement of wharves and docks, the construction of bulkheads and all work appurtenant or adjacent thereto 3,500,000

Toward the construction, equipment and extensions to buildings under the control of the Department of Public Health ... 1,130,000

Toward the erection and construction of the main building of the Free Library of Philadelphia, to be used in addition to funds heretofore borrowed and such other moneys as may hereafter be authorized to be borrowed therefor 1,000,000

Toward the acquisition of property for and construction of City Hall Annex 1,000,000

Toward construction of Art Museum 1,500,000

Toward the preparation of plans, the acquisition of land and the construction and erection of the Delaware River Bridge and the approaches thereto...... 500,000

Toward the construction of building or buildings for the Juvenile, Domestic Relations and other branches of the Municipal Court 1,000,000

To pay for damages for opening, widening and change of grades of streets, construction of sewers and condemnation of property for other purposes 2,000,000

Toward improvement of parks under the care of Fairmount Park Commission 400,000

Total $33,000,000

8

BUSINESS

IPAL RESEARCH

FRANKLIN BANK BUILDING
AS SECOND CLASS MATTER
OFFICE AT PHILADELPHIA,
AUGUST 24TH, 1912 —
DOLLAR THE YEAR

Council Do
t It?

November 4, 1920

e commission's program of
now rests almost entirely
will council take?

of playgrounds, park:
centres in the conge
populated parts of the
bounded by Susquehan;
ington avenue, Broad
Delaware River .....

Construction of and impro
ings at Brown's Farm

Purchase and equipment of
for children ....

Toward the construction
of wharves and docks,
of bulkheads and all
or adjacent thereto ...

Toward the construction, e
tensions to buildings ι
of the Department of l

Toward the erection and c
main building of the
Philadelphia, to be us
funds heretofore bor;
other moneys as m;
authorized to be borrov

Toward the acquisition of
construction of City H

Toward construction of Ar

Toward the preparation o
quisition of land and
and erection of the
Bridge and the approa

Toward the construction
buildings for the Ju
Relations and other
Municipal Court ......

To pay for damages for c
and change of grades
struction of sewers and
property for other pur

Toward improvement of par
of Fairmount Park Cor

Total ....

CITIZENS' BUSINESS

BUREAU OF MUNICIPAL RESEARCH

ISSUED WEEKLY AT 805 FRANKLIN BANK BUILDING
PHILADELPHIA—ENTERED AS SECOND CLASS MATTER
JUNE 7, 1913 AT THE POST OFFICE AT PHILADELPHIA,
PA., UNDER THE ACT OF AUGUST 24TH, 1912—
SUBSCRIPTION ONE DOLLAR THE YEAR–

What Will Council Do About It?

No. 441   November 4, 1920

The fate of the civil service commission's program of employment standardization now rests almost entirely with council. What action will council take?

The Question at Issue

What action shall be taken on the report of the civil service commission on employment standardization?

No other question now confronting our city administration is so far-reaching in its importance to the administrative efficiency of the various municipal departments, nor so vitally related to the welfare of upwards of 12,000 of our city employes. The commission's report aims, among other things, to correct the existing inequalities in compensation and in working conditions in the city service, *to insure equal pay for equal work, to establish definite lines of promotion,* and to make salaries and wages more nearly adequate to the demands of the present high cost of living. If the proposals in this report are put into effect, these aims will be largely realized; if the proposals are not put into effect, all the existing inequalities and other handicaps to morale and efficiency will be continued.

A Bit of Background

A brief review of recent events may help to clarify the present situation. Early in August, and coincident with the piecemeal completion of the civil service commission's work on classification and standardization, the various city departments began the preparation of their 1921 budget estimates. In order to facilitate the application of the commission's recommendations to next year's municipal payroll, the mayor, on August 12, issued instructions to all departments asking them to incorporate the new standard titles of positions and the new standard rates of pay in their estimates for personal service. These instructions in the main were faithfully carried out and the departmental estimates were forwarded to the mayor.

On October 13, when the mayor transmitted his budget to council, he announced that in order to stay within the city's next year's revenue under the existing tax rate it had been necessary to lay aside the recommendations of the civil service commission with regard to salary increases, and that "with a few minor exceptions," only policemen and firemen were to receive a substantial increase in pay. The new standard titles had also been stricken from the budget estimates and the old titles had been restored. In effect, this was a complete repudiation by the mayor of the recommendations of the civil service commission. Their fate now rests with council.

The Cost Objection Considered

When council comes to a consideration of this problem there are several important facts that should be taken seriously into account. In the first place, the mayor has not found any fault with the *recommendations* of the civil service commission, but feels that at the present time the city is not financially able to bear the *added cost*. According to the consulting firm retained by the commission for the technical work on classification and standardization, this added cost for 1921, for those branches of the city service covered by the classification, would be approximately $1,800,000 and would represent an increase over the existing salary and wage schedule of between 10 and 11 per cent. This amount is less than a million dollars in excess of the increase to which the mayor himself is committed in his recommendation that policemen and firemen be paid a minimum wage of five dollars a day. The cost objection to the initiation of the standardization program in 1921 would therefore not appear to be overwhelming.

Present City Pay Inadequate

In the second place there is the fact that most city salaries and wages are inadequate and ought to be increased. Although the cost of living since 1914 has gone up at least 100 per cent, during the same period the average compensation of those city employes who are paid by the day has advanced only 47 per cent and that of salaried employes has advanced only 34.4 per cent. Not only have municipal salaries and wages failed to keep pace with the rising cost of living, *but they have failed also to hold their own in comparison with standards of compensation in private employment.* The vast majority of city employes are receiving less than their fellows who are rendering corresponding services in local commercial and industrial establishments. As a result the labor turnover in the city service has been abnormally high, fewer and fewer persons have been applying to the civil service commission for municipal positions, for many examinations not a single applicant has appeared, vacancies in the various departments have become increasingly difficult to fill, and in some of the departments it has not been at all possible to secure urgently needed workers even after civil service restrictions had been waived.

How Will Council Meet the Issue?

In view of these conditions it is unlikely that council will refuse to make any increases in the payroll except for policemen and firemen, *nor would it be fair to refuse.* It is also highly improbable that such increases will be less in aggregate amount than those recommended by the civil service commission. The question therefore, resolves itself as follows: Shall these increases be made by rule-of-thumb methods, or in accordance with a scientific plan? Shall they be made on the old and inequitable basis, or on the new and equitable basis? Shall they be made so as to aggravate existing inequalities in the service, or so as to remove these inequalities?

There would seem to be but one answer. *What answer will council give?*

CITIZENS' BUSINESS

BUREAU OF MUNICIPAL RESEARCH

ISSUED WEEKLY AT 805 FRANKLIN BANK BUILDING
PHILADELPHIA ENTERED AS SECOND CLASS MATTER
JUNE 7, 1913 AT THE POST OFFICE AT PHILADELPHIA
PA., UNDER THE ACT OF AUGUST 24TH, 1912—
SUBSCRIPTION ONE DOLLAR THE YEAR-

Transit Issues

No. 442   November 11, 1920

This bulletin reviews briefly some of the
legal aspects of the Philadelphia transit
situation.

The Fare Increase and the 1907 Contract

The agreement of 1907 between the city and the Philadelphia Rapid Transit Company stipulated that rates of fares could be changed, "but only with the consent of both parties." The city has not consented to a change. Nevertheless, with the approval of the public service commission the transit company has been collecting increased fares since November 1.

The appellate courts of this state have held that although a utility promises not to exceed a certain rate if granted a franchise by a municipality, the public service commission may allow an increase if the rate agreed upon proves inadequate. These decisions are based substantially upon the ground that to allow a municipality to cripple the service of a public utility by denying it adequate revenue would be to violate section 3 of article XVI of the state constitution, which provides that "the exercise of the police power of the state shall never be abridged or so construed as to permit corporations to conduct their business in such manner as to infringe the equal rights of individuals or the general well-being of the state."

Contract or No Contract?

It was apparently assumed by the public service commission that the doctrine of these cases was broad enough to justify it in ignoring the 1907 contract. That the assumption is warranted is not universally conceded. It is pointed out that the agreement of 1907 is not simply an ordinance granting a franchise. It was negotiated under the authority of the legislature, conferred by the act of April 15, 1907, P. L. 80. The supreme court has construed it in several cases in which its validity seems to have been taken for granted. In Brode v. Philadelphia, 230 Pa. 434, (1911) the supreme court expressly sustained its validity. That the creation of the public service commission invalidated the contract, or that it deprived the city of the benefit of the fare clause without invalidating other provisions of benefit to the transit company, is seriously questioned in some quarters.

At this writing no appeal from the public service commission's order has been entered either by the city or by the transit company.

Broad Powers of the Public Service Commission

The fare increase authorized by the commission was not that asked for by the transit company. The public service company law, however, does not require that it should be. The transit company asked for a straight five cent fare with the abolition of transfers and exchanges. It was directed to charge a seven cent fare, sell four tickets for a quarter, and to leave unchanged the existing transfer and exchange privileges. The order states that the increase is temporary and that a permanent rate will not be fixed until the completion of the valuation of the transit company's property. The transit company has filed its inventory with the commission, but has submitted no appraisal. The city's engineers have been checking the inventory for about a month.

In addition to authorizing fare increases, the public service commission ordered its bureau of engineering, in association with the engineers of the transit company and the city's engineers, to make an investigation looking to the improvement of the service, necessary extensions to the system, additional equipment. and to submit "recommendations for the elimination of such skip-stops as are unduly burdensome and dangerous to the public." Upon submission of the findings of the engineers, the commission has power to specify "the just reasonable, safe, adequate and sufficient ser-

vices, facilities, rules, regulations or practices thereafter to be put in force."

The Underlying Companies in Court

The complaint of the United Business Men's Association has been appealed from the public service
commission to the superior court, which has not yet
rendered its decision. This complaint, in substance,
alleges that the underlying companies are receiving
excessive rentals, and asks the commission to ascertain the value of their properties for the purpose of
determining the rates to be charged the public by the
underlying companies, or by their agents or lessees,
for the service actually being furnished for public use.
Whether the proceedings before the commission had
reached the stage at which they could be appealed
from, and whether the underlying companies are
"public service corporations" "doing business" within
the intent of the public service company law are the
principal issues in the superior court.

Interesting Constitutional Questions

To the lay mind it will be interesting to learn from
the courts the answer to the question: Is it permissible
for the state to inquire whether the underlying companies are "conducting their business in such manner
as to infringe the general well-being of the state,"
within the meaning of the section of the state constitution quoted above? If the state courts decide
that the underlying companies are subject to the public
service company law and the public service commission
should order a reduction of the rentals, another issue
will be raised—whether the public service company
law as interpreted by the state courts violates the
prohibition of the federal constitution against state
laws impairing the obligation of contracts.

H. Sei

CITIZENS' BUSINESS

BUREAU OF MUNICIPAL RESEARCH

ISSUED WEEKLY AT 805 FRANKLIN BANK BUILDING
PHILADELPHIA—ENTERED AS SECOND CLASS MATTER
JUNE 7, 1913 AT THE POST OFFICE AT PHILADELPHIA,
PA., UNDER THE ACT OF AUGUST 24TH, 1912—
SUBSCRIPTION ONE DOLLAR THE YEAR—

How Our City Government Pays Its Workers

Number 1

No. 443   November 18, 1920

In this and in subsequent numbers of CITIZENS' BUSINESS the reader will find significant facts bearing upon the salary and wage situation in the city service.

Employment Standardization Gaining Strength

The cause of classification of positions and standardization of salaries under the city government appears to be gaining strength as the recommendations of the civil service commission are becoming more generally understood. This was to be expected. No one would deliberately oppose a plan with such commendable purposes as the one now before council. Who could object to establishing equal pay for equal work? Who could protest for one moment against the elimination of the existing jumble of uninforming and misleading titles of positions and the substitution of really informing standard titles? Yet these are two of the primary purposes which the recommendations of the civil service commission to council seek to accomplish.

The Problem before Council

At this juncture council seems to be ready to accept the new standard titles, but does not yet see its way clear to the adoption of the standard rates of pay. The departmental budget requests for next year are far in excess of the estimated revenues under the existing tax rate, and council is determined not to adopt a budget that will require a higher tax rate. It therefore becomes a question whether sufficient reductions can be made in other requests to make possible an addition of slightly less than $1,800,000 to the city payroll which the adoption of the standard salary and wage rates would entail. Since the mayor has already committed himself to an increase of almost $1,000,000 in his recommendation that firemen and policemen be paid five dollars a day, the net cutting of other items that will have to be done on behalf of the standardization plan amounts to less than $800,000.

Weighing the Relative Needs of the City

In the process of reducing the 1921 budget, council will be obliged to weigh the relative importance of the various needs of the city government and to meet them accordingly. To what extent the personal service needs will be met, will depend very largely upon the importance that councilmen attach to them as compared with other needs. In forming their judgment, councilmen, in common with citizens generally, will be materially influenced by their knowledge of the actual conditions of compensation under which city employes are working.

Tests of Adequacy of Present City Pay

With this thought in mind, the Bureau of Municipal Research has examined into these conditions from a number of different angles and is planning to place its findings before council and the public. Among other things, the Bureau has compared existing rates of pay in the city service with corresponding rates in local private establishments as shown by the data collected last summer by the classification staff of the civil service commission. It has compared the increase in the general level of city pay since 1914 with the increase in the cost of living since that date. It has compared present city pay with the 1920 equivalent of the rates paid in 1915 by other city governments and by local private employers. It also has compared present city pay with the cost of maintaining a fair standard of living at present prices.

A Few Concrete Generalities

As a result of these comparisons the following general statements may be made at this time, to be followed later by supporting details:

1. The overwhelming majority of city employes other than policemen and firemen receive less pay than corresponding workers in conservative local private establishments,

4

2. Since 1914 the general level of city pay has increased about 43 per cent whereas the cost of living has increased more than 100 per cent.

3. In 1914 and 1915, the average municipal pay in thirteen other large cities in the United States was about 11 per cent higher than the average pay in the city service of Philadelphia.

4. If our city government were to pay its employes according to the standards that obtained in local private establishments in 1915, it would have to raise the general level of city pay at least 18 per cent.

5. If our city government were to pay its employes according to the standards that obtained in thirteen other large cities in the United States in 1914 and 1915, it would have to raise the general level of city pay at least 55 per cent.

6. The majority of city employes are now receiving less than a living wage.

City Pay Compared with Private Pay

In this number of CITIZENS' BUSINESS we are setting forth some of our findings in comparing present rates of pay in the city service with corresponding rates of pay in private establishments in and near Philadelphia.

The information upon which these findings are based consists (1) of the classified lists of city positions and salaries compiled by the classification staff of the civil service commission and (2) of rates of pay for corresponding classes of work obtained by the classification staff from local private employers, including "banks, railroad companies, insurance companies, contractors, public utilities, hospitals, mercantile concerns, manufacturers, and other establishments."

The General Level of Private Pay Higher

A careful examination of this information discloses that according to a conservative estimate fully 90 per cent of the different classes of workers in the city service that are comparable with corresponding classes in private service are receiving lower compensation than private employers are paying. This fact gains in significance when it is borne in mind that even in private service salaried employes and also many classes of wage earners have suffered an actual reduction in the purchasing power of their incomes since the beginning of the great upheaval in prices. If these groups of workers should soon regain their pre-war standards of compensation in private employment as is highly probable, then the city government, in order to compete successfully with private employers, will have to make at least corresponding advances in its standards of compensation.

6

Specific Examples of Underpayment

A more concrete idea of the relative underpayment of city employes may be gained from the few typical examples listed below:

Classes	Average Annual Compensation		Excess of Private Pay over City Pay	
	In private service	In the city service	Amount	Per cent
Asst. electrical engineer	$2741	$2000	$741	37.1
Asst. mechanical engineer	2488	2180	308	14.1
Asst. structural engineer	3033	2556	477	18.7
Blacksmith	1837	1381	456	33.0
Boiler inspector	1800	1680	120	7.1
Boilermaker	2239	1767	472	26.7
Chauffeur	1565	1206	359	29.7
Electrical worker	1603	1475	128	8.7
Elevator repairman ...	2572	1299	1273	98.0
Engineering field aid ..	1646	1413	233	16.5
Head engineman	2370	1823	547	30.0
Junior engineering aid.	1351	1078	273	25.3
Laboratory assistant ..	1413	1231	182	14.8
Laborer (general)	1258	1118	140	12.5
Office boy	638	540	98	18.1
Registered nurse	1115	761	354	46.5
Senior electrical engineer	3600	2300	1300	56.5
Senior assistant structural engineer	3972	3106	866	27.9
Sheet metal worker ...	1768	1580	188	11.9
Surveys engineer	6240	4500	1740	38.7

Speedy Action Needed

That this condition of underpayment ought to be corrected, and speedily, would appear to be self-evident. It is unfair to the employes of the city, and it is ruinous to the efficiency of the

7

service. **Whether we as taxpayers realize it or not it is a most expensive form of economy.** The bureau of surveys, for example, is unable with its depleted corps of technical men to keep abreast with its important current work. Our municipal hospitals are inadequately staffed. Owing to the high turnover in the service some departments and bureaus are greatly handicapped by having their working forces composed too largely of new appointees. The men and women who resign to seek employment elsewhere, we may be sure, are more likely to be the best equipped workers than those of only mediocre ability.

While Increasing the Pay, Let's Correct the Inequalities

If we are going to correct this condition as we doubtless should do, isn't it better to follow a carefully prepared plan than merely to add to the payroll in the haphazard manner of former years? The salary and wage recommendations of the civil service commission doubtless are not perfect and will need to be revised in places, but at any rate they have been logically conceived and, if adopted, will remove the existing inequalities in compensation throughout the service. By no other method ready to hand can we hope to receive an equal return in the increased efficiency of our municipal workers for the same amount of increase in our municipal payroll.

CITIZENS' BUSINESS

BUREAU OF MUNICIPAL RESEARCH

ISSUED WEEKLY AT 805 FRANKLIN BANK BUILDING
PHILADELPHIA ENTERED AS SECOND CLASS MATTER
JUNE 7, 1913 AT THE POST OFFICE AT PHILADELPHIA,
PA., UNDER THE ACT OF AUGUST 24TH, 1912 —
SUBSCRIPTION ONE DOLLAR THE YEAR

How Our City Government Pays Its Workers

Number 2

No. 444   November 25, 1920

In this number of CITIZENS' BUSINESS a significant comparison is made between the increase in
municipal salaries and wages since 1914 and the increase in the cost of living during the same period.

IN last week's CITIZENS' BUSINESS were shown some of the findings of the Bureau of Municipal Research in comparing present rates of pay in the city service with corresponding rates of pay in private establishments in and near Philadelphia. It was pointed out, among other things, that the overwhelming majority of city employes other than policemen and firemen receive less pay than workers performing similar duties in private establishments.

This week we are publishing some of the Bureau's findings in comparing the increase in the general level of city pay since 1914 with the increase in the cost of living since that date.

Philadelphia as Paymaster Six Years Ago

In order to catch the full significance of the facts set forth below it should be recalled that even in 1914 Philadelphia was not a generous paymaster as compared with other large cities throughout the country. From comparative salary and wage data collected by the Bureau of Municipal Research about five years ago from the payrolls of fourteen American cities, including New York, Philadelphia, Detroit, Cleveland, Boston, Baltimore, Pittsburgh, Los Angeles, San Francisco, Buffalo, Milwaukee,

Cincinnati, Minneapolis and Birmingham, it appears that while Philadelphia ranked second in population it stood eleventh in point of compensation standards in its civil service. Only Baltimore, Milwaukee and Birmingham paid their municipal employes at lower average rates than did Philadelphia. All the other cities paid higher rates. The general average pay in *all* of the thirteen cities with which comparison was made was about 11 per cent higher than the average pay in Philadelphia.

What the H C L Hath Wrought

Since 1914 the cost of living has more than doubled and standards of compensation in local private establishments appear to have advanced about 73 per cent, but the general level of pay in our city service has gone up only about 43 per cent. If we were now to undertake to restore the 1914 purchasing power of municipal salaries and wages, we should be obliged to increase them by almost 40 per cent. The wage earners in the service, that is, the employes who are paid on a daily basis, would require an average increase of 36 per cent; and the salaried employes, those who are paid on a monthly or an annual basis, would require an average increase of 48 per cent.

Be it remembered in this connection that the

recommendations of the civil service commission propose nothing so drastic as an increase that would restore the 1914 purchasing power of municipal salaries and wages, but pursue the more moderate course of suggesting an advance for 1921 of only about 10 per cent over the existing schedule!

How the Comparison Was Made

The figures in the following tables were derived from a comparison of the rates of pay in the various city departments in January 1914 with the corresponding rates in November 1920. In making this comparison we confined ourselves strictly to those positions that were continuous throughout the entire period between these two dates. In the case of salaried positions the actual number of incumbents at the different rates of pay was taken into account in calculating the average increases, but in the case of per diem employments the number of incumbents could not be definitely ascertained from the appropriation ordinances, so the various wage scales were rated as equally important. However, since the number of employes paid by the day is considerably larger than the number paid on a salary basis, the two groups were weighted eight and three respectively in calculating the general average increase for all positions in the service. In all cases the bonus was considered a part of the present rates of compensation.

The first column of figures in all the tables shows the percentage of increase that has taken place since January 1914 in the average rates of pay for the various groups of municipal workers, and the second column shows the further increase still necessary to make the purchasing power of existing salaries and wages equal to the purchasing power of the salaries and wages of January 1914.

TABLE SHOWING INCREASE IN COMPENSATION FROM JANUARY 1914 TO NOVEMBER 1920 IN SALARIED POSITIONS THAT WERE CONTINUOUS DURING THIS PERIOD, AND SHOWING ALSO THE INCREASE STILL NECESSARY TO MAKE THE NOVEMBER 1920 COMPENSATION EQUAL IN PURCHASING POWER TO THAT OF 1914. BY SERVICE GROUPS.*

| | PERCENTAGE OF INCREASE | |
| | From January 1914 to November 1920 | Still necessary to restore 1914 purchasing power |
SERVICE GROUPS		
All groups	34.4	48.8
Custodial (caretakers, janitors, storekeepers, watchmen, etc.)	48.5	34.7
Unskilled labor	46.3	36.7
Skilled labor	44.6	38.3
Protectional (salaried policemen, firemen and guards) ...	40.7	42.2
Miscellaneous	33.8	49.5
Clerical	27.	57.5
Professional and scientific....	25.	60.
Inspectional	22.6	63.1
Executive	5.4	89.8

TABLE SHOWING INCREASE IN COMPENSATION FROM JANU-
ARY 1914 TO NOVEMBER 1920 IN SALARIED POSITIONS
THAT WERE CONTINUOUS DURING THIS PERIOD, AND
SHOWING ALSO THE INCREASE STILL NECESSARY TO
MAKE THE NOVEMBER 1920 COMPENSATION EQUAL IN
PURCHASING POWER TO THAT OF 1914. BY OCCUPA-
TIONAL GROUPS.*

OCCUPATIONAL GROUPS	PERCENTAGE OF INCREASE From January 1914 to November 1920	Still necessary to restore 1914 purchasing power
All groups	34.4	48.8
Housekeepers	86.2	7.4
Riggers	63.2	22.6
Civil service examiners	60.7	24.5
Miscellaneous skilled workers	57.4	27.1
Watchmen	56.	28.2
Caretakers and janitors	54.4	29.5
Enginemen	53.1	30.6
Laborers	46.3	36.7
Guards	46.	37.
Police matrons	45.	37.9
Hostlers and drivers	44.5	38.4
Firemen	44.3	38.6
Drawbridge operators	44.	38.9
Woodworkers	43.2	40.
Blacksmiths	40.5	42.4
Storekeepers and yardmen	40.5	42.4
Bookkeepers	40.3	42.6
Machinists	40.	42.9
Superintendents and foremen	39.1	43.8
Telephone operators	38.6	44.3
Electrical workers	37.9	45.
Electrical inspectors	35.3	47.8
Food inspector	35.3	47.8
Laboratory assistants	35.3	47.8
Painters	35.	48.1
Plumbers and steamfitters	35.	48.1
Miscellaneous professional and scientific	33.8	49.5

Occupational Groups	Percentage of Increase From January 1914 to November 1920	Still necessary to restore 1914 purchasing power
Motor drivers	33.7	49.6
Inspectors of lighting service.	33.6	49.7
Miscellaneous inspectors	33.6	49.7
Recreation instructors	32.6	50.8
Statisticians	32.3	51.2
Policemen (above rank of patrolmen)	31.8	51.7
Photographers	31.5	52.1
Messengers	30.6	53.1
Disinfectors	30.5	53.3
Marine workers	29.8	54.1
Draftsmen	29.7	54.2
Stenographers and typists ...	29.7	54.2
Chemists	28.6	55.5
Otherwise unclassified	27.6	56.7
Institutional attendants	26.	58.7
Bakers	25.9	58.9
Engineers	25.9	58.9
Clerks	25.4	59.5
Inspectors of public works....	25.1	59.9
Nurses	24.5	60.6
Dentists	24.3	60.9
Detectives	23.5	61.9
Bacteriologists	23.2	62.3
Water service inspectors	23.	62.6
Fire prevention inspectors	21.8	64.2
Inspectors of supplies	20.	66.7
Medical inspectors	19.4	67.5
Inspectors of steam engines and boilers	19.1	67.9
Inspectors of buildings	13.7	75.9
Private secretaries	13.6	76.
Physicians	12.8	77.3
Lawyers	10.4	81.2
Bureau chiefs or heads	5.4	89.8
Executive secretaries	3.3	93.6
Department officials	1.4	97.2

TABLE SHOWING INCREASE IN WAGE SCALES UNDER THE
CITY GOVERNMENT FROM JANUARY 1914 TO NOVEMBER
1920, AND SHOWING ALSO THE INCREASE STILL NECES-
SARY TO MAKE THE NOVEMBER 1920 WAGE SCALE
EQUAL IN PURCHASING POWER TO THAT OF 1914. BY
OCCUPATIONAL GROUPS.*

| OCCUPATIONAL GROUPS | PERCENTAGE OF INCREASE | |
	From January 1914 to November 1920	Still necessary to restore 1914 purchasing power
All groups	47.	36.
Metal workers	72.	16.3
Blacksmiths	70.9	17.
Hostlers and drivers	70.2	17.5
Machinists	66.7	20.
Guards	64.4	21.7
Laborers	57.3	27.1
Boilermakers	57.1	27.3
Enginemen	53.8	30.
Miscellaneous skilled workers.	53.8	30.
Electrical workers	50.9	32.5
Patrolmen	47.3	35.8
Plumbers and steamfitters ...	44.1	38.8
Woodworkers	41.3	41.5
Bricklayers	37.4	45.6
Stonemasons	35.	48.1
Elevator operators	34.2	49.
Structural iron workers	33.3	50.
Painters	31.5	52.1
Marine workers	30.	53.8
Riggers	22.7	63.

* Because of difficulties in making comparisons it has not
been possible to include in these tables all of the divisions and
bureaus in the departments under city government. The following, however, have been included: Mayor's office; Civil
Service Commission; Purchasing Agent; Art Jury; Department of Law; Department of City Transit; Department of
Wharves, Docks and Ferries; Department of Public Safety;
Department of Public Works (excluding Bureau of Gas);
Department of Public Health (excluding Bureau of Hospitals);
and Department of Public Welfare (excluding the director's
office, Bureau of Constructive Social Service and Bureau of
Legal Aid).

Vol. XXI.

CITIZENS' BUSINESS

BUREAU OF MUNICIPAL RESEARCH

ISSUED WEEKLY AT 805 FRANKLIN BANK BUILDING
PHILADELPHIA ENTERED AS SECOND CLASS MATTER
JUNE 7, 1913 AT THE POST OFFICE AT PHILADELPHIA,
PA., UNDER THE ACT OF AUGUST 24TH, 1912 —
SUBSCRIPTION ONE DOLLAR THE YEAR

How Our City Government Pays Its Workers

Number 3

No. 445   December 2, 1920

If we wish our city government to be a model employer, can we permit the majority of municipal workers to serve us at less than a living wage?

PRACTICALLY 8000 of the 12000 employes in the departments of the city government under the mayor are receiving less than a living wage!

This may prove shocking to many Philadelphians who are not closely in touch with conditions in our city service, but it is true nevertheless. In fact the statement above is conservative in every respect. It understates rather than overstates the gravity of the actual situation.

A Living Wage Today

As shown by the Bureau of Municipal Research in CITIZENS' BUSINESS No. 433 on September 9, the annual cost of a workingmen's standard of living in Philadelphia at August 1920 prices was $1988.32. This standard, by the way, was anything but a luxurious one and has been publicly criticised in many quarters for its meagerness. Since August, it is true, there has been a slight decline in retail prices, but as yet, the effect upon the household budget has been hardly appreciable. If we reduce our figure from $1988.32 to $1900, we are probably making ample allowance for such decline in the cost of living as has taken place from August of this year to date.

Our City Payroll Cautiously Examined

Assuming therefore that $1900 is a living wage at present prices, let us see to what extent our city employes are now receiving a living wage. Since the figure we are using applies to a family rather than to a single person, we are confining ourselves to those classes of work that are usually performed by men of mature years. Positions likely to be held by women or by single young men are not included in our count. All classes of work with regard to which there may be doubt are also excluded. In order that we may not be drawn into error by the misleading titles on our municipal payroll, we are using instead the classified lists of positions and salaries prepared by the classification staff of the civil service commission.

What We Found

Our findings are as follows:

1. At least 7,979 out of a total of slightly over 12,000 employes in the departments under the mayor are engaged in classes of work usually performed by mature men and are paid less than $1900 a year.

2. Of this number 6,968 employes are paid less than $1600 a year and 1,498 employes are paid less than $1300 a year.

In other words almost two-thirds of our municipal workers are receiving less than a living wage and over half of them do not come within $300 of receiving a living wage!

Is this condition to be regarded with indifference?

One of the Results of Underpayment

We all subscribe to the motto "The best shall serve the state." Perhaps we can agree also to the proposition that the state, or the city, is more likely to secure "the best" when it can choose from among a large number of competitors for public place than when it must choose from a smaller number. With this in mind let us scan the table below showing the number of persons who have attended the entrance examinations of the civil service commission during each year since 1914.

TABLE SHOWING THE NUMBER OF ENTRANCE EXAMINATIONS AND THE NUMBER OF PERSONS ATTENDING THEM FOR EACH YEAR FROM 1915 TO DATE.

Year	Number of examinations	Number of persons who attended	Average number per examination
1915	183	5945	32.5
1916	201	5046	25.
1917	175	2822	16.
1918	325	2771	8.5
1919	322	2844	8.8
1920 to date	408*	2740	6.7

A Few High Spots

While examining this table, dear reader, please note the rapid falling off in the average number of persons attending the examinations, from 32.5 in 1915 to 6.7 in 1920. Doesn't it appear to have a striking relation to the shrinking value of the dollar during that same period? In the case of 84 of the 408 examinations in 1920, it should be added, only one applicant appeared, and *in the case of sixty of these examinations no applicant at all appeared!*

Under such conditions how can we expect to get "the best" to serve our city?

---

* This includes all entrance examinations that had been held and for which the eligible lists had been published on or before November 26.

CITIZENS' BUSINESS

Sci.

BUREAU OF MUNICIPAL RESEARCH

ISSUED WEEKLY AT 805 FRANKLIN BANK BUILDING
PHILADELPHIA ENTERED AS SECOND CLASS MATTER
JUNE 7, 1913 AT THE POST OFFICE AT PHILADELPHIA,
PA., UNDER THE ACT OF AUGUST 24TH, 1912 —
SUBSCRIPTION ONE DOLLAR THE YEAR

Bond Issues for Repaving

No. 446   December 9, 1920

The Bureau's stand on a proposed amendment of
the new city charter is briefly set forth herein.

Sound Public Policy

Nowadays almost everyone would admit that it is bad public policy for a city or other local government to meet any of its current expenses (as distinguished from "capital outlays") out of borrowed money. In fact, it is now almost universally taken for granted, as a canon of sound and equitable public finance, that a city should keep its expenses within its revenue or income, or, in other words, should raise at least sufficient revenue to cover its expenses.

What the Charter Committee Sought

Realizing the extent to which the city had been borrowing money on 30-year bonds to meet its current expenses, and thoroughly sensing the injustice which this short-sighted policy was rapidly pyramiding on the taxpayers and citizens of future years, the framers of the new city charter determined from the very first to put a stop to this objectionable practice.

Accordingly, they framed a set of provisions which were calculated to put the city on a real pay-as-you-go basis, and which, in addition, would have enabled the city to conduct its financing on a much more flexible, simple, and economical plan than had ever before been possible.

Compromise, Yet Victory

Partly because of a hesitancy on the part of the powers that be to depart from the way things have always been done, but largely because of arbitrary opposition from certain local officials, the charter committee's original proposals were supplanted at the eleventh hour by compromise and patchwork provisions along the lines of the unsatisfactory and oft-circumvented act of 1879. Nevertheless, the substituted provisions contained much of both the letter and the spirit of the charter committee's own draft, with the result that distinct progress was made.

What the New City Charter Says

As finally enacted into law, the new city charter permits the borrowing of money through "emergency loans" for any municipal purpose whatever; but at no time may the aggregate of emergency loans then outstanding exceed $2,000,000, nor may any emergency loan be created for a period in excess of one year. Other than this, no money may be borrowed for current expenses, or for repaving; and no money may be borrowed for any capital outlay, unless prior to the authorization of the loan the city controller certifies to council that all the expenditures proposed to be met out of the loan are "capital expenditures as distinguished from current expenses."

The Point

If the charter did not contain its specific prohibition against the borrowing of money for repaving, there is no doubt but that most of the city's repaving would be viewed by the city controller as a proper expenditure to be met out of loans.

The Bureau's Stand

In our opinion, most of the city's repaving may properly be viewed as capital outlay; and so long as other non-revenue producing capital outlays of a probable useful life to the city of no greater duration may be met out of loans, capital outlays for repaving may without impropriety also be chargeable against loans.

Philadelphia for many years has followed so low a

standard in the matter of borrowings, and there are so many accumulated demands for urgent non-revenue producing capital outlays, including from $15,000,000 to $20,000,000 worth of needed repaving, that it seems to this Bureau, as it did when the charter was in the making, that it would work too great a hardship on the taxpayers to compel them to finance out of current revenue any considerable portion of these outlays at this time.

The Bureau is not responsible for the prohibition against borrowing for repaving that was inserted in the charter during the last hour compromises. It is, however, responsible for the prohibition against borrowing for other than capital outlays, and for the provision that the city controller is to be the sole and final judge as to whether or not a proposed expenditure is a capital outlay.

In view of the situation referred to above, we felt then, and still feel, that a prohibition against borrowing for current expenses, and the requirement that loans be repaid within the probable useful life to the city of the asset acquired, constitute as high a standard as Philadelphia was able to adopt at the time. The first part of this moderate standard became law with the approval of the charter; the second part—which is an essential of all true pay-as-you-go plans—needs still to be incorporated in the city's organic law.

We Will Help

We are ready to lend our support to the movement that is to be made to strike from the charter the restriction against borrowing for repaving, but we shall urge that all loans be limited to the probable useful life of the asset or improvement acquired, and also that all loans be payable on the serial plan.

CITIZENS' BUSINESS

BUREAU OF MUNICIPAL RESEARCH

ISSUED WEEKLY AT 805 FRANKLIN BANK BUILDING
PHILADELPHIA ENTERED AS SECOND CLASS MATTER
JUNE 7, 1913 AT THE POST OFFICE AT PHILADELPHIA,
PA., UNDER THE ACT OF AUGUST 24TH, 1912 —
SUBSCRIPTION ONE DOLLAR THE YEAR

A Change in Gas Standard

No. 447   December 16, 1920

If the candle power standard is no longer necessary
or advisable, the new heat unit standard should be
established with justice to both the city and the company.

By the ordinance of November 12, 1897 the mayor of Philadelphia was authorized to execute a contract with the United Gas Improvement Company for the lease of the city owned gas works during a period of thirty years terminating December 31, 1927.

Candle Power Standard Originally Specified

The lease required the company to "supply gas of good quality of not less than twenty-two (22) candle power, daily average" subject to a penalty of $500 for noncompliance, except when such noncompliance was due to causes beyond the control of the company.

British Thermal Unit Standard Temporarily Adopted

At the request of the company for the establishment of the British Thermal Unit standard to diminish the use of gas oil and to reduce the cost of the manufacture of gas, the twenty-two candle power standard was suspended until January 1, 1921 by an agreement entered into by the mayor under authority of an ordinance of council approved July 19, 1920. This agreement specified a standard of 530 British Thermal Units as a minimum requirement. In so doing it temporarily changed the basis for the determination of the quality of the gas from the intensity of light produced in an open-flame burner to the amount of heat produced.

A Gas Survey Proposed

In order to have the advice of experts and the benefit of a general survey of the gas situation before taking action either to establish permanently or to discontinue the temporary British Thermal Unit standard, council provided by an ordinance passed October 5 for the employment of three competent public utility experts to make such a survey under the direction of the mayor. This original ordinance was vetoed by the mayor. Later, however, it was reintroduced with an amendment authorizing the addition to the surveying body of other persons not exceeding two in number, and the employment of an accountant and other assistants, and was passed by council on November 30. At the time of going to press this ordinance had not been approved by the mayor.

Company Reports An Operating Loss Even Under the Temporary Standard

The issue is further complicated by the statement of the president of the company in a letter to the mayor under date of November 17, 1920 (Appendix No. 240 to the Journal of Council) that the company was losing $10,000 a day even under the temporary 530 British Thermal Unit standard, with a probable loss in 1920 of $3,000,000. He states that "the first and most important step is to put into effect those economies in the manufacture of gas as cannot be put into effect until a British Thermal Unit standard is permanently established." He urges the city to take immediate steps through a commission of impartial men to verify the statements made and to recommend what action should be taken to adjust the situation.

How the Use for Lighting Is Affected

To the extent that the gas now supplied under the British Thermal Unit standard is of less than twenty-two candle power, it is less efficient for lighting use by the open-flame burner, but not by the incandescent or "thrift burner" which depends upon heat units in the gas for the intensity of illumination. If the actual use of gas for illumination in open-flame burners is now reduced to an inappreciable quantity and if incandescent burners can be substituted where open-flame burners are still used, the abolition of the candle power standard resolves itself into a consideration of the number of British Thermal Units to be specified in the new standard adopted.

How the Use for Heating and Cooking is Affected

It is pertinent to note that although the high candle power standard may not be so necessary now as formerly, the consumer has become accustomed to using a high-grade gas for heating purposes. While candle power tests have been the basis of the determination of the quality of the gas, heat producing tests also have been made. The reports of the bureau of gas for the eight years from 1912 to 1919 show that the average candle power was slightly above twenty-two in each year except 1918, but that the average content of British Thermal Units was above 600 each year. To the extent that the gas now being supplied contains less than the average content of heat units during past years, it would appear to be less efficient for all heating purposes, including lighting by incandescent burners, than the gas supplied under the twenty-two candle power standard. This is a question on which the city should have the advice of gas experts.

Equal Heating Value or Contract Concessions?

It is quite essential for the public to know in what ways the permanent substitution of the present temporary standard would modify the value of the gas for heating purposes. If a lower heating value is authorized, its adoption must be clearly justified. While the cost of gas manufacture has recently been excessively high and the company reports an operating loss, it must be ascertained whether the profits of the company during the fat years are not sufficient to offset the losses of recent lean years. If abnormal conditions require concessions to prevent a collapse of the company, such concessions should be so given as to permit their cancellation when the abnormal conditions cease to exist.

The Relative Value of "Lean" Gas

Recently the Pennsylvania Gas Association has petitioned the Public Service Commission for a reduction of the British Thermal Unit standard which is used throughout the state except in Philadelphia. The claim has been made by the Association that "lean" gas—that is, gas low in British Thermal Units—is more useful to the consumer, that it contains less dirt, and that its distribution is much easier. Undoubtedly the question of supplying a lean gas will enter into the determination of the standard to be adopted in Philadelphia if the candle power standard is permanently discontinued. It would then be quite necessary that the relative value of the lean gas to the consumer should be determined by the proposed investigators so that the price can be adjusted accordingly.

CITIZENS' BUSINESS

BUREAU OF MUNICIPAL RESEARCH

ISSUED WEEKLY AT 805 FRANKLIN BANK BUILDING
PHILADELPHIA ENTERED AS SECOND CLASS MATTER
JUNE 7, 1913 AT THE POST OFFICE AT PHILADELPHIA,
PA., UNDER THE ACT OF AUGUST 24TH, 1912 —
SUBSCRIPTION ONE DOLLAR THE YEAR-

The Gas Survey

No. 448   **December 23, 1920**

The ordinance authorizing the gas survey has been
approved by the mayor. The next step now is to secure
all the facts with regard to the twenty-three years'
operation of the gas works under the existing lease.

IN last week's issue of CITIZENS' BUSINESS were discussed the several phases of the gas situation as affected by the proposed permanent change from the twenty-two candle standard to a British Thermal Unit standard. The present bulletin deals primarily with the question of the facilities used by the company.

Company to Extend and Improve the Facilities

The ordinance of councils of November 12, 1897, authorizing the gas lease, states that the unavailability of public funds to expand the facilities owned by the city made it advisable to contract for the operation and development of the gas works for a period of years, at the end of which the city should resume possession of the facilities, modernized and fully equipped.

To that end the lease provided that the company should expend five million dollars within three years in improvements and extensions and such sums of money in each subsequent year as would be necessary to provide for the growth of the business, but not less than a total of fifteen million dollars during the thirty years of the lease. The company was further required to "maintain said gas works in first-class condition, with the best and most economical processes in use that are customary in the best regulated gas works."

Complete Facilities to Become Property of City Without Payment

It is the expressed intent of the agreement that the city shall receive in first class condition without charge or cost on December 31, 1927, all of the facilities employed by the company, including all extensions, enlargements, improvements and betterments made by the company, together with the right to use all processes in the manufacture of gas then established and in use at any of the works.

Financial Return to the City

In consideration for the privileges conferred by the lease, the company agreed to furnish gas free of charge for illuminating purposes in public buildings along the line of its mains, and to supply free gas to a specified extent to street lamps. The company was also required to pay to the city all sums received from the consumers in excess of certain stated minimum rates. Under this provision the city now receives twenty-five cents on each thousand feet of gas sold, and this income is turned into the general fund and helps to defray the city's expenses.

But no less important, in computing the financial return to the city, than free gas and yearly cash payments is the equity which is being built up in gas facilities by the payments of the gas consuming public and which becomes the property of the city without cost when the lease expires.

What is the Condition of the Gas Facilities

Since the lease will remain in effect only seven more years, it is a question of grave concern to the city whether the facilities are being maintained "in first class condition, with the best and most economical processes in use that are customary in the best regulated works." Obviously an examination of the condition of the works to ascertain their fitness for supplying an adequate quantity and a proper quality of gas is a task for gas experts such as are provided for under the ordinance just approved.

Let's Have the Facts First

The first step to be undertaken in the gas survey is to secure all of the facts concerning the twenty-three years' operation of the gas lease. The information now in the hands of the city is very meagre indeed, for the bureau of gas has been operated primarily to test the quality of the gas but not to secure the fulfillment of all of the terms of the lease, nor to examine the records of expenditures for improvements and extensions. The assembling of the facts must be made with all the cards on the table, and the tone of the company's letters to the mayor would seem to indicate that the company is willing to cooperate fully in the survey.

Matters for Consideration When the Facts Are Secured

After the facts have been secured in regard to past years' operation and the financial condition of the company, the survey board will be in a position to suggest a permanent adjustment in the gas standard and in the price of gas in accordance with a new standard. If a new standard should be required sooner or later, its adoption now would secure for the city the greatest benefit from extensions and betterments to be made during the remaining seven years of the lease, and therefore the maximum equity in gas facilities when the lease expires.

CITIZENS' BUSINESS

BUREAU OF MUNICIPAL RESEARCH

ISSUED WEEKLY AT 805 FRANKLIN BANK BUILDING
PHILADELPHIA ENTERED AS SECOND CLASS MATTER
JUNE 7, 1913 AT THE POST OFFICE AT PHILADELPHIA,
PA., UNDER THE ACT OF AUGUST 24TH, 1912 —
SUBSCRIPTION ONE DOLLAR THE YEAR

Making Bricks without Straw

No. 449   December 30, 1920

Let us not expect our civil service commission to do
the impossible. If we want a high standard of employment administration in the city service we must provide
the necessary funds.

The Pros and Cons of Civil Service

Within the last few weeks we have heard a great deal *pro* and *con* on the subject of civil service. There are *pros* and *cons*, of course, to nearly every question of social or political expediency; but however many *cons* we may discover on the subject of civil service, one needs only to get a glimpse of the most likely alternative to civil service, the spoils system, to become convinced that the *pros* have the better of the argument.

The Proof of the Pudding

It is not enough, however, to win in argument. A system or a plan may be ever so desirable in itself, and yet its execution may be wholly disappointing. We must not rest content with having placed upon the statute books a civil service law that is excellent; we must strive on to secure an equally excellent administration of that law. In the last analysis the merit system will be judged by its administration rather than by its original design. This is true particularly at a time when opposing forces are in the field seeking to curb, if not to overthrow, the system itself.

Civil Service Efficiency and the Purse Strings

An old proverb tells us that there are other ways of killing a cat besides choking it with butter. So also are there other means of scrapping civil service than that of direct frontal attack in the legislature. There is such a thing as nullifying and discrediting a civil service law by merely starving the official body charged with its administration.

Conversely, one of the most effective ways of maintaining the merit system intact is to make possible a high standard of employment administration by providing the civil service commission with the wherewithal to do the work. And this is the point we wish at this time to bring to the attention of the citizens of Philadelphia.

The Commission's Inadequate Examining Staff

The most important function of the commission is the examination of applicants for employment. If the examining staff is inadequate it is not possible to meet the demands of the various departments for eligibles to fill vacancies, nor is it possible to give to each examination the care in preparation that is necessary. In 1915 the commission had a regular examining staff of five persons. That was before the classified service had been enlarged by the organization of the new division of housing and sanitation, by the creation of the department of public welfare, and by the taking over by the city of the garbage reduction plant and the street cleaning work in the central section. That, too, was before the commission had seriously undertaken the task of reclassification and standardization which the new charter has made mandatory. That was, moreover, during a period when the turnover in the service was relatively low and examinations were required to be held less than half so frequently as at present. The expansion of the city service since that time and the growth of the examining work of the commission, in the ordinary course of things, would have been met by a corresponding enlargement of the examining staff. But the contrary has proved to be the case. Since 1915 the number of regular examiners provided for in the budget appropriations has been reduced from five to three!

Additional Examiners Denied by Mayor and Council

Early in the year the civil service commission realized how inadequate was the examining staff for the work that was required. Accordingly, on March 18, 1920, the commission asked council for two additional examiners and for three classifiers. Council, however, allowed only one additional examiner and only one classifier. And then the mayor vetoed the additional examiner and the classifier, so that the net increase in the commission's examining force was zero!

In making its 1921 budget request, the commission again asked for an examining and classification staff of eight persons, but again the request was denied and only three examiners were allowed.

Let's Give the Commission the "Straw"

This is not a criticism of the work the civil service commission has been doing. As a matter of fact, it is a marvel what the commission has been able to do with such an inadequate appropriation. Better work, however, can be done if the commission is given more adequate support; and the people of Philadelphia are entitled to a better administration of its civil service law. The Bureau of Municipal Research therefore urges upon the mayor and council that action be taken at the earliest date possible increasing the appropriation to the civil service commission and giving the commission an examining and classification staff adequate to the needs of the ensuing year.

The Season's Best Wishes to all our readers!

Lightning Source UK Ltd.
Milton Keynes UK
UKHW022230280119
336364UK00008B/952/P